D1590999

Two Peacemakers in Paris

02850

Two Peacemakers in Paris

THE HOOVER-WILSON POST-ARMISTICE
LETTERS 1918–1920

Edited and with Commentaries by

FRANCIS WILLIAM O'BRIEN

Texas A&M University Press

COLLEGE STATION AND LONDON

Copyright © 1978 by Francis William O'Brien

All rights reserved

Library of Congress Cataloging in Publication Data

Hoover, Herbert Clark, Pres. U.S., 1874–1964.
    Two peacemakers in Paris.

    Continues the author's the Hoover-Wilson wartime
correspondence, September 24, 1914, to November 11,
1918.
       Bibliography: p.
       Includes index.
       1. Hoover, Herbert Clark, Pres. U.S., 1874–1964.
2. Wilson, Woodrow, Pres. U.S., 1856–1924. 3. Reconstruction (1914–1939)—Sources. 4. United States. Food
Administration. 5. Paris. Peace Conference, 1919. I. Wilson, Woodrow, Pres. U.S., 1856–1924. II. O'Brien, Francis William, 1917–   III. Title.
E802.A4   1978   973.91'3   77-99273
ISBN 0-89096-051-8

Manufactured in the United States of America

FIRST EDITION

Contents

42830

4585)

Preface

In 1974 *The Hoover-Wilson Wartime Correspondence, September 24, 1914, to November 11, 1918* was published. All the three hundred letters known to have passed between President Wilson and Herbert Hoover from the beginning of World War I to the Armistice are contained in that book. No part of any letter was deleted. In addition, commentary was supplied for most of the correspondence, placing the letters in their settings to make them more intelligible for the reader.

The present work contains the letters exchanged by Hoover and Wilson after November 11, 1918. Soon after this date Hoover left for Europe to undertake the reconstruction of the several nations ravished or adversely affected by four years of armed hostilities. Some three weeks later, Wilson arrived in Paris.

Hoover's reputation as a humanitarian, a brilliant administrator, a knowledgeable expert in the area of foreign affairs, and a trusted Wilson confidant rested on several foundations. For three years he had headed the Commission for Belgian Relief. Upon the active entrance of America into the war he became U.S. Food Administrator, directly responsible to President Wilson. Prior to undertaking these positions, he had lived for years in several foreign countries as an engineer for various mining companies.

Because of the experience Hoover had gained in these several capacities, Wilson relied heavily on him while the two were in Paris during the Peace Conference. In the French capital the Food Administrator acquired a new title, that of Director General of Relief and Reconstruction of Europe; and in the performance of his new duties he made valuable contacts throughout the Continent. Thus he was able to channel reliable information to the President on matters of the highest importance. Many major decisions that he personally made for the President or in close consultation with him have had effects of immeasurable proportions.

Actually, little happened in any part of Europe in which Hoover did not have the keenest interest. Though his earlier letters as Food Administrator often treated lackluster matters, his work in Europe was always of great importance and frequently had touches of high drama. His letters to Wilson dealt with the Bolshevist movement in Russia; the Communist takeover in Hungary; the Separatist movement in Germany; and freedom for Poland, Finland, and the Baltic States. He clashed with Clemenceau and Lloyd George over the continuation of the blockade of Germany and cascaded Wilson with letters on the subject. He had ink to spare to write memorandums on conditions in what was then part of Austria-Hungary, now Yugoslavia. He had his own definite views on the question of German reparations. Indeed, he did not hesitate to bring to the very door of Wilson's chambers his sharp criticism of the final draft of the peace treaty itself because the treaty clashed with these views.

The President read Hoover's letters with great attention and relied heavily on the judgment of his adviser. Lack of time usually prevented his writing lengthy replies. Indeed, he often was compelled to have his confidential secretary, Gilbert F. Close, respond for him. But he frequently met personally with Hoover, and many of the actions he took and the directives he gave to others clearly indicate that the President was greatly influenced by the head of European relief.

In view of the importance to history of this relationship, it seemed desirable to prepare this second volume of Hoover-Wilson correspondence, *Two Peacemakers in Paris: The Hoover-Wilson Post-Armistice Letters, November 11, 1918, to July 10, 1920,* containing all known correspondence exchanged by the two men after the Armistice. The majority of letters originated in Paris, a limited number were written just prior to Hoover's sailing for Europe on November 17, and a few were penned after Hoover's return to the States in mid-September of 1919. Nonetheless, all—with the rarest exception—deal with the subject of peacemaking and problems relating to the Peace Conference. With publication of these two volumes, readers may be assured that they have at hand a record of all the correspondence exchanged from 1914 to 1920 by two of the world's most influential twentieth-century figures.

As in the earlier book, historical commentary has been supplied for each letter that appears to require it; some letters need none since they contain sufficient material themselves to be understandable to the reader. A general introduction is included to provide background on the times and organization of the Peace Conference. This should be read in advance. Readers will also profit from frequent references to this introduction while perusing the correspondence. The commentaries are not intended to be anything like a history of the Peace Conference. They are, along with the letters, one modest source of information about that epochal event. For more background, scholars and interested readers are advised to consult the many excellent relevant books available.

Textual note: Handwritten signatures and notes appear in *italics*; other signatures appear in either capital and lower case or all capital letters.

FRANCIS WILLIAM O'BRIEN

Sources

The Letters

As far as can be ascertained, all letters in the Hoover-Wilson correspondence and public statements of the two men are now housed in four documentary depositories: the Hoover Presidential Library, West Branch, Iowa; the Hoover Institution on War, Revolution and Peace, Stanford University; the Firestone Library, Princeton University; and the Library of Congress. The Hoover Institution and the Library of Congress possess the original letters. I visited all four depositories and arranged to supplement the earlier collection at the Hoover Presidential Library so as to have at hand the needed matter for the volumes on the Hoover-Wilson correspondence. As a result, the Hoover Presidential Library now has a complete collection of all the letters exchanged between these two former presidents. *Two Peacemakers in Paris* is based on this collection. The *List of Letters* indicates at which institution copies were made through use of a duplication machine. The list identifies the writer of each letter as either Wilson or Hoover, although the persons who actually performed the task of composing many items were really confidential secretaries and not the men whose ideas they communicated. This was especially true in the case of President Wilson.

Although the effort to produce the Hoover-Wilson correspondence in its entirety has meant the inclusion of several letters and notes on apparently trivial and inconsequential matters, it is hoped that even these will assist readers in appreciating the type of activities that consumed the daily hours of these two men and the character of the relationship that existed between them.

Secondary Sources

The following list of books is modest indeed and makes no pretense at being exhaustive. Nonetheless, it should prove sufficient for most readers interested in delving more deeply into the many problems discussed by Hoover and Wilson in their Paris correspondence.

In presenting the letters and in writing the introductory discussions, no effort was made to document every controversial statement or incident mentioned. Even in places where references seemed advisable, footnotes have been avoided and the briefest form of citation possible has been employed within the text of the commentaries. This practice, it is hoped, will supply adequate documentation for most readers without distracting them from the text itself.

Brief Reference Form	*Source*
Administration	William C. Mullendore. *History of the United States Food Administration, 1917–1918.* Stanford: Stanford Univ. Press, 1941.
Aftermath	Daniel M. Smith. *Aftermath of War: Colby and Wilsonian Diplomacy, 1920–1921.* Philadelphia: American Philosophical Society, 1970.
Bridge to France	E. N. Hurley. *The Bridge to France.* New York: Lippincott, 1927.
Bullitt	William Bullitt. *The Bullitt Mission to Russia.* New York: Huelsh, 1919.
Carthaginian	Etienne Mantoux. *The Carthaginian Peace.* Pittsburgh: Univ. Pittsburgh Press, 1965.
Chronicle	Ray Stannard Baker. *American Chronicle.* New York: Scribner, 1945.
Conference	N. Gordon Levin, Jr., ed. *Woodrow Wilson and the Paris Peace Conference.* 2d ed. Lexingington, Mass.: Heath, 1972.
Consequences	John Maynard Keynes. *The Economic Consequences of the Peace.* New York: Scribner, 1919.
Correspondence	Francis William O'Brien. *The Hoover-Wilson Wartime Correspondence: September 24, 1914, to November 11, 1918.* Ames: Iowa State Univ. Press, 1974.
Daniels Diaries	E. David Cronon, ed. *The Cabinet Diaries of Josephus Daniels, 1913–1921.* Lincoln: Univ. Nebraska Press, 1963.

Brief Reference Form	*Source*
Diplomatist	Arthur S. Link. *Wilson the Diplomatist: A Look at His Major Foreign Policies.* Baltimore: Johns Hopkins Univ. Press, 1957.
Economic Council	Supreme Economic Council. Minutes and Documents. Paris, 1919. Typed, unpubl. 9 vols. Hoover Presidential Library, West Branch, Iowa.
Eight Years	David F. Houston. *Eight Years with Wilson's Cabinet.* 2 vols. New York: Doubleday, 1926.
Epic	Herbert Hoover. *An American Epic.* 4 vols. Chicago: Regnery, 1959–1964.
F.R., P.C.	*Papers Relating to the Foreign Relations of the United States, Paris Peace Conference.* 13 vols. Washington, D.C.: USGPO, 1942.
F.R., Russia	*Papers Relating to the Foreign Relations of the United States, 1919, Russia.* Washington, D.C.: USGPO, 1932.
First Crusade	Herbert Hoover, *America's First Crusade.* New York: Scribner, 1942.
George Memoirs	David Lloyd George. *Memoirs of the Peace Conference.* 2 vols. New Haven: Yale Univ. Press, 1939.
Grain Trade	Frank M. Surface. *The Grain Trade During the World War.* New York: Macmillan, 1928.
Grandeur	Georges Clemenceau. *Grandeur and Misery of Victory.* New York: Harcourt, Brace, and Co., 1930.
Harding	Robert K. Murray. *The Harding Era.* Minneapolis: Univ. Minnesota Press, 1969.
Hoover	Eugene Lyons. *Herbert Hoover: A Biography.* 2d ed. Garden City, N.Y.: Doubleday, 1964.
Hoover and Germany	Louis P. Lochner. *Herbert Hoover and Germany.* New York: Macmillan, 1960.
Inquiry	Lawrence E. Gelfand. *The Inquiry: American Preparations for Peace.* New Haven: Yale Univ. Press, 1963.
Intimate Papers	Charles Seymour. *The Intimate Papers of Colonel House.* 3 vols. Boston: Houghton Mifflin, 1926.
Ledger	*Philadelphia Ledger.*
Life and Letters	Ray Stannard Baker. *Woodrow Wilson, Life and Letters.* 8 vols. Garden City, N.Y.: Doubleday, 1927–1939.

xiv / *Sources*

Brief Reference Form	Source
Lost Peace	Thomas A. Bailey. *Woodrow Wilson and the Lost Peace.* New York: Macmillan, 1944.
McCormick Diary	McCormick Diary, 1919. Paris. Typed, unpubl. Hoover Presidential Library, West Branch, Iowa.
Memoirs	Herbert Hoover. *The Memoirs of Herbert Hoover.* 3 vols. New York: Macmillan, 1951–1952.
Men	Lewis L. Strauss. *Men and Decisions.* Garden City, N.Y.: Doubleday, 1962.
Messages	Albert Shaw. *The Messages and Papers of Woodrow Wilson.* New York: Review of Reviews Corp., 1924.
Negotiations	Robert Lansing. *The Peace Negotiations: A Personal Narrative.* Boston: Houghton Mifflin, 1921.
Ordeal	Herbert Hoover. *The Ordeal of Woodrow Wilson.* New York: McGraw-Hill, 1958.
Organization	Suda L. Bane and Ralph H. Lutz, eds. *Organization of American Relief in Europe, 1918–1919.* Stanford: Stanford Univ. Press, 1942.
Peacemaking	Harold Nicholson. *Peacemaking 1919.* New York: Grosset & Dunlap, Universal Library Ed., 1965.
Poland	Louis L. Gerson. *Woodrow Wilson and the Rebirth of Poland.* New Haven: Yale Univ. Press, 1953.
Politics, Diplomacy	Arno Mayer. *Politics and Diplomacy of Peacemaking: Containment and Counterrevolution at Versailles, 1918–1919.* New York: Knopf, 1967.
Pork	Frank M. Surface. *American Pork Production in the World War.* Chicago: Shaw & Co., 1926.
Post	*Washington Post.*
Pre-Commerce Papers	Pre-Commerce Papers. Hoover-Wilson Correspondence, Hoover Presidential Library, West Branch, Iowa.
Public Years	Bernard Baruch. *The Public Years.* New York: Holt, 1957.
Russian Prisoners	Willis F. Edward. *Herbert Hoover and the Russian Prisoners of World War I.* Stanford: Stanford Univ. Press, 1951.
Senate	Henry Cabot Lodge. *The Senate and the League of Nations.* New York: Scribner, 1925.

Brief Reference Form	Source
Soviet-American	George Kennan. *Soviet-American Relations: The Decision to Intervene*. Princeton: Princeton Univ. Press, 1956.
Supply and Relief	Supreme Council of Supply and Relief. Minutes and Documents. Paris, 1919. Typed, unpubl. 9 vols. Hoover Presidential Library, West Branch, Iowa.
Times	*New York Times*.
Tragedy	William Appleman Williams. *The Tragedy of American Diplomacy*. New York: World, 1959.
Truth	Andre Tardieu. *The Truth about the Treaty*. Indianapolis: Bobbs-Merrill, 1921.
Unfinished	Stephan Bonsal. *Unfinished Business*. New York: Doubleday, 1944.
War Memoirs	David Lloyd George. *War Memoirs*. 6 vols. Boston: Little, Brown, 1933–1937.
What Happened	Edward House and Charles Seymour, eds. *What Really Happened at Paris: The Peace Conference*. New York: Scribner, 1921.
What Wilson Did	Ray Stannard Baker. *What Wilson Did at Paris*. New York: Doubleday, 1922.
Wilson	Arthur S. Link. *Wilson*, vols. 3–5. Princeton: Princeton Univ. Press, 1960, 1964, 1965.
Woodrow Wilson	Charles Seymour, ed. *Woodrow Wilson and the World War*. New Haven: Yale Univ. Press, 1921.
World Settlement	Ray Stannard Baker. *Woodrow Wilson and World Settlement*. 3 vols. New York: Doubleday, 1922–1923.

Acknowledgments

I am grateful for a grant from the Earhart Foundation, which helped to make the publication of this book possible.

I acknowledge the assistance I have received in various ways from B. Joe Colwell, Gayle Cooper, Ruth Dennis, Betty Gallagher, Lawrence Gelfand, John Henry, Janet Kephart, Mrs. Crone Kernke, Franz Lassner, John T. McCarty, Mildred Mather, Dale Mayer, Dwight Miller, Mrs. Dorothy Secor, Kate Stewart, Thomas Thalken, Mrs. Kathleen Todd, Elizabeth K. Webb, Patrick Wildenberg, and Robert Wood.

List of Letters

*Hoover appears to have composed most of the letters which bear his signature. On the other hand, Wilson while in Paris very often left letterwriting to his confidential secretary. The letters themselves give no indication which might be the products of rough drafts, notes, or verbal instructions from Wilson or Hoover, as the case may be. Indeed, it is highly probable that in some instances the secretaries were given broad discretionary powers to write letters in accordance with their own intepretation of Wilson's or Hoover's mind on the matter under consideration. In any event, on many occasions the private secretaries actually signed the letters exchanged by the two men. After doing so, the secretaries usually typed these words on the carbon copies: "[signed, Wilson's secretary]" or "[signed, Hoover's secretary]." These carbon copies were then filed away. Every letter presented in this volume is a faithful copy of the letter just as it is to be found—usually among the Wilson Papers in the Manuscript Division of the Library of Congress or among the Hoover Papers in the Hoover Institution on War, Revolution and Peace at Stanford University.

† The Hoover Presidential Library has the only complete set of Hoover-Wilson letters, but most are duplicates made from the copies housed either in the Hoover Institution on War, Revolution and Peace at Sanford (HIS) or in the Wilson Papers in the Manuscript Division of the Library of Congress (LC). The initials will indicate where the letters printed in this book were located and photocopied.

List of Letters / xxi

Date		Writer*	Subject Matter	Source†	Page

An explanation is called for on the policy followed as concerns the inclusion in this volume of the enclosures which Wilson and Hoover often sent to one another along with their letters. In those instances where the enclosures seemed to be of particular significance, they have been reproduced in their entirety. In other in-

stances, the contents of the enclosures have been briefly summarized
in the introduction to the letter under consideration. In cases where
the enclosures were missing, this fact has been noted in the introduction. One might reasonably conclude that Hoover and Wilson
sent many such enclosures on to third parties for whom they had a
particular interest.

Introduction

On October 6, 1918, the German government announced its unqualified acceptance of Wilson's Fourteen Points and his several subsequent declarations as a basis for peace. Toward the end of the same month, the President sent Colonel Edward M. House to Paris as his personal representative, and from October 29 until November 4 House met with the Allied prime ministers in an effort to draw up terms for the approaching Armistice. Finally an agreement was reached stipulating the acceptance by the Allies of the Fourteen Points and Wilson's additional declarations—with certain reservations of France and Great Britain. Marshal Foch and his advisers had also drawn up extensive naval and military provisions. These, along with the above-mentioned agreement, provided substantially the matter debated at Paris from January to June 1919.

From May 1917 Herbert Hoover had been serving in Washington as the American Food Administrator, and in this capacity he had coordinated the production and distribution of food for the Allied and neutral nations. When hostilities came to an end, he quickly concluded his work in Washington and within five days left the capital. On November 17, 1918, he boarded the *Olympic* for London to aid in the economic reconstruction of Europe. He reached London on November 24 and went on to Paris the following day.

During the ensuing three weeks Hoover shuttled between London and Paris; but on December 12 he moved into his permanent Paris office at 51 Rue Montaigne where fifty rooms were available for his staff, whose task was the economic rehabilitation of a prostrate continent. From the day of his arrival in Europe, Hoover had been meeting with scores of representatives of the British, French, and Italian governments. He discovered that their plans for the restoration of war-battered Europe differed sharply from that envisaged by himself and approved in general by President Wilson. Hoover parried the thrusts of his European peers and thus was able to deliver considerable food to the famished nations even during the days of his preliminary disillusionment with the masters of European power politics.

President Wilson finally reached Paris on December 14, whereupon Hoover and Colonel House immediately acquainted him with the frustrating situation. Without delay Wilson personally intervened with Prime Ministers Georges Clemenceau, David Lloyd George, and Vittorio Orlando. From their consultations came a ready agreement that Hoover should be appointed sole director of relief and rehabilitation. The Big Four (representing the United States, France, England, and Italy) also accepted Hoover's proposal for establishment of an advisory council in Paris with representatives of their governments, plus Belgium. These men would be concerned with questions of supplies, credit, military affairs, shipping, and the food blockade. Invested now with solid authority and assured of the sources of necessary information, Hoover felt better equipped to carry on his work of feeding Europe and restoring a semblance of economic order.

The Peace Conference itself did not begin until January 12, 1919. In the meantime, President Wilson visited London, Manchester, Rome, Milan, and, of course, Paris. In these metropolitan centers, he met with the world's highest dignitaries and spoke before enthusiastic throngs of people who received him as their messiah.

Since the Armistice was signed, two months had elapsed; and one month had passed since the arrival of the U.S.S. *George Washington* at Brest. Only then did the leaders of the world begin their deliberations over the multifarious problems facing Europe. Originally, Geneva, Lausanne, Brussels, or The Hague had been seriously considered as suitable sites for this world assemblage. The French capital was finally chosen, and most of the sessions actually were held there. Had Wilson really insisted, Switzerland might have become the center for the drafters of the peace. With the advantage of hindsight, critics can convincingly argue that this would have been the happier choice, for the charged atmosphere of Paris was really not conducive to the calm and dispassionate deliberations so sorely needed for the shaping of a just and enduring peace.

People from some twenty-seven Allied and Associated powers, plus the five British dominions, made their way to Paris in mid-January, many expecting to become active members of the most august world parliament ever assembled in the history of mankind. Fortunately, the realists quickly perceived that a body of several hundred delegates was far too unwieldly, too loquacious, and too mercurial for expediting the delicate business of the Peace Conference. Thus the plenary sessions were of slight importance and did little more than rubber-stamp decisions made by the smaller groups.

At the beginning, the most important body was the Supreme Council, which evolved from the Supreme Inter-Allied War Council established at Versailles during the last part of the war to direct Allied military policy.[1] In January 1919 it became known as the Council of Ten because it consisted of two delegates from Italy, France, Great Britain, Japan, and the United States. Each of the first four was represented by its prime minister and its minister of foreign affairs; the United States was represented by President Wilson and Secretary of State Robert Lansing. The Council of Ten met with great formality in the study of the French foreign minister in the palace on the Quai d'Orsay, with Clemenceau as presiding officer. For two months the Council of Ten was universally recognized as the official source of authority of the entire Conference. It was the Council that called the plenary assembly into being, reviewed its decisions, and regulated its activities. It was the Council that created the many commissions set up to study special problems that needed men with particular expertise.

However, it was soon evident to all that the Council was too large, for usually some thirty people, counting interpreters and secretaries, attended its meetings. Moreover, it was ill equipped to handle the many details involved in most matters or even to decide the general policies for legions of problems that were necessarily the specialties of highly trained experts. Therefore, the Council was soon compelled to establish a number of commissions—committees of specialists to investigate these problems and propose acceptable solutions.

[1] For a description of the organization of the Peace Conference, see Clive Day in Edward House and Charles Seymour, eds., *What Really Happened at Paris: The Peace Conference* (New York: Scribner, 1921), pp. 16–36.

Some writers highly praise the work of these commissions. Others describe the Paris situation in general as one of "indescribable confusion and disorganization,"[2] little relieved by the commission system.[3] Between fifty-two and sixty commissions operated during the course of the Conference, and altogether they held 1,643 sessions.[4] Nevertheless, none can discount the importance and indispensability of such commissions as the one on reparations or the commission on the League of Nations presided over by President Wilson. In his writings Hoover generally refers to these groups as committees, councils, or boards[5] and sometimes speaks of them in almost contemptuous language.[6] Hoover states that he was a member of twenty of the sixty commissions, or inter-Allied councils, and chairman of six.

Early in January 1919 Hoover approached President Wilson with a plan that somewhat coordinated the activities of the many Americans who sat as representatives on the approximately sixty commissions.[7] Wilson approved, and accordingly the President's Committee of Economic Advisers was established, with Hoover, Bernard Baruch, Vance McCormick, Edward N. Hurley, Norman Davis, Admiral William Benson, General Tasker Bliss, Colonel Edward House, and President Wilson as members.[8] The latter was chairman, and in his absence House presided over the meetings. Henry M. Robinson was given a place after Hurley returned to America. The meetings were quite informal, held usually at lunch, and no minutes or records were kept except for what McCormick wrote in his diary.[9]

Hoover implies that this committee performed many valuable

[2] Thomas A. Bailey, *Woodrow Wilson and the Lost Peace* (New York: Macmillan, 1944), p. 134.
[3] Ibid., p. 135. See also Harold Nicholson, *Peacemaking 1919* (New York: Grosset & Dunlap, Universal Library Ed., 1965), pp. 7, 104–31.
[4] House and Seymour, *What Happened*, p. 26.
[5] Herbert Hoover, *An American Epic*, 4 vols. (Chicago: Regnery, 1960), vol. 2, p. 294; Herbert Hoover, *The Ordeal of Woodrow Wilson* (New York: McGraw-Hill, 1958), p. 83.
[6] Herbert Hoover, *The Memoirs of Herbert Hoover*, 3 vols. (New York: Macmillan, 1951–1952), vol. 1, pp. 297–98, n. 1.
[7] Hoover, *Ordeal*, pp. 84–85.
[8] Ibid., p. 84.
[9] Ibid.

functions.[10] But the most prestigious agency on which Hoover sat was the Supreme Economic Council created about January 11, 1919, to coordinate the numerous inter-Allied economic organizations.[11] It was originally called the Supreme Council of Supply and Relief, but so many assistants and advisers were allowed at the meetings that they soon became mere talkfests, a fact that encouraged most American members to stay home. Accordingly, Hoover persuaded Wilson to have this agency abolished for a tighter organization entitled the Supreme Economic Council whose constitution was the handiwork of Hoover himself.[12] On February 8 Wilson secured the approval from the Council of Ten for this agency.[13]

The jurisdiction of this new council was wide, covering such matters as finance, food, blockade control, shipping, and raw materials—things "not primarily of military character." Membership was limited to five delegates each from the "interested governments." This appears to have meant only France, Great Britain, Italy, and the United States.[14] However, by late April 1919 Belgium began to be represented by at least one person at most meetings.[15] The American members appointed by Wilson on February 13 were Baruch, Davis, Hoover, McCormick, and Robinson.

The ineffectual parent organization seems to have held twelve meetings between January 19 and February 24.[16] Its successor actually began to operate on February 17 and thereafter gathered twenty-nine times until August 2, 1919.[17] This does not include the many additional meetings of subcommittees. The meetings of the Supreme Economic Council were held at least twice each week under a rotating chairman.

10 Ibid., pp. 84, 146–49; Hoover, *Epic*, vol. 2, p. 293.

11 Hoover, *Ordeal*, p. 86.

12 Ibid.

13 Ibid. See also Hoover, *Memoirs*, vol. 1, pp. 297–99.

14 For this and other related matters, see the nine volumes of typed minutes and documents catalogued under Supreme Economic Council (Paris, 1917) in the Hoover Presidential Library, West Branch, Iowa (hereafter cited as HPL).

15 Ibid., vol. 2, p. 69.

16 Supreme Council of Supply and Relief, Minutes and Documents (Paris, 1919), vol. 1, p. 1. A typed copy is in the HPL.

17 Actually, the organization continued to limp along (even after the American members left in August) as an adjunct of the Supreme War Council and then kept it in touch with the economic organs of the League of Nations.

On the importance of this organization, Ray Stannard Baker has written as follows:

> [T]he Supreme Economic Council . . . [was] for a brief time a kind of economic government: the greatest experiment ever made in the correlation, control, and direction, in time of peace, of international trade and finance. In some ways it was the most interesting and significant, because it was the newest of the Paris Conference. Military and political alliances and cooperation are not new in the world, but such a degree of economic cooperation never before existed.[18]

According to Baker, it built up "the spirit of international cooperation" and persuaded nations of diverse traditions and interests "to make the necessary individual sacrifices in order to promote the common good of the world."[19] Its practical achievements were "great and notable."[20] At first the Supreme Economic Council submitted its resolutions to the Council of Ten before putting them into effect. However, on March 5 this body ruled, on Arthur Balfour's initiative, that the Economic Council needed no further authorization for implementing its own economic decisions. Thereafter, the two bodies consulted only when an economic question involved some important political matter.

In detailing some of the concrete achievements of the Supreme Economic Council, Baker observes that "the bulk of all this work fell upon the Food Section, of which Hoover was chief."[21] Strangely enough, Hoover has written rather cynically of this organization. Indeed, he almost seems to damn it with slight praise when he observes that "the 'Supreme Economic Council' . . . was of some purpose—at least for letting off steam."[22]

Actually, one gets the distinct impression that Hoover regarded his principal source of power at Paris as deriving from his position as Food Administrator and secondarily as Director General of Relief and Reconstruction of Europe. In these two posts he was not ham-

[18] Ray Stannard Baker, *Woodrow Wilson and World Settlement*, 3 vols. (New York: Doubleday, 1922–1923), vol. 2, p. 335.
[19] Ibid., p. 342.
[20] Ibid.
[21] Ibid., p. 341.
[22] Hoover, *Memoirs*, vol. 1, pp. 298–99, n. 1; cf. Hoover, *Ordeal*, pp. 86–87, which, however, was published seven years after *Memoirs*.

strung by boards or commissions; he was the sole authority under only Wilson and the Big Four. In addition, Hoover was still chairman of the United States Grain Corporation, chairman of the Sugar Equalization Board, head of the committee for all food purchases in the United States, and chairman of the Belgian Relief Commission. His performance in Washington during the war in these various capacities had won worldwide acclaim. More important still, his activities there had brought him into close contact with President Wilson, who soon learned to place the highest possible value on his judgments.[23]

At that time, except for Wilson, Hoover was perhaps the one American most loved and respected by Europeans. Moreover, his practical knowledge of Great Britain and the nations of the Continent was immense. From September 1914 to May 1917 he had lived mostly in Belgium, France, and London while directing the relief of occupied Belgium. During these years he had been allowed to travel behind the German lines even to Berlin, and of necessity he had often spoken with scores of German officials. As Food Administrator after 1917 he had many dealings with the neutral countries as well as with the Allies. Long before the war Hoover had worked as a mining engineer, and because of activities related to this profession he had circled the globe five times.[24] He had lived in such places as Australia, New Zealand, China, India, Canada, Africa, Egypt, Burma, Japan, Italy, the Hawaiian Islands, the Malay States, and Russia.

Wilson knew European culture and its traditions as a scholarly professor. He had often visited England, but he had toured the Continent only once, for some three weeks in September 1903.[25] Thus his practical knowledge of the world and of Russia and western continental Europe—something highly significant to the Peace Conference —was inferior to that of Hoover.[26] Wilson was indeed surrounded

---

[23] Francis William O'Brien, *The Hoover-Wilson Wartime Correspondence: September 24, 1914, to November 11, 1918* (Ames: Iowa State Univ. Press, 1974). Wilson's high esteem for Hoover is revealed in nearly all his letters to the Food Administrator.

[24] For details on these travels, see Hoover, *Memoirs*, vol. 1, pp. 74–78.

[25] O'Brien, *Correspondence*, p. 293. Hoover himself touches on Wilson's knowledge of Europe as contrasted with his own (*Ordeal*, p. 72).

[26] This is not to say that Wilson and his staff came unprepared to the

by a host of learned experts[27]—many of them professors like him-self—but Hoover commanded a staff of some four thousand who seemed to know every European railroad line and city (almost every village street) and to understand clearly how they would be affected by pen strokes of high dignitaries in Paris as they drew new bound-aries for old nations or acted as midwives at the birth of new ones.

It was partly in recognition of Hoover's great reservoir of in-formation that Wilson kept in such close contact with him. During 1917 and 1918 the two had carried on a voluminous correspondence and met at least once each week in Washington.[28] In Paris they con-sulted at least twice weekly, even daily when critical issues were at stake.[29] In addition, Hoover wrote lengthy letters to Wilson on a multitude of weighty problems involving European restoration.

On many other occasions Hoover appeared before the Council of Ten or the Big Four to present special reports. Between 1914 and 1919 he had a number of sessions with Lloyd George.[30] Thus it is evident that Hoover was in the vortex of the many storms that kept Paris in constant agitation during those fateful months of 1919. In addition, Hoover spent much of his time in an office in the Hotel Crillon, the Paris residence of Colonel House, Secretary of State Robert Lansing, and General Tasker Bliss—three of the four persons who, with Wilson, were the official American plenipotentiaries at the Peace Conference. Hoover spoke daily with such highly placed sources.[31] On January 21, Vance McCormick noted in his unpub-lished diary that he had seen Wilson that day and suggested "the importance of his having weekly conferences with his advisers simi-lar to the War Cabinet meetings in Washington. He agreed to start them this week" (typed copy in HPL, p. 32). Indeed, not a few

---

Conference. See Daniel M. Smith, "The Struggle for an Enduring Peace," in *Woodrow Wilson and the Paris Peace Conference*, ed. N. Gordon Levin, Jr., 2d ed. (Lexington, Mass.: Heath, 1972), pp. 7–8.

[27] Lawrence E. Gelfand, *The Inquiry: American Preparations for Peace* (New Haven: Yale Univ. Press, 1963), points out the virtues as well as the many serious shortcomings of Wilson's staff of experts. See pp. 315–33.

[28] O'Brien, *Correspondence*, p. 165.

[29] Hoover, *Ordeal*, p. 90.

[30] Herbert Hoover, *America's First Crusade* (New York: Scribner, 1942), p. 30.

[31] Ibid., p. 31. The fifth plenipotentiary, or commissioner, was Henry White.

writers have suggested that Hoover should have been chosen as a plenipotentiary.[32] But it is also possible that with this obligation he might have found his activities more restricted and his influence actually less than it was as Director General of Relief and Reconstruction.

It is impossible here to give a complete picture of the extraordinary problems faced by Hoover and the skillful organization he built to circumvent or overcome them. Even after Armistice Day there was no real restoration of telegraph and telephone communications between the Allied countries and their former enemies.[33] Hoover prevailed upon Admiral William Benson of the United States Navy to place an American destroyer or cruiser equipped with wireless in every important seaport in Europe. Arrangements were also made to establish wireless offices for Hoover's use in Berlin, Vienna, and other inland cities. When the navy withdrew in February 1919, Hoover asked all the European governments, except the Allies and some neutrals, to assign him two telegraph circuits. General Pershing then furnished army operators from the Army Signal Service, which managed the whole operation. One major obstacle was France, which insisted that Hoover's communications must travel from Paris to the frontier through the regular French censorship system. This would have made the transmission of messages slower than if sent by mail. Pershing solved the problem by having his own men build a line connecting Hoover's Paris office with his French headquarters, which had its own line direct to Cologne in Germany. From Cologne, Hoover was thus connected with all his continental circuits.

The problem of getting all the necessary passports to cross the borders of some twenty-seven nations could have been another intolerable burden.[34] Hoover prevailed upon all these governments—Britain and France excepted—to allow him to sign passports for his staff, thus freeing them from the need for visas and relieving them of the insufferable delays from searches at every frontier.

Countless other problems were far less amenable to Hoover's persuasive supplication or to his skillful engineering. When hostilities ceased on November 11, 1918, the railway system of Europe was

[32] See, for instance, Bailey, *Lost Peace*, p. 91. See also n. 42 below.
[33] Hoover, *Memoirs*, vol. 1, pp. 306–8.
[34] Ibid., pp. 308–9.

in shambles. Many cars and locomotives had been completely destroyed; others were badly damaged. Hoover possessed no magic wand to call new ones into being and no powers to restore rolling stock rendered completely useless during the war.

Adding to these problems was the fact that new boundaries were being drawn daily and new countries being brought into existence. Previously, the old Austrian, German, and Russian empires had consolidated government-owned railroads that served central Europe well.[35] Now each new nation jealously guarded its own railway system and placed barriers against the flow of foreign commerce over its lines. The free flow of raw materials and finished products via great inland waterways like the Danube suffered in a similar manner from the knives of the diplomats who were cutting central Europe into several parts.

One reason Wilson stayed in Washington for three weeks after the Armistice was signed was his desire to present the annual State of the Union Message to Congress at the opening of its new session on December 2, 1918. However, this could have been dispensed with in favor of a written message. As a matter of fact, from the time of Jefferson's presidency in 1801 this had been the unbroken custom; it was only in 1913 that Wilson had revived the earlier tradition of Presidents Washington and Adams. Thus, not until December 4 was Wilson able to sail for Europe, reaching Paris on December 14. Two days later he had an interview with Hoover who painted a picture of Europe in darkest terms. The President, however, was filled with a great hope that the spirit of the prostrate peoples would soon be restored, and thus he was somewhat unimpressed by Hoover's grim portrayal.[36] Wilson's hopes rose even higher in the next three weeks during his trips throughout France, England, and Italy where he was welcomed with boundless enthusiasm.

The first meeting of the Council of Ten took place on January 12, 1919, but the first plenary session was not held until January 18. Possibly Wilson could have speeded up the opening of the Peace Conference and thus prevented a number of untoward developments throughout war-weary Europe in the two months immediately after

[35] Hoover, *First Crusade*, p. 29; Hoover, *Ordeal*, p. 68.
[36] Hoover, *Ordeal*, p. 68.

the Armstice. Clemenceau was president of the Council of Ten; and when Wilson gave his address on January 18, he proposed the French prime minister as permanent chairman of the Conference. "The Tiger" was thus in a position to control the machinery of the peace congress. His native instinct was to pursue a severe policy toward Germany. Moreover, his own Chamber of Deputies had given him a vote of confidence based solely on an assurance that the pursuit of such a policy would be relentless.

On December 14, 1918, Lloyd George's coalition government had been returned to power in a general election, and during the tough campaign the prime minister had pledged that he too would demand a victor's terms from a vanquished foe. Wilson, on the other hand, had suffered a personal and a party defeat in November 1918 following his intervention in the midterm elections. This put him at a distinct disadvantage vis-à-vis his two peers at Paris.

In the meantime, the existence of a number of secret treaties involving France, Britain, Russia, Rumania, Italy, and Germany had come to light. These treaties had been consummated between 1915 and 1917 and envisaged the carving up of Europe and the transfer of colonies in a manner wholly inconsistent with principles enunciated in Wilson's Fourteen Points of January 1918 and in the several additions he made in four subsequent addresses of the same year. This is not the place to enter into the debate over whether Wilson had previous knowledge of the existence of these treaties. Even if he had known of them, it is indeed possible to argue that he believed the "27 points" had abrogated most such agreements. That the Allies and the Central Powers had accepted these points as the basis for the Armistice and the peace treaty seems beyond dispute.

It was perhaps possible to view the "27 points" merely as general principles capable of a variety of interpretations. However, it is not expedient to discuss here all these "points" and their several possible interpretations. Suffice it to say that Wilson's three major Paris colleagues had no intention of implementing them in a manner consistent with the mind of their drafter.

In the beginning, the Council of Ten was the supreme source of authority. But, although the Council held 72 sessions, it soon became evident that most grave issues were too difficult and delicate for expeditious handling by this body. Thereupon Wilson, Lloyd George,

Clemenceau, and Orlando withdrew and began to meet by themselves. Thus by March 14 the Peace Conference was in the hands of the Big Four. They held 149 sessions—many purely personal and informal—with no more than an interpreter and a secretary to assist them. The old Council continued to function, but with greatly diminished prestige, as did the Council of Five—the foreign ministers of Britain, France, Italy, Japan, and the United States.

Perhaps there was an excessive number of commissions and sessions (some 1,643 in all). But many of them performed most meritorious services for the Conference by the special studies they conducted—many on the spot. The resulting reports—accepted verbatim and without change—make up the bulk of the treaty. The commissions on territorial questions, reparations, international legislation on labor, and preparing a charter for the League of Nations were particularly important.

Wilson was named chairman of the commission on the League of Nations, which the Council of Ten established in late January 1919. The President labored with extraordinary devotion—generally after his other daily work on the Council and often late at night—and on February 14 he was able to submit a draft of the Covenant of the League to a plenary conference. Wilson was adamant on two general issues: first, the League must be an integral part of the treaty itself; second, the League was to be an alliance of all nations, victors and vanquished alike, relying upon the cooperation of sovereign states and the opinion of mankind for its effectiveness. Clemenceau, on the contrary, envisaged the League to be a mere alliance of victors supported by a large international army and organized to guarantee the domination of the Continent by France.

Wilson was successful in winning support for a League constructed almost exactly as he desired. He scored an additional triumph by getting the Covenant of the League firmly embedded in the peace treaty itself. But to gain these goals, he was forced to make a number of consequential concessions to members of the Big Four. Thus the treaty—and Wilson personally—became targets for many embittered critics who felt that the rights of their countries had been denied.

Wilson sailed from France for the United States on February 14, 1919. As chief executive, duties of a domestic nature begged for his attention. Bills had to be signed, and in addition, his fellow citizens were eager to hear a first-hand report on the state of affairs in the French capital. The President experienced considerable chagrin to learn that a great many of his fellow citizens were puzzled by the sluggish pace of the Paris peacemakers. More, including some high and mighty, were disquieted by certain features of the Covenant of the League. The complaints of such critics were still ringing in his ears when he arrived back in Paris on March 14.

In his absence the defenders of the "old order" had attempted to undo much that he had previously accomplished. Wilson acted with dispatch to restore his painfully acquired gains.[37] This was a task demanding herculean effort, for the European diplomats had so distorted the text and the spirit of the Fourteen Points that they bore little resemblance to those conceived by Wilson. On April 3 Wilson fell seriously ill; and on April 7, his patience at an end, he ordered the *George Washington* readied to take him back to the United States. This bold and dramatic gesture had a sobering effect on the whole conference. Clemenceau's posturing and obdurate spirit became somewhat more relaxed.

The correspondence between Hoover and Wilson reveals their mutual concern and agreement on remedies for many serious problems. Weeks before either had reached Paris, the Allies had proposed a continuation of the wartime pool of Allied food. Hoover and Wilson immediately uttered a vigorous "no." They both deplored the continued imposition of the blockade by the Allies. They both firmly resisted the refusal of France and Great Britain to provide food for the German people. They both opposed the tenets of Bolshevism and viewed with great alarm its spread into central European countries.

The two men also entertained similar misgivings about the use of arms to stem the Communist threat. Hoover and Wilson believed it would be far more desirable to supply the affected countries with food and clothing and to make other visible manifestations of support to their embryonic democratic governments. Thus the Allies might shore up the sinking morale of a dispirited and famished people and leave them less vulnerable to the blandishments of the Bol-

[37] Baker, *World Settlement*, vol. 2, pp. 25–26.

sheviks. It was vital, Wilson and Hoover thought, that the former enemies be permitted to become productive once more and thereby capable of commerce with other nations. For this to be possible, the victors could not drain the vanquished nations of the means of production or demand intolerable reparations. Nor could the Central Powers be so dismembered that their industrial capacity would be virtually destroyed.

On the latter point, Hoover and Wilson were in general agreement, although the President did ultimately compromise on the Saar and the Rhineland. Moreover, the Wilson principle of self-determination helped fuel the flames of extreme nationalism in many ethnic groups who demanded some rather bizarre boundaries, thus creating several independent countries deemed by Hoover to be economically nonviable.

As to German reparations, Wilson in Hoover's opinion yielded far too much to the unrelenting insistence of the Allies, especially the French. This resulted in imposition of a burden that was self-defeating: it destroyed German capacity to repay even a reasonable sum and it prepared an embittered people ultimately to accept Hitler with his promise of redress of grievances.

The idea of mandates has been called by some a great Wilson victory because, so they state, it eventually resulted in the end of colonialism.[38] Hoover, however, thought the President was "just fooled" and that the mandate system simply dispensed great colonial wealth to the benefit of the victorious powers.[39] In any event, if mandates were to be awarded and other trophies of war distributed to the victors, the highly practical Hoover thought Wilson himself should have picked up a share of the spoils so dearly earned by the war effort of the American people and then used them as bargaining items to win from the Allies a few concessions to his own views on the peace treaty.[40] But apparently Wilson's Calvinist conscience could countenance no such horse trading.

The treaty was signed on June 28, 1919, in the Hall of Mirrors

[38] Arthur S. Link, *Wilson the Diplomatist: A Look at His Major Foreign Policies* (Baltimore: Johns Hopkins Univ. Press, 1957), p. 113; Manley O. Hudson in House and Seymour, *What Happened*, pp. 228–30; Bailey, *Lost Peace*, p. 172.
[39] Hoover, *Ordeal*, p. 225.
[40] Hoover, *Memoirs*, vol. 1, p. 451.

at Versailles.[41] Both Wilson and Hoover entertained similar misgivings about much contained in that heavy document, though Hoover's disappointment was deeper and more pervasive. Shortly thereafter, on June 28, the President left Paris for Brest and the United States where he engaged in gallant but ineffectual battle with the Senate over ratification of the treaty and the League. Hoover remained in Europe for another eight weeks. His correspondence with the President continued on many matters of importance. But the letters soon grew fewer in number until they ceased entirely several months before the election of 1920.

The account given here is merely a sketch of the relations between Hoover and Wilson during the post-Armistice period. However, the description of such things as the organization of the Paris Conference is sufficient to guide the reader through the letters and the introductory notes. The footnotes will put the reader in contact with primary documents and works by many gifted scholars and writers who treat in detail the interesting and consequential drama that began in November 1918 and reached its denouement in November two years later.

A final precautionary note should be added. These few pages merely touch upon affairs that have provided material for hundreds of tomes by highly qualified authors. Controversy has characterized much of the writings, for the Paris Peace Conference dealt with thousands of explosive and controversial questions. In addition, both Hoover and Wilson were among the most controversial figures in the French capital.

This book—certainly this Introduction—is not meant to be a history of the Peace Conference. The purpose is to present the correspondence of two men who played leading roles in Paris while attempting to bring peace and order to Europe after World War I.[42]

[41] Actually, a total of five treaties with the Central Powers was drafted at Paris in 1919–1920.

[42] Although Hoover was not one of the five plenipotentiaries, or commissioners, who headed the American delegation to the Paris Peace Conference, his contribution to the work there was most consequential. Indeed, many knowledgeable persons then judged that he should have been chosen (Edward House, Diary MSS, Dec. 3, 1918, Yale University, as quoted in Gelfand, *Inquiry*, p. 159, n. 7).

But scholars as well as the average reader interested in this titanic enterprise should find it a service to have available one single volume containing every known letter included in the Hoover-Wilson correspondence related to the Conference.

Readers will undoubtedly be impressed by the bulk of the Hoover side of the exchange and the number of subjects his letters cover, as indeed his contemporaries were greatly impressed. Bernard Baruch remarked that "to Hoover's brain, facts are water to a sponge," while some years later Hoover's Secretary of State, Henry L. Stimson, observed that "he has the greatest capacity for assimilating and organizing material of any man I ever knew."[43]

The frequency with which Hoover's presentations won the approval of President Wilson should be especially noted. Indeed, often he simply wrote on the bottom of a Hoover letter the words "Approved Woodrow Wilson." Only rarely did he reject outright any Hoover proposal. The President's stand on many consequential matters seems attributable largely to arguments advanced by Hoover. These include the proposal for an inter-Allied food pool; the establishment of the President's Committee of Economic Advisers; the establishment of the American Relief Administration for Europe; the American position relative to the Bolshevik government in Russia; the use of food to fight Communism; the stand against the French attempts to sever Bavaria from Germany; the Nansen food mission to Russia; and the recognition of Finland. In addition, Wilson's judgment was influenced by Hoover on important matters affecting the blockade in general, Poland, the Baltic countries, Trieste, and Danzig.

Hoover did fail to move the President on at least two matters that have had the most profound consequences for the entire world. In spite of vigorous last-minute appeals in June of 1919, he was unable to convince Wilson to join with the British to attempt a revision in the treaty of the extremely harsh terms to be imposed on Germany. His efforts were likewise abortive when in November he pleaded with Wilson to accept some of the amendments of the res-

---

[43] Quoted in Louis W. Koenig, *The Chief Executive*, rev. ed. (New York: Harcourt, Brace & World, 1968), p. 367.

ervationists in order to win Senate approval for American participation in the League of Nations.

These observations must surely prompt readers to speculate on the outcome at Paris if Wilson had stayed in Washington and Hoover had been one of the American plenipotentiaries at the Peace Conference. Even at the time many men close to the President judged that his decision to attend the Conference was a serious mistake. Critics likewise thought that the four who accompanied him were by no means the most suitable men available for the delicate tasks of treaty making.

One might even question Wilson's credentials for negotiating peace terms that were to have such worldwide repercussions since his only personal contact with continental Europe had come from a three-week tourist trip in 1903. Arthur Link, the foremost Wilson biographer, has observed that in *Congressional Government*, published in 1885, Wilson made only a passing reference to foreign affairs, while his 1889 book, *The State*, devotes only a page and a half to international law out of more than one hundred pages on law and legal institutions.[44] Link also quotes Wilson as he stood on the threshold of the presidency as saying, "It would be an irony of fate if my administration had to deal with foreign affairs."[45]

One contemporary who thought Wilson should have chosen Hoover as a plenipotentiary was House, who wrote thus:

> I wish to my soul the President had appointed me as Chairman of the Peace Conference with McAdoo and Hoover as my associates. I could have attended to the political end, McAdoo to the financial end, and Hoover to the economic end. . . . If I could have had these two men as associates and only these, I would have been willing to guarantee results.[46]

John Maynard Keynes, distinguished economist and British delegate at the peace conference, has lamented in these words:

> Hoover was the only man who emerged from the ordeal of Paris with an enhanced reputation. . . . [H]e imported into the Councils of Paris, when he took part in them, precisely that atmosphere of re-

[44] Link, *Diplomatist*, p. 4.
[45] Ibid., p. 5.
[46] House, Diary, Dec. 3, 1918.

ality, knowledge, magnanimity, and disinterestedness which, if they had been found in other quarters also, would have given us the Good Peace.[47]

Some respected scholars deny that Wilson failed or that his training and interests left him unqualified in foreign affairs. These supporters affirm that, given the spirit prevailing in Paris and the temper of his counterparts at the Conference, he succeeded at least as well as any other American negotiator might have. Perhaps this is correct. And insofar as there were failures, they can surely be related partially to Wilson's weakened physical condition, especially in the critical weeks of April and May. Wilson had a disciplined mind and was capable of intense concentration; but he required relaxation, distraction, and physical exercise. One is surprised at the time given to golf, the theatre, and motor outings with his wife during his first five years in Washington. No such pleasures were his while in Paris, and his illnesses in the French capital—some say a stroke—were undoubtedly attributable to the accumulation of tensions for which there was no refreshing release.

Hoover, on the other hand, was a prodigious worker who apparently needed neither regular exercise nor mental distractions. He was also doggedly determined whenever he strove to achieve his objectives. And as the Hoover-Wilson correspondence reveals, he could marshall masses of detailed information to reinforce his positions. Thus, if Hoover had been one of the principal negotiators at the Peace Conference, it is interesting to conjecture about the outcome of his encounters with the skilled European diplomats.

However, there are limits to such sterile speculation. Perhaps readers are better advised to address themselves immediately to the Hoover-Wilson correspondence with the expectation of viewing two distinguished Americans in the pursuit of establishing a new order of justice after a cataclysmic world conflict.

But it would perhaps be wise to tarry a moment longer within this Introduction in order to anticipate questions which thoughtful writers will surely pose by the time they have concluded reading this collection of letters.

[47] Quoted in Eugene Lyons, *Herbert Hoover: A Biography*, 2d. ed. (Garden City, N.Y.: Doubleday, 1964), p. 118.

This book, of course, concerns itself almost exclusively with the Hoover-Wilson relationship as that relationship is revealed in their exchange of letters. But many readers will understandably be prompted to ask questions touching on the relationship which these two Americans established with such history-making Europeans as Clemenceau, Lloyd George, and Orlando.

At the outset it must be frankly confessed that the Hoover-Wilson correspondence will be perused in vain for anything more than a faint hint of an answer to questions of this nature. But without going too far afield, readers can learn something relative to this subject from sources other than the Hoover-Wilson letters.

Prior to the Paris Peace Conference, Hoover, first as head of the Commission for Belgium Relief and later on as United States Food Administrator, had already come into close contact with David Lloyd George. Forty years later, in his *Memoirs*, Hoover wrote thus of the British leader:

> I had scores of sessions with David Lloyd George extending from 1915 to 1919. His official and unofficial character has been amply discussed and will no doubt continue to be discussed by historians. I may say at once that he gave great weight to my views at all times on matters in which I was concerned. He had a quick, adroit mind and was instinctively sympathetic to human suffering. He had full moral courage and a driving physical energy. He was possessed of great administrative ability. He was a man of great oratorical powers, a magnificent leader of the mob. Instinctively he adopted any cause that led up the political ladder of the day. When the interest of Britain was at stake the end always justified the means. He was as nimble as the pea in a shell-game. His major principle was expediency. He had two fine qualities in that he was not personally malicious or vindictive.
>
> President Wilson's passionate devotion to truth in international relations made him an easy prey for such adroitness. Lloyd George had the delicate job of modifying the twenty-five points and establishing the secret treaties and the harvesting of the victory. And making it all look nice and idealistic to Mr. Wilson.[48]

When Hoover was about to leave Paris, Lloyd George sent him the following message:

> At the moment when you are relinquishing your official duties to

[48] *Memoirs*, vol. 2, p. 449.

return to the United States I wish to express to you on behalf of the British Government their warm thanks and their great appreciation of the work you have done for the Allied and Associated Powers. The ability and energy which you have shown in directing the economic relief of the population stricken by . . . [famine] has been of inestimable value. They have earned for you the lasting gratitude of the people of Europe.[49]

On the other hand, Lloyd George's own memoirs carry several adverse remarks about Hoover. In the passage below he is recounting the persistence with which Hoover and House pressed their demands that the Allies supply Germany with food.

> Mr. Hoover, who organised the distribution, seemed to have ruffled French susceptibilities by his manner of extracting money from them. He had a surliness of mien and a peremptoriness of speech which provoked a negative answer to any request he made. He did not mean it. But how were foreigners to know that? The French are a humane people with generous instincts, but they were in a mood of natural exasperation when they saw the ruin which had been wrought in their finest provinces and when they contemplated the sorrow brought to myriads of their homes. It needed tact to handle any appeal for help to those who had been the perpetrators of all this misery. Mr. Hoover has many great qualities, but tact is not one of them.[50]

The above, plus other less direct remarks, must lead one to conclude that Hoover and Lloyd George did not like one another—much as they might have recognized each other's extraordinary talents. But there appears to have been a much better rapprochement between Hoover and the cynical and sharp-tongued Clemenceau. This may seem strange because on many occasions in 1919 Hoover was compelled to break a lance with the French leader during controversies over peace settlements with the Central Powers. Four decades later, as Hoover reflected upon that highly charged period, he wrote thus: "at the Peace Conference, that fierce old tiger . . . demanded every device for dismembering Germany in order to keep a reunited Germany from attacking France again."[51] But in the same

[49] Hoover, *Epic*, vol. 3, p. 227 (1961).
[50] David Lloyd George, *Memoirs of the Peace Conference*, 2 vols. (New Haven: Yale Univ. Press, 1939), vol. 1, p. 199.
[51] Hoover, *Epic*, vol. 3, p. 89.

work Hoover observed that "Clemenceau was absolutely unfailing in his support of the C.R.B. [Commission for the Relief of Belgium], even during the low part of France during the war."[52] Again, when Hoover was pressing for the recognition of a free and independent Finland, Wilson suggested that he "discuss the matter with Premier Clemenceau."[53] Hoover puts this gloss on the ensuing interview: "As always with me, the Premier was most considerate. He agreed with my proposals and at once instructed the French Minister of Foreign Affairs accordingly."[54]

In the same work Hoover seems actually to be indulging in some rather fond recollection of a respected friend when he wrote that "my last call before leaving France was upon Premier Clemenceau to express my appreciation for his undeviating support."[55] But in his *Memoirs*, Hoover gives this long and rather sober appraisal of "the old Tiger":

> Clemenceau was the most utterly realistic, blunt statesman at the Peace Table. His soul contained to his dying day all the bitterness of the sufferings of the French people. The widows, orphans, and ruined homes of France were the lenses he looked through. To him the turn of Germany to democracy was a fraud; the only way to deal with Germans was to make them impotent forever. As the sole victor in the war he would have taken Carthage as the only adequate historic precedent for action. He treated the "New Order" and the twenty-five points as a joke on history. His essential creed as far as he may have had one was that force always triumphed over abstract justice. He in fact believed that the strong ought to direct the weak. He had no belief that right would prevail without plenty of force. Personally he had a fine sense of humor, a biting wit and little regard for the feelings of other men. The consideration with which he treated me at all times, however, leaves only a grateful memory of this rugged son of France. He never did understand Mr. Wilson. I don't think he tried to.[56]

Gallons of ink have been utilized by writers describing the Wilson–Clemenceau–Lloyd George relationship. In his 1958 *The Or-*

[52] Ibid., vol. 1, p. 46.
[53] Ibid., vol. 3, p. 35.
[54] Ibid.
[55] Ibid., vol. 3, p. 232.
[56] Hoover, *Memoirs*, vol. 2, p. 449.

deal of Woodrow Wilson, Hoover quotes these pungent words of
the British Prime Minister:

> He [Wilson] was the most extraordinary compound I have ever
> encountered of the noble visionary, the implacable and unscrupulous
> partisan, the exalted idealist and the man of rather petty personal
> rancours.[57]

In 1963 Lord Beaverbrook wrote thus of Clemenceau:

> [Clemenceau] reserved his savage criticism for Wilson, who he
> said, talked like Jesus and acted like Lloyd George. When Wilson
> was speaking Clemenceau pretended to be asleep. Wilson accused
> him and Clemenceau replied: And it would have been better for the
> Peace Conference had you slept instead of talking.[58]

President Wilson, for his part, undoubtedly expressed his opinion of the French Premier to a host of people, but it is not the purpose of this book to conduct the poll necessary to record such an
opinion. But in the research for the present volume, this author discovered that on one occasion, May 15, 1919, Wilson remarked to
Hoover, Bernard Baruch, Vance McCormick, and Norman Davis that
his European counterparts were "mad men, particularly Clemenceau."[59]

It would be interesting to explore the mind of Clemenceau as he
formed his opinion of Hoover. He put little in writing. But in 1930
he recalled simply "the stiffness of the man whose nerves are at the
end of their tether."[60]

Did Hoover ever realize what Clemenceau and Lloyd George
had written about him? It would be difficult to say. But in his 1961
Epic, he recalls "vivid memories . . . of Lloyd George—adroit, yet
gentle to suffering; Clemenceau 'the old Tiger,' . . . always considerate of me and our work."[61]

Orlando was a relatively minor figure in comparison with Clem-

[57] Hoover, *Ordeal,* p. 254, quoting from Lloyd George's, *The Truth about the Peace Treaties.*

[58] Lord Beaverbrook, *The Decline and Fall of Lloyd George* (New York:
Duell, Sloan and Pearce, 1963), pp. 143–44.

[59] Vance C. McCormick, Diary, 1919 (typewritten MS, HPL).

[60] Georges Clemenceau, *Grandeur and Misery of Victory* (New York: Harcourt, Brace and Co., 1930), p. 149.

[61] Hoover, *Epic,* vol. 3, p. 536.

enceau or Lloyd George. Thus neither Hoover nor Wilson had as many confrontations with him as they had with the French or the British leader. In his *Memoirs*, Hoover observes that "Orlando was a polished gentleman with just one mission," which was to secure all that France and Great Britain had promised to Italy in the secret Treaty of London of 1915.[62] Wilson was "greatly outraged" when he learned of these promises, and thus, to quote Hoover once again, Orlando "was at times a difficult member of the Supreme Council."[63] This appears somewhat of an understatement in view of Hoover's and Wilson's sharp controversies with Italy over such things as the control and ultimate disposition of Trieste and Fiume.

But more than enough space has already been given to this subsidiary question of the relationship of Hoover and Wilson with the principal European leaders at the Peace Conference. It is now time to release readers from further pursuit of this subject and to direct them immediately to the Hoover-Wilson post-Armistice correspondence itself.[64]

[62] Hoover, *Memoirs*, vol. 2, p. 450.
[63] Ibid.
[64] In the following pages the phrases "allied governments" and "associated governments" appear interchangeably. President Wilson preferred the latter when the phrase was intended to include the United States.

Letters

WITH INTRODUCTORY COMMENTARIES

1918

Hoover Objection to Food Pool

In mid-October 1918, nearly a month before the Armistice, the British, French, and Italian governments had presented the United States with their agreement whereby after the war ended the Allies were to pool all credit, food, raw materials, ships, and coal for a period of years. The organization, based in London, would operate by majority rule. The United States would have only one vote but would be the major contributor.

On October 24 Hoover wrote to Wilson that he opposed such a pooling of resources after hostilities had ceased. He also cabled Joseph P. Cotton, the Food Administration's representative in Europe, that he should abstain from any action that might even appear to commit the United States to such a plan. But the representative in London was of a different mind and he revealed his views in two cables he sent to Hoover on November 7. In one Cotton expressed himself in favor of American participation in the inter-Allied food pool. In another he urged that Hoover promptly communicate his ideas on the postwar feeding of the people on the Continent and not wait until his arrival in Europe before disclosing his plans.

Hoover was with Wilson at the White House at 2:30 on Wednesday, November 13. Possibly the two discussed the contents of these cables on that occasion. In any event, on November 14 Hoover sent the President a short note in which he wrote, "I enclose herewith copy of the cablegram which I have dispatched to Mr. Cotton in accordance with your suggestion." In this cable of November 13, Hoover reaffirmed his opposition to the pool plan and restated his position that any decision involving American food or credit must wait upon his arrival in Europe. Two days later he departed for Europe accompanied by Robert Taft, Lewis Strauss, Alonzo Taylor, and Julius Barnes (*Organization*, p. 41). He arrived in London on November 24 and left for Paris on November 25.

The following letter of November 11 is a clear statement of Hoover's mind on this subject. That he had the firm backing of Wilson on the matter is evident from an earlier letter to Secretary of State Robert Lansing in which Hoover advised Lansing that no arrangements for handling food for liberated people should be made until he had arrived in Europe. On November 7 Wilson wrote to Lansing thus: "I think the suggestions of Mr. Hoover . . . should be complied with, and I would be glad if you would convey our attitude in this matter to House" (*Life and Letters*, vol. 8, p. 572).

Washington, 11 November, 1918

Dear Mr. President:

I enclose herewith two cables which I would be grateful if you could find time to peruse.

The first, with regard to our entering into a joint inter-Allied pool for the purpose of distributing all of the world's wheat until the middle of 1920, fills me with complete horror. Of all the import wheat in the world, seventy per cent must come from the Western Hemisphere and I assume that we would be called upon to finance it and to place the distribution of it in the hands of a body that we could not control.

I can see no objective in such a plan as I believe there is sufficient wheat for the world to get through with, unless it is the intention to use this control of the prime necessity of life to dominate other measures in the world.

As to the second telegram on the subject of arrangements which the English may set up in London for provisioning the world with our foodstuffs and on our credit, I have a similar reaction.

Both of these telegrams bring me to express to you the urgency of a definition of our principles in these matters, to be conveyed to the Allied governments in order that I and the other agents of the government in Europe may be able to act in entire unison with your own views.

If I might make a suggestion in this direction, it would be on the line that we consider ourselves as trustees of our surplus production of all kinds for the benefit of the most necessitous and the most deserving. We feel that we must ourselves execute this trusteeship; that we are not unmindful of the obligation which we have to the sustenance of those who have fought with us against Germany and that, together with the necessities of those populations released from the German yoke, we feel that they may well deserve a priority in our distribution. On the other hand, we cannot undertake any co-operative arrangements that look to the control of our exports after peace and furthermore—and equally important—that the inter-Allied councils hitherto set up in Europe were entirely for the purpose of guiding inter-Allied relations during the period of the war and that any extension of their functions either by way of their control of our relations to other nations or the extension of their present functions beyond peace, cannot be entertained by us; that all relationship involving the use of American food or credit for the people of other nations than the Allies themselves, must await Mr. Hoover's arrival in Europe, so far as any such supplies or interest of the United States is concerned.

I believe that the settlement of this question requires some specific statement from you.

Yours faithfully,
Herbert Hoover

Relief for Formerly Occupied Countries

This memorandum contains many plans already agreed upon by Hoover and Wilson. At an October meeting of the War Council, or "war cabinet," it was settled that Hoover would proceed immediately to Europe to organize the relief and restoration of Europe. On November 7 Wilson had given Hoover complete authorization to control the rehabilitation of Belgium. Paragraph 6 in the memorandum is simply a restatement of the firm resolve of the two that American representatives in Europe were to await Hoover's arrival and to take no action themselves as to the distribution of American food.

Washington, 12 November 1918.

Dear Mr. President:

Please find enclosed herewith a memorandum agreed this morning between Mr. Baker, Mr. Hurley and myself.

I should be glad to know if it meets with your approval.

Yours faithfully,
Herbert Hoover

Enclosure

12-November-1918

MEMORANDUM OF ARRANGEMENTS WITH REGARD TO
PROVISIONING THE POPULATIONS WHICH
ARE NOW OR HAVE BEEN UNDER THE
DOMINATION OF THE CENTRAL EMPIRES

1. Mr. Hoover, as United States Food Administrator will proceed at once to Europe to determine what action is required from the United States and what extensions of the Food Administration organization or otherwise are necessary in order to carry out the work of the participation of the United States Government in this matter, and to take such steps as are necessary in temporary relief.

2. In order to expedite the movement of foodstuffs towards Europe, the War Department will undertake to purchase in the usual co-ordination through the Food Administration during the next twenty days, 120,000 tons of flour and from 30,000,000 to 40,000,000 pounds of pork products. These foodstuffs to be shipped by the diversion of Army tonnage at the earliest possible moment that the Shipping Board arranges and to be consigned to French ports for re-consignment or storage.

3. This foodstuff and any other suitable surplus supplies of the Quartermaster in Europe to be made available for distribution at Mr. Hoover's direction, it being understood that if it proves infeasiable [*sic*] to re-ship or re-direct the steamers to the territories lately held by the Central Empires, Mr. Hoover will make arrangements for the re-sale of the foodstuffs to the Allied governments or, alternatively, to the Belgian Relief.

4. In order to facilitate administration in Washington, Mr. Hoover will set up a preliminary committee to assist the Food Administration, comprising

Mr. Theodore Whitmarsh, of the Food Administration, who will act as Chairman in Mr. Hoover's absence.
Mr. F. S. Snyder, of the Meat Division of the Food Administration.
Mr. Julius H. Barnes, of the Cereal Division of the Food Administration.

General R. E. Wood, Quartermaster General, representing the War
Department.

Mr. John Beaver White, representing the War Trade Board.

Mr. Prentiss N. Gray, representing the Shipping Board.

These gentlemen to take in hand the general directions of these operations through the various government agencies concerned.

5. The War Department is to purchase, inspect, pay for, load and
ship these foodstuffs in the usual manner of transmission of Quartermaster's supplies and upon transfer from the Quartermaster's Department in Europe they are to be paid for by the buyer.

6. The American representatives in Europe are to be at once instructed by cable that the whole of the matter of the American food
supplies and the establishment of a more permanent organization
are to be settled by Mr. Hoover on his arrival in Europe and that
the United States will take no participation in any arrangements
made pending that time.

APPROVED

WOODROW WILSON

Authorizing Rickard to Act for Hoover

> The executive order mentioned here was signed on November 16
> and sent to the State Department on November 18.

Washington, 13 November 1918

Dear Mr. President:

On the occasion of my absence in Europe last summer, you delegated the authority to Mr. Edgar Rickard to act in my stead, and I
assume that you will approve the same arrangement at this date. I
am enclosing an Executive Order drawn up in the same form as the
one that you signed in July, which will cover the existing situation.

Yours faithfully,

Herbert Hoover

Cable on Inter-Allied Food Pool

Washington, 14-November-1918

Dear Mr. President:

I enclose herewith copy of the cablegram which I have dispatched to Mr. Cotton in accordance with your suggestion.

Faithfully yours,
Herbert Hoover

Cablegram

With regard to various telegrams yourself and Cravath on Relief to areas lately under German control on further consultation with President he authorized the following further statement to be made to our officials in Europe for their guidance but not for communication and asks that a copy should be sent to Colonel House and Cravath—statement begins—we consider ourselves as trustees of our surplus production of all kinds for the benefit of the most necessitous and the most deserving. We feel that we must ourselves execute this trusteeship, that we are not unmindful of the obligation which we have to the sustenance of those who have fought with us against Germany and that together with the necessities of those populations released from the German yoke we feel that they may well deserve a priority in our distribution. On the other hand we cannot undertake any cooperative arrangements that look to the control of our exports after peace and furthermore and equally important that the interallied councils hitherto set up in Europe were entirely for the purpose of guiding interallied relations during the period of the war and that any extension of their functions either by way of their control of our relations to other nations or the extension of their present functions beyond peace cannot be entertained by us. All relationship involving the use of American food or credit for the people of other nations than the Allies themselves must await Mr. Hoover's arrival in Europe so far as any such supplies or interest of the United States is concerned in which we will coordinate in every proper way (end of statement). You can inform Sir Worthington Evans that the form of organization involving coordination of the United States Government for distributing its food commodities arising in the

United States through the various parts of Europe lately under German subjection can only be settled upon my arrival that the United States Food Administration is taking steps to at once largely increase the volume of American food stores at various points in Europe in order that the material may be available for earliest possible action after my arrival and that we have every desire for proper coordination of all efforts.

Herbert Hoover

Need of Ships for European Relief

Washington, 14 November 1918

Dear Mr. President:

The general food situation in Europe looms more strongly hour by hour through the various reports and telegrams that we are receiving.

In accordance with the arrangements made with your approval, the War Department is to give us shipping for 140,000 or 150,000 tons at once which foodstuffs they will advance to carry into French stocks or southern European ports for re-distribution on methods that may be determined on my arrival.

In addition to this, and in view of the serious situation in Northern Europe, I am—in accordance with our discussions of yesterday —instructing the Grain Corporation to purchase and ship to English ports for re-direction, another 125,000 to 140,000 tons of food to be used, probably in Northern Europe. We can finance this through the Grain Corporation up to the point of sale.

The ability to perform the measure will depend of course on our ability to secure the shipping. Mr. Hurley is making arrangements to divert to us if possible some boats outside of the Army programme but if this should fail I am anxious that the Army should make other sacrifices of its munitions programme to enable this to be carried out at once. I am confident that if we can have started to Europe 350,000 to 400,000 tons of food for these special purposes within the next ten or fifteen days and I can inform the various governments—especially some of the Northern Neutrals—of positive arrivals that will be placed at their disposal, it would enable them to increase rations from their present stocks and probably keep their boats from rocking.

I have had an opportunity this morning to discuss with a group of Senators the question of the provision of an appropriation for working capital to cover these operations. Some of them, especially Senators Pittman and Kellogg, are prepared to place themselves at your disposal, to forward any appropriation for this purpose. On the other hand, I find that amongst some of them bitterness is so great that they would raise strong opposition to raising an appropriation that they thought might be used for feeding Germany. I do believe that appropriation of a revolving fund could be obtained for providing food to the liberated peoples and neutrals and that it might be well to limit this legislation to these purposes: because through such agencies as the Army and the Grain Corporation, with perhaps your Presidential fund, we could probably manage to handle the German problem in itself.

While it should be clear in such appropriation that it is not a gift, but to provide a revolving fund to enable us to carry on relief commerce, it should have a special provision that the foodstuffs may be used for philanthropic purposes if necessary, for the populations of Belgium and Serbia.

Yours faithfully,
Herbert Hoover

Objections to Shipping Plans

Washington, 14 November 1918.

Dear Mr. President:

I have, unfortunately, to lay before you at the last moment one of these awkward priorities. I supposed we were all in agreement that shipping should at once be diverted from the transportation of Army engineering supplies to Europe and devoted to food. Secretary Baker and I were in complete agreement in this matter but the General Staff does not think it is justified in accepting the responsibility for altering their shipping programme until notified by General Pershing. The consequence is that the shipping authorities are handling large quantities of engineering materials to France instead of food supplies, which I believe are more vital now in order to get peace than the munitions of the armies.

This is one of these differences in view in which there is no question of the desire of both interests to do the utmost service, but it appears to me that it will require a decision and direction by yourself.

Faithfully yours,
Herbert Hoover

Appeal to Women on Food

Washington, November 15th, 1918.

Dear Mr. President:

In a message of 1917, you made a statement which has lived in the United States and which has had most unusual and beneficial results. It was as follows:—

> Every housewife who practices strict economy has put herself in the ranks of those who serve the nation. This is the time for America to correct her unpardonable fault of wastefulness and extravagance. Let every man and every woman assume the duty of careful, provident use and expenditure as a public duty, as a dictate of patriotism which no one can now ever be excused or forgiven for ignoring.

With the signing of the armistice and preparations for peace, which situation requires the sending of a larger quantity of food than in previous years to the Allies and the liberated millions, we must ask the American housewife to continue in her efforts for conservation. This is based upon the appeal to humanity rather than the winning of the war. In our Campaign Week of December first, we shall have on Wednesday a Woman's Organization Day.

The members of my staff who are in charge of this program are very anxious that I should, if possible, secure from you a statement which will be kept for this day to be read in all the women's organizations in the country as an appeal to a continued mobilization for service to the government. You will state what I know is your appreciation of the loyalty of the American housewife to her government and the desire that she shall continue to practice economy and to apply intelligence in the management of her household.

Faithfully yours,

[signed, Hoover's secretary]

To the Women of the United States

You have been in the front lines of defenses. You pledged the resources of time and skill to the releasing of our food supplies to the end that, as a nation, we have been able to sustain the morale of the Allies, until the day of victory.

Not in khaki nor in camp, not by military enlistment, but by the intelligent reduction of food consumption (to the minimum point of health and strength), you of the family have enabled us to fulfill our promises to feed the allied nations. They counted on these promises and we have not failed them. Only when a country has lacked food has it succumbed.

The call of hungry millions is an appeal to you to stand mobilized to help these who are hurt by the war. Our greatest enemy may be selfish greed and luxurious living, unless we perform a greater sacrifice of our time, our food and our skill to relieve famine, to restore blighted homes and to conquer anarchy.

Shall we as a nation receive the blessings of sacrifice and build for the common good, which is as broad as humanity? As long as hungry hands are stretched toward our continent we must help by simple living. This demands the thoughtful attention of all consumers, but particularly of those who manage the family expenditure.

Your economy of resources in the individual family is our great hope of fulfilling our duty to starving nations. I ask you to remain recruited until our great tasks are done and liberated millions can help themselves.

Funds for European Relief

The cable below seems to be the first message sent to Wilson by Hoover after he arrived in Paris on November 25. Hoover had reached London on November 22 and conferred there with Allied representatives. (Also on that day the Communist Russian government began publication of a number of secret treaties manifestly to discomfort and embarrass the Allies.) The next day Hoover met with Hugh Gibson who had been loaned to Hoover by the State Department. A passage from Gibson's diary reveals that some American representatives in Europe had already been attempting to undermine Hoover's relief plans by falsely stating that the plans did not really emanate from Wilson (*Ordeal*, p. 95). Hoover then went on to Paris where on November 26 he saw Colonel House for whom he drafted a report, which House cabled to Wilson the next day with an urgent plea that he immediately inform the foreign ministers of the Big Three of American plans for European relief. Wilson did so, sending them a cable through House on December 1. In the meantime Hoover returned to London, visited Brussels, and thence returned to Paris on November 30.

Wilson's plan, when finally unveiled, called for the appointment of a Director General of Relief with broad authority over aid for Germany and Austria, the neutrals, and nations recently under German occupation. Hoover was appointed to this position on January 4, 1919.

The following cable was dispatched by Hoover, apparently through House to the State Department which sent it on to Wilson.

Paris, December 1, 1918

For the President from Hoover. "In order to give a working capital to the relief, we consider it will *not* be necessary to set up some agreement of Treasury participation and possibly request Congressional appropriation. In the meantime, that we may proceed in urgent matters, I am anxious to know if you could appropriate to this purpose five million dollars from your Presidential fund. I could later supplement this by dividends to you from Sugar Equalization Board and might avoid appropriations and consequent discussions altogether. Would it be possible to settle this before your departure. Hoover."

Serbia, Yugoslavia, Austria Relief

The subject of this letter—the relief of peoples under the Serbian government—was one of the many topics Hoover discussed with Wilson the day after the President's arrival in Paris. The letter and enclosed telegrams likely were delivered by Hoover personally and signed by Wilson immediately (*Ordeal*, pp. 100–2).

As for the five enclosures, Hoover may have drafted all of them himself, even those ostensibly written by Norman Davis, who served with Hoover as a member of the President's Committee of Economic Advisers (see Introduction, p. xxx). Davis was also a Paris representative of the Treasury Department.

The Hoover letter of December 16 was probably a review of matters Hoover and Wilson had discussed earlier. Also on December 15 or 16 Hoover had analyzed the proposed food pool for House. In approving Hoover's letter, Wilson authorized Hoover to dispatch the cables and letters, drafts of which were enclosed in the letter; Hoover did this immediately. It appears that during the conversation Hoover also tendered his resignation, to be effective after the relief organization had been set up and Belgian restoration turned over to other hands. But Wilson's manifest distress compelled Hoover to reconsider and to accept his fate (*Ordeal*, p. 101). Ten days earlier rumors of Hoover's prospective resignation were adrift and he had denied them (*Times*, Dec. 5, 1918, p. 7).

Paris, 16 December 1918.

Dear Mr. President:

SERBIAN RELIEF

In the matter of the relief of populations under the Serbian Government, I enclose herewith a letter from Mr. Norman H. Davis, who is, as you know, the special representative of the Treasury in matters connected with relief, which it is proposed to be despatched to the Secretary of the Treasury, if it meets with your approval, and I also enclose herewith, for your signature and delivery to Mr. Davis, a proposed letter which he has addressed to the Secretary of the Treasury. These arrangements provide Treasury advances for this purpose.

JUGO-SLAV & SOUTH AUSTRIA

In respect to relief of other populations of southern Austria, as I recounted to you last evening, there are certain populations in South, or Old Austria, which as yet are of doubtful national destination whose food situation is extremely pressing and the relief of which we cannot financially see daylight through any normal government advances. Also, there is [*sic*] the expenses of the Food Administration's activities in Europe to cover these relief measures. It is for this purpose that I requested from you an allocation from your fund for the National Security and Defense of $5,000,000 to be paid directly to the Grain Corporation. I am in hopes that we can yet devise relief measures which will transform this fund merely into working capital which will be recoverable, and, in any event, we will take some kind of obligations for it, except for such minor amounts as may be used in administration. I do not, however, wish to guarantee that we can save this entire sum, but the question of human life and the necessity of maintaining military stability is such that I am sure it is an entirely appropriate use of the funds appropriated. I therefore enclose herewith a draft cable for despatch to the Secretary of the Treasury, directing him to pay to the United States Grain Corporation this sum of money from your blanket fund.

U.S. ARMY OFFICERS

As to the use of United States Army Officers, I am informing General Pershing that you are in accord with his delegating to my service such officers as he can spare, they to remain for the present in the army service, their status to be cleared up at as early a date as possible after our organization is established.

WAR DEPARTMENT

In regard to War Department supplies, as you are aware, before I left Washington, Mr. Secretary Baker and myself arranged with your approval to ship a matter of 20 shiploads of foodstuffs to Europe temporarily for account of the Quartermaster General. These ships have begun to arrive at Gibraltar and I have temporarily arranged with the Quartermaster General to forward them to Adriatic ports, to be discharged at these ports for his account and his care. Mr. Secretary Baker has cabled that he approves this arrangement as to the boats arriving pending your arrival in Europe, and that it requires your authorization for him to continue this program. In accordance with our conversations last evening, I have drafted the enclosed cable for the Secretary of War, to be sent to you. The effect of this is that the Quartermaster Department carries temporarily the financial load involved in the transit of these foodstuffs from United States to Adriatic ports and holds them in storage at these ports until such time as they are released for relief, and upon their release from the stores at Adriatic ports, they will be paid for by the Grain Corporation in the United States from the funds provided in the previous paragraphs, or from such moneys as we may be able to collect from the sale of these foodstuffs to such positions as the City of Vienna. In any event, there is no real risk in the matter, because in the worst event, we can stop the flow of foodstuffs from the United States to Italy and divert these stocks to the Italian Government, that is, assuming the whole of relief measures were to break down. The great assistance of these matters is that it enables us to carry the relief of southern Europe with much less sum invested than would otherwise be the case.

I am, my dear Mr. President,

Respectfully yours,
Herbert Hoover

Approved
Woodrow Wilson

Enclosures: (1) Letter from Mr. Davis
(2) Cable Mr. Davis proposes to dispatch relating to Servia[1] if approved by the President.
(3) Letter to the Secretary of the Treasury to be signed by the President if he approves.
(4) Cable authorizing payment of $5,000,000 from fund for National Security and Defense.
(5) Cable to the Secretary of War authorizing the continuance of cargo dispatch.

---

[1] Servia was an earlier name for Serbia, which in 1918 became part of the newly created Yugoslavia.

Enclosure 1

16 December 1918.

Dear Mr. President:

The Secretary of the Treasury requested me to come to Europe as special representative of the Treasury to take up with Mr. Hoover the various financial questions arising in relation to relief in Europe.

As you are aware, the only method by which the Treasury Department can give financial assistance even for such purposes is by way of the establishment of credits and subsequent advances to Governments at war with the enemy. The regular procedure, of course, is for the Secretary of the Treasury with your approval, to establish such credits and make such advances. Mr. Hoover has reported to me his conversations with you regarding the proposed emergency measures and has also informed me of the financial assistance immediately required in respect to Servia and the larger portion of Jugo-Slavia, for which the relief would have to be furnished through advances to the Servian Government. On account of the urgency of the situation, I have drafted a cable to the Secretary of the Treasury, which is enclosed herewith, to be sent if it meets with your approval. May I also ask that you sign the enclosed letter addressed to the Secretary of the Treasury if the plan proposed meets with your approval.

I am, my dear Mr. President,

Very respectfully,
Norman Davis

Enclosure 2

Hoover reports that to meet urgent requirements for relief to Serbia, including that portion of Jugo-Slavia under the Serbian Government, would require 30,000 to 40,000 tons of food per month until next harvest, but that internal transportation will probably not permit the execution of this whole program. In meantime, however, in order to meet emergency and to start operations, he recommends that Treasury, upon request of Serbian Government, establish a credit for $15,000,000, to be paid through the Serbian Minister directly to the Grain Corporation. Hoover's idea is that $10,000,000 of this would be required for working capital, and $5,000,000 as the value of the first month's food delivered, which food is already arriving at Adriatic ports at risk of Grain Corporation or Food Administration.

In addition to above, he recommends the establishment of credit for $5,000,000 monthly for four months, making a total altogether of $35,000,000. At present, it is impossible to be more precise. The entire amount may not be required, but will only be used under the direction of Hoover who will direct and supervise distribution. He recommends that the Treasury Department have a representative over here probably in Servia to collaborate with his representatives.

Agreement has not yet been reached with Allied Governments as to the general plan for food relief in Europe, but this situation seems extremely pressing and of great importance in order to save life and maintain stability in military situation. Whatever is done will be upon the understanding that any arrangements which may be later arrived at with the Allied Governments will be retroactive, so far as any expenses or advances made by us are concerned, and upon the arrangements which may be made will depend, more or less, the use of subsequent credits [I] have referred to. I have submitted this cable to the President who strongly approved and who has handed me the following communication addressed to you: QUOTE Paris, 16th December, 1918, The Honorable, The Secretary of the Treasury, Dear Mr. Secretary: Mr. Hoover informs me that situation in Serbia and Jugo Slavia is such that food supplies should be sent in there immediately in order to save life and maintain stability in the military situation, and Mr. Davis has shown me his proposed cable to you explaining the situation, and suggesting the establishment of a credit of $35,000,000 in favor of the Serbian Government to be used for relief of Servians and Jugo Slavs under Servian Government, provided the Serbian Government makes application for such credit and agrees to turn over the funds to the Food Administration or the Grain Corporation for the purchase, delivery, and distribution of the supplies in question. If you therefore desire to establish this credit and to make advances thereunder as above indicated you may consider this as my full approval. Cordially yours

Woodrow Wilson

APPROVED

Enclosure 3

16th December, 1918.

Dear Mr. Secretary:

Mr. Hoover informs me that situation in Serbia and Jugo Slavia is such that food supplies should be sent there immediately in order to save life and maintain stability in the military situation, and Mr. Davis has shown me his proposed cable to you explaining the situation, in favor of the Serbian Government to be used for relief of Servians and Jugo Slavs under the Servian Government, provided the Serbian Government makes application for such credit and agrees to turn over the funds to the Food Administration or the Grain Corporation for the purchase, delivery, and distribution of the supplies in question. If you therefore desire to establish this credit and to make advances thereunder as above indicated you may consider this as my full approval.

Cordially yours,
[President Wilson]

Enclosure 4 (for Secretary of the Treasury)

Please pay at once to the U.S. Food Administration Grain Corporation five million dollars from my fund for National Security and Defense.

Woodrow Wilson

APPROVED

Enclosure 5

16 December, 1918.

(For Secretary of War)

In respect to the foodstuffs being shipped by the War Department for direction of Mr. Hoover, I would be indeed obliged if you would continue to forward these foodstuffs to such ports as Mr. Hoover may direct, and that the War Department continue to take care of the discharge and custody of these foodstuffs at these ports. The foodstuffs will not be released by the Quartermaster General's representatives, except as paid for by the Food Administration in Washington, arrangements for which are now being completed.

WOODROW WILSON

Tumulty Cable on Breweries

Tumulty sent this cable to Wilson on December 17. The President's personal secretary, who stayed on in Washington during the Paris Peace Conference, requested the President to consult Hoover on the matter. This Wilson did and Hoover immediately responded, giving the impression that he too may have received a cable from Tumulty.

Paris, 18 December 1918

My dear Mr. Hoover,

The President has asked me to refer to you the enclosed cable from Mr. Tumulty, regarding the modification of order issued on September 16th, 1918, prohibiting the use of grain in the manufacture of soft drinks.

The President would appreciate it if you would give him your advice in this matter.

Sincerely yours,
Gilbert F. Close
Confidential Secretary to the President

Cablegram

For: The President of United States, Paris.
The labor [forces] urgently ask modification of order issued by you Sept. 16 1918 prohibiting use of grain in manufacture of soft drinks. Baruch and Garfield in favor but other members of Board opposed. Since you left this office has received numerous telegrams from leading citizens, Bankers and others. Resolutions passed by Chamber of Commerce and other business organizations requesting order prohibiting manufacture of non-intoxication soft beverages be removed. Manufacturers have on hand ample supply of coal and raw materials for their purposes; therefore granting this request will not effect [*sic*] food or coal supply. Understand materials used in manufacture of these beverages are now exported to Canada, France, and England. Unless order is rescinded approximately six thousand men will be thrown out of employment during winter months in St. Louis alone and just at this time men formerly engaged in munition factories there are solely [*sic*] to need of continuing employment of men in winter time and not throwing them out of employment in competition with returning soldiers and discharged munition workers. Labor Leaders and organizations have materially supplemented this appeal of business.

TUMULTY

Ask Herbert Hoover.

Advice on Opening Breweries

19 December, 1918.

Dear Mr. President:

I am in receipt of a cable from Mr. Tumulty with regard to the re-opening of brewing in the United States, and have also received direct cables from our own office to the same effect.

It appears to me that the matter has several phases: The first is that as quickly as shipping becomes more available for exports from the United States, which is not likely to be more than 30 days hence, the real situation with regard to feeding stuffs for animals will quickly develop. The world is entirely short of these grains, and from a point of view of food conservation, there can be no question as to the desirability of the cessation of brewing.

The matter, however, is one that has many internal moral and economic complexities which I do not pretend to judge at this distance. I may mention, however, that in addition to the very difficult internal problems involved, there is a tendency to expand brewing in Europe, under the same types of pressure.

You will of course realize that under the new Congressional Act, brewing would in any event cease on the first of July, and that the labor difficulties cannot be so great now as they will be at that time when there is a larger demobilization.

It would generally appear to me that, if you do not wish yourself to make a decision on a matter so difficult to determine from this end, it is a matter which should be settled by the Cabinet as a whole.

Yours faithfully,

[signed, Hoover's secretary]

Bolshevism and German Separatism

Article 26 of the Armistice Convention of November 11, 1918, read in part that "[T]he Allies and the United States contemplate the provisioning of Germany during the Armistice as may be found necessary." Hoover accepted these words as a pledge to be honored for humanitarian reasons as well as for the protection of Central Europe from engulfment by Bolshevism. He feared this was a lively possibility for desperate and famished people who might embrace any new movement that promised relief. In this letter, Hoover asks Wilson for a statement from the United States and the Allies that they cannot hope to feed Germany unless a stable government is in power. He also asks the President to tell the Germans that supplies will not be channeled through leaders of a Bolshevik regime. In addition Hoover expresses his deep concern over a Separatist movement in Germany. Should such develop, he thought that provisioning the conquered nation would become a problem of immeasurable proportions.

20 December, 1918.

Dear Mr. President:

Soon after the Armistice, you took one or two occasions to make clear that the maintenance of order in Germany by the German people was a prime requisite to food-stuffs and to peace, and that the necessity of feeding Germany arose not only out of humanity but out of its fundamental necessity to prevent anarchy.

It would seem that these warnings have a little worn off and I have a feeling that it would be desirable if some joint and very pointed statement could be made by the four associated governments on the positive subject of Bolshevism in Germany.

As you are aware there is incipient or practical Bolshevist control in many of the large centres; there is also a Separatist movement in progress amongst the German States, arising somewhat from fear of Bolshevism; there is also—apparently largely supported—a movement towards the election of a constitutional assembly of some kind.

Viewing the German Empire from a food point of view, there will be no hope of saving these people from starvation if Bolshevist activities extend over the Empire in a similar manner to Russia, with its sequent break down in commercial distribution and in the control and distribution of existing food. The extremes to which such a situation can extend are well exemplified by the already practical depopulation of the cities of Moscow and Petrograd, and such a situation would not be confined to two cities as in Russia, but to thirty cities in Germany, and the saving of the German people would be absolutely hopeless if the normal commercial and distributive functions and food control should cease, as it certainly would under a Bolshevist regime.

Again a political Separatist movement amongst the German

States would produce the same situation that we have in the old Austrian Empire, where some sections of the Empire have a surplus of food and by practical embargoes are creating food debacles in other centres. We must maintain a liquidity of the existing food stocks in Germany over the whole Empire, or again the situation will become almost unsolvable.

In order to visualise to you somewhat the problem, if we say that the normal consumption of the German people, without restraint, is 100, the German Empire within its old boundaries must possess today somewhere about 60% of this quantity. If there is distribution and control, the population can probably go through without starvation on something like 80% of normal, and therefore the problem is to find 20% by ways of imports. If there is an extension of the Bolshevist movement or extension of the Separatist movement, so far as food is concerned, we shall have some localities consuming 100 out of their local supplies and feeding any surplus to animals. The problem will be unsolvable by way of the available supplies in the world for import because the total consumption under such conditions would run a great deal more than 80% and all this aside from the almost impossible completion of dealing with distribution in the hands of such highly incompetent agencies as Bolshevist Committees.

It would appear to me therefore that some announcement with regard to the food policies in Germany is critically necessary, and at once. If that announcement could be made something on the line that the United States and Allies could only hope to solve the food difficulties in Germany until next harvest through the hands of a stable and experienced government based on an expressed popular will, and a hint be given that the Allies cannot anticipate furnishing the food assistance to Germany through the hands of Bolshevist elements, it would at once strengthen the whole situation in Germany and probably entirely eliminate the incipient Bolsheviem [sic] in progress, and make possible the hope of saving their food situation. I realize that this is a suggestion of some delicacy, but I feel that I should present it to you.

Yours faithfully,
[signed, Hoover's secretary]

Turnbull Letter on Germany

Paris, 21 December, 1918.

My dear Mr. Hoover:

At the suggestion of the President I am taking the liberty of enclosing herewithin a statement from Mr. Arthur Turnbull (I don't know who he is) which purports to give some facts and information about food supplies in Germany. The President thought that you might be interested in it.

Sincerely yours,
[signed, Wilson's secretary]
Confidential Secretary to the President

Stockpiling Food in Europe

For five weeks Hoover had been arguing, with little success, against a continuance of the blockade. On December 22 a slight relaxation occurred, but on December 31 the blockade was strictly reimposed. Two days before, Hoover had been made privy to this action. Immediately he called a meeting of the principal Americans affiliated with the different economic organizations in Paris. General Tasker Bliss, a member of the five-man American peace delegation, was unable to attend but on the following day he wrote Hoover of his opposition to the blockade. Soon thereafter the group discussed the matter with Wilson who asked Hoover to supply him with a memorandum on the controversial subject. The memorandum was prepared and given to Wilson who immediately approved it shortly before he left Paris for a week's tour in Italy (*Memoirs*, vol. 1, pp. 338–39).

Paris, 23rd December 1918.

Dear Mr. President:

In order to adequately handle the problem of European food relief, it is necessary that we should establish stocks of food, particularly cereals and fats, at certain strategic ports, these stocks to be drawn upon for the supply of different countries from time to time. Such an arrangement enables us to maintain constant transport and a regular drain of our food supplies from the United States. This arrangement, together with many political considerations involved, require [sic] that the foodstuffs in transit and in storage at these bases of supplies should remain in the name and possession of the United States Government. The War Department, with your approval, is now performing this function in respect to certain stocks in the Adriatic, but I assume that their action is only for the emergency, and beyond this it is necessary for us to establish further such stocks at points like Rotterdam, possibly at Gutenberg,[1] and even at German ports.

The United States Food Administration has the right to buy and sell foodstuffs as may be required in the common defense. The appropriations to the Food Administration for these purposes lie entirely in the Food Administration Grain Corporation, of which you are the sole stockholder. The Directors of the Grain Corporation feel that, as a corporation, they should have your approval to this extension of their operations outside of United States territory. There is no reason either in law or in the purposes of the United States to maintain the common defense that does not warrant such action, and there is abundant actual reason why this action should be taken as a part of the necessity of the United States to maintain tranquillity in Europe while its armies are entangled here.

It is not proposed to part with any of the foodstuffs thus belonging to the Grain Corporation without prior payment. There is, of course, some commercial risk in the matter, also there might be further outbreak of hostilities in Europe that some of our bases of supplies might be involved. This, however, I regard as a risk of war that cannot be avoided.

I would, therefore, be glad to know if you authorize the Grain Corporation to extend its operations to the extent of establishing these stocks and carrying them on the capital and credit which it possesses.

Yours faithfully,
Herbert Hoover

Approved, 23 December, 1918.
Woodrow Wilson

---

[1] Probably Gothenberg (or Göteborg) in Sweden.

1919

Organization of Relief

This memorandum begins with the words "From Pres. to H.H."
However, the author appears to have been Hoover himself. He frequently wrote such memorandums and even "Dear Mr. Hoover"
letters that Wilson signed and returned to the original composer. It
was an approved and simple expedient utilized by Hoover for obtaining authorization for the many plans he conceived. The short document should be read alongside the Hoover letter that follows immediately.

[January ?] 1919

(FROM PRES. TO H.H.)

Many million people in Central Europe surrounding Germany
are today faced with starvation and from starvation flows anarchy
and chaos. In order that the United States may not be behind in
organization of charity and proper relief, I desire that all American
effort should be co-ordinated to meet this situation. Certain powers
have been conferred upon me by Congress for the disposal on credit
of our surplus wheat and flour; large charity has been organized by
the European Children's Fund now feeding over 2,500,000 starving
children in Europe. The Near East Committee in conjunction with
the European Children's Fund are caring for the suffering Armenians
in the Caucasus and Turkey. The Jewish Joint Distribution Committee has provided large funds for the care of Jews. Many other funds
exist, some of them of great purpose. In order to secure the most
efficient use of all such funds, I would be glad if you would consult
the Treasury and the Wheat Director and the larger relief activities
and nominate to me gentlemen who would act under your chairmanship to form a non-partisan American Economic Relief Council.

I would propose to ask that all American activities co-operate under the authority of such a council, and to authorize the Wheat Director to supply surplus wheat or flour on credit for relief as recommended by this council.

Coordination of American Action

An extended discussion of the origin of the organization mentioned in this statement is given in the Introduction, p. xxx. This statement most likely was prepared very early in January and should be read in conjunction with the document given immediately above (*Ordeal*, pp. 83–86).

Hoover to Wilson

[January ?, 1919]

1. As you are aware, our Government has been represented in Europe upon various inter-Allied councils, relating to finance, food, shipping, and raw materials, war trade measures, etc. The purpose of these councils is rapidly changing and the American attitude toward them and the problems they represent must change. The matters involved are much interlocked and up to the time of the Armistice were co-ordinated through the Council sitting under your chairmanship. Messrs. Hoover, Hurley, Baruch, and McCormick are, or will soon be, in Europe. The working of these bodies still needs co-ordination by the heads of the departments concerned, who will be in Europe together with the chief representatives here of the departments whose heads are still in Washington.

2. This same group are essential in determination of policies to be pursued by our Government in the peace negotiations.

3. It is recommended that a council be set up, comprising Messrs. Hoover, Hurley, Baruch, and McCormick and Davis, with a Treasury representative to be appointed by Mr. Glass, under your chairmanship, to discuss and decide such joint policies as are necessary in both these phases and to co-ordinate it with the Peace Commission by inclusion of Colonel House, General Bliss, and Admiral Benson, Colonel House to act as Chairman in your absence or inability to find time.

Herbert Hoover

Approved: W.W.

Dropping Food Licenses

Paris, January 7, 1919.

Dear Mr. President:

I am enclosing herewith an Executive order for the dropping of the License Provision under the Food Act on a number of Food trades and in respect to a number of commodities.

We are proposing this in accordance with the policy laid down by your [sic] to re-establish as fast as can safely be done the normal basis of trade. The shortening of war demands on our food supplies convince [sic] us that it is no longer necessary to maintain these licenses and we think it is desirable they should be brought to an end.

I would be glad indeed if you could sign the proclamation which I enclose and we will advise Washington by cable at the signature.

Yours faithfully,
[signed, Hoover's secretary]

Executive Order on Licenses

Paris, 7 January 1919.

My dear Mr. Hoover:

I am returning herewith the Executive Order for the dropping of the License Provision under the Food Act, which was enclosed with your letter of January 7th to the President and which the President has signed.

Will you not be kind enough to send me a copy of this proclamation for our files?

Sincerely yours,
[signed, Wilson's secretary]
Confidential Secretary to the President

Polk Letter on Food Bill

Hoover and Wilson at this time were encouraging Congress to enact an appropriation bill of $100,000,000 for food relief in Europe. On

January 4 Wilson had cabled Congress of the need for such a bill. To muster arguments for the request, Hoover on January 6 sent an "urgent" telegram to Ira Nelson Morris, the American Minister to Stockholm, asking him to collate and forward information on the food needs in Finland and the Baltic states to the Secretary of State. Also on January 6, Hoover cabled an "urgent, please rush" message to the Food Administration in Washington on the desperate situation in fourteen European countries (Pre-Commerce Papers, box 8; and *Times*, Jan. 8, 1919, p. 18).

Congress, however, was first interested in learning what England, France, and Italy intended to contribute to the relief fund. They thus approached Frank Polk, acting Secretary of State, and on January 3 he conveyed to Wilson their inquiry into this matter. The Senator Martin mentioned in this letter was Thomas Martin, Democrat from Virginia. Congressman Joseph Swagar Sherley was a lame-duck Democrat from Kentucky who held the deciding vote in the House committee then considering the relevant bill.

No evidence exists that Hoover furnished the requested information in writing. He may have informed Wilson in a personal conversation or he may have delegated another to do this for him. More likely, he simply referred the President to relevant material in the January 5 cablegram Hoover sent to Rickard of the Food Administration. On January 7, a cablegram to Polk—presumably from the President's office in reply to a Polk cable of January 4—states that the information sought was included (Wilson Papers, Ser. B, LC MSS div.). The January 7 cable says: "See Hoover's one seventy three to Food Administration which explains situation rather fully." It then addresses itself to the pertinent matter in these words:

> The Allies are already furnishing relief but it is impossible to make any definite proposals or arrangements with them until we are in position to act. It is believed however that England, France and probably Italy would be willing to agree to participate in the relief for a fixed percentage of the whole contributing, to the extent of their available resources in transportation, clothing, expenses which can be paid in their currencies and such minor amounts of food as they may have in surplus provided we are prepared to agree to advance any dollars required to complete their fixed contribution—but understand Secretary of Treasury does not favor advancing funds to Allies for payment of American food to be supplied by them to other countries.

On January 9 Hoover sent another "urgent" cable to the Food Administration in Washington, giving a graphic picture of the desperate situation in Vienna as presented by his three chief relief representatives in Austria. Hoover concluded his message: "Please give a copy to Shirley [Sherley]" (Wilson Papers, Ser. B, LC MSS div.).

Polk's cable with its message from Martin and Sherley, mentioned below in Wilson's note, is not printed here.

Paris, 7 January 1919.

My Dear Mr. Hoover:

The President has asked me to refer to you the enclosed copy of a cable from Mr. Polk, the acting Secretary of State, containing a message from Senator Martin and Congressman Sherley asking information as to the amount of money which England and France will provide and also information as [to] Italy, in connection with the proposed food appropriation. The President asks if you will not be kind enough to secure the necessary information so that the message may be answered promptly.

> Sincerely yours,
> [signed, Wilson's secretary]
> Confidential Secretary to the President

British and American Farm Products

During the war the Allies importuned Hoover time and again to supply them with more food. To fulfill these urgent requests Hoover used every expedient to encourage increased farm production; the expedient that proved most effective was a government guaranteed price. When the war ended, the Allies no longer needed the same quantities of food from the United States, and, moreover, their ships were free to tap the vast resources in the Indies and the Southern Hemisphere. Thus the British announced in early January that they were withdrawing their orders from American farm products that had been accumulated in vast stockpiles on the other side of the Atlantic (see also *Memoirs*, vol. 1, pp. 329–34).

Wilson was apparently impressed with Hoover's letter and memorandum on the problem thus created, for on January 9 he cabled both to the Secretary of War in Washington. His message, which went out at 5 P.M., carried this prefix:

The Food Administration will present to you the situation produced by army reduction in pork purchases and the situation generally arising out of changed currents of trade due to the armistice and the action of the British authorities.

42830

I have received the following letter from Hoover with its memorandum which latter I propose [to] present to early meeting with Allied premiers. As this latter may not succeed, I would like at once the views of yourself and colleagues as to whether, in the interest of peace, the safety of our army from rising anarchy, and the protection of our producers, the War Department should not make the necessary purchases to protect the American situation and ship the material to Europe for distribution under their direction as a military measure. (Pre-Commerce Papers, box 8.)

January 8th, 1919.

My dear Mr. President:

I have cablegrams this morning, copies of which are enclosed, stating that the whole of the customary monthly orders from the British buying organizations on behalf of the Allied Governments have been withdrawn. I am informed by the French and Italian officials that it is untrue that they have not withdrawn their share of the orders and I am endeavoring to restore them.

The Allied food necessities have been outlined from time to time by a series of programmes made up by the Inter-Allied Food Council, the latest of these programmes is as recent as the 15th of December and calls for our entire January surplus. Our manufacturers have provided the particular types of manufacture required by each of these Governments and have enormous [sic] stocks of these materials in hand ready for delivery in accordance with the indicated programmes above mentioned.

While we can protect our assurances given producers in many commodities the most acute situation is in pork products which are perishable and must be exported. We have in January a surplus of about 400,000,000 pounds and the French, Italian and Belgian Relief and other customary orders when restored will cover 60% of such. The British orders at the rate indicated in their official programmes would have been 140,000,000 pounds and covered our deficiency plus some help I am giving from the relief. The British position is that they have sufficient supplies to last them for some weeks and that they wish to reduce their stocks.

If there should be no remedy to this situation we shall have a debacle in the American markets and with the advances of several hundred million dollars now outstanding from the banks to these pork product industry [*sic*] we shall not only be precipitated into a financial crisis but shall betray the American farmer who has engaged himself to these ends. The surplus is so large that there can be no absorption of it in the United States and it, being a perishable, will go to waste.

You will recollect that measures are before the Congress providing for appropriations for further economic assistance to the Allied Governments and I am confident that with the disclosure of this situation and the apparent desire of certain parties in England to break the American market [these conditions] will cause a re-action in the United States that will destroy the possibility of this economic support. In the face of this, the demand of liberated, neutral and enemy populations in Europe as to fats is beyond the ability of the United States to supply, and the need from the point of view of preserving order and laying the foundation of peace is absolutely instant in its insistence.

Mr. Davis and I have endeavored for the last six weeks to arrange at [*sic*] some co-operative action with the British agencies to forefend this situation and, as indicated above, the final result had been the refusal on their part to co-operate. We have suggested that the British Government should join with ourselves in the purchase of the necessary amounts of fats at our assured price to be resold to the liberated and enemy territories in order to prevent the above debacle and in this they have finally refused. I wish to assure you again that the prices which we are maintaining are the very minimum on which our American producers can come out whole on the effort they have made in the Allied cause and I cannot impress upon you too strongly the reaction that will arise in the United States if this situation falls to the ground.

With Mr. Davis I have prepared the attached memorandum which I would like to suggest should be presented by you to the Allied Premiers at the earliest possible moment as I cannot conceive that men with their vision as to the present situation will tolerate for one moment the attitude taken.

> Faithfully yours,
> [signed, Hoover's secretary]

Memorandum

January 8, 1919

Memorandum for agreement with Allied Premiers to comprise a direction to their various Government Departments. It is impossible to discuss the peace of the world until adequate measures have been taken to alleviate the fear of hunger, its attendant anarchy and its danger of possible further military operations. Therefore, before these peace negotiations can be opened auspiciously, it is essential to have the better feeding of the liberated, neutral and enemy territories of Europe in actual progress as the foundation of stability in government antecedent to the settlement of the great problems that will come before the Conference. It is therefore agreed by the Allied and the United States Governments that each shall, without further delay, furnish every possible assistance and facility required for carrying out the undertakings as to European Relief.

The United States has, in order to support the Allied Governments in war, provided large supplies of food stuffs, many of them perishable, which would have been required by the Allies had hostilities continued. In order to accumulate these supplies, the American Government has given assurances and guarantees to their producers. The Allied Governments, as a result of the cessation of hostilities and the opening of other markets, no longer require the same amount of supplies from the United States as they have from time to time indicated by their programmes.

This surplus is now required to meet the necessities of Europe and it is most fortunate that the surplus is available for these purposes. It would be disaster to the objects of the Associated Governments if the congestion in the United States should not be relieved so as to save waste and to meet the assurances given to the United States Government, and the Allied Governments agree to at once direct their departments to co-operate with the United States Food Administration to support these assurances, and the application of these foodstuffs to the needs of liberated, neutral and enemy peoples.

Pending the more mature plans and settlements of the Relief Administration as to food, shipping, and finance, it is directed that immediate provision should be made from any available source of food supplies for provisions to points of acute need in the Balkan

States, the liberated peoples of Turkey, Austria, to Belgium and Poland, that such provision shall be retroactively the obligation of the four Governments pending more definite arrangements.

It is desirable that the Associated Governments should show their good will toward the neutral countries of Europe by the immediate increase in the permitted importation of the surplus food commodities to these neutrals at once, being such amounts as the United States shall declare to be in surplus.

That it is necessary to at once give evidence of progress in the matter of food supplies to Germany and South Europe, and to this end the British, French and United States Governments will each at once give cabled orders for the shipment during the month of January of 30,000 tons of such fats (in addition to their orders for home consumption) as the United States shall declare available for these relief purposes. These foodstuffs shall be subsequently offered to Germany, subject to payment therefor and on other conditions that the Associated Governments may impose. That the Allied Governments and the United States will co-operate in the securing of such payment in a manner acceptable to each of the Associated Governments, and for providing the transportation of such foodstuffs. Before these supplies can arrive, the Relief Administration is expected to be working and to decide the conditions of distribution of payment and of further supplies and shipping.

These arrangements are declared binding upon all departments of the Allied and the United States Governments and shall be given immediate execution.

Walscheid Letter on Germany

Paris, 10 January 1919

My dear Mr. Hoover:

I am taking the liberty of referring to you the enclosed letter from Mr. Otto W. Walscheid with reference to food conditions in Germany.

Sincerely yours,
[signed, Wilson's secretary]
Confidential Secretary to the President

Appointment as Relief Director

For some time Hoover must have been aware that he would be appointed Director General of Relief for Europe, thus this letter probably did not surprise him. The Council mentioned in Wilson's letter was originally called the Inter-Allied Supreme Council for Supply and Relief; within five weeks it developed into the Supreme Economic Council (see Introduction, p. xxxi).

Paris, 11 January 1919.

Dear Mr. Hoover:

I desire to confirm your appointment as Director General of Relief in Europe, in accordance with the understandings with the Allied Governments with which you are familiar.

I also confirm your appointment as one of the representatives of the United States Government upon the Council of the Associated Governments which is to deal with the various questions involved in this matter.

Cordially yours,
Woodrow Wilson

Minutes from Relief Council

At 2:30 P.M. on Monday, January 13, the Supreme War Council met at the Quai d'Orsay in the office of the French Minister of Foreign Affairs. Lloyd George, Clemenceau, Wilson, and Hoover were among those present. It appears that the substance of the minutes mentioned in Hoover's letter of January 12 were given approval (F.R., P.C., vol. 3, pp. 552–53).

Paris, January 12, 1919.

Dear Mr. President:

Please find enclosed herewith extracts from the minutes of the 'Supreme Council for Supply and Relief' which were agreed to today by the representatives of all four Governments. It is of the utmost importance that these minutes should be brought before the Supreme War Council for ratification in order that they may become binding on their Governments and Departments.

Yours faithfully,
Herbert Hoover

Enclosure

I. RELIEF OF LIBERATED TERRITORIES

1. That it is imperative in the interest of humanity and for the maintenance of orderly government that relief should be given to certain European countries. It is provisionally estimated that for the furnishing of this relief till next harvest a minimum sum of 300 million dollars may be necessary apart from the requirements of Germany which will be separately examined.

2. The Council is of opinion that this sum of 300 million dollars should be placed at its disposal by the four associated Governments.

3. That the financial representatives of the four Governments should consider and make recommendations to meet this expenditure.

4. If these recommendations be accepted by the Council they should then be referred to the respective Governments for their approval.

II. GERMAN SHIPPING

The Supreme Council of General Supply believes that it is indispensable that the Associated Governments recommend to their representatives on the Naval Armistice Commission, which is sitting in London under the chairmanship of Admiral Weymis, that they should insert among the clauses of the new Armistice Treaty which is to be signed with Germany, a provision to the effect that the German passenger and cargo fleet shall be at the disposition of the Associated Governments to be operated through the intermediary of the Allied Maritime Transport Council, for the purpose of augmenting the sum total of the world's tonnage, from which there may be drawn the tonnage necessary for the supply and relief of Europe.

III. FOOD SUPPLIES TO GERMANY

1. The Council has given consideration to the measures already in progress for the relief of the allied, liberated and neutral territories, and is taking steps to provide and expedite such relief.

2. The Council has formed the opinion upon the material already in its possession (which is necessarily incomplete) that additional supply of food will be required in Germany before the next harvest is gathered.

For the purpose of obtaining more precise information the Council is making further investigation.

3. The Council recommends to the Supreme War Council that if the German cargo and passenger fleet is placed at the disposal of the associated Governments, the associated Governments should permit Germany to import a prescribed quantity of foodstuffs so limited as not to interfere in any way with the priority of supply which must be assured to Allied, liberated and neutral countries.

4. Under the conditions indicated, the Council would recommend that in the first instance the following supply should be permitted: 200,000 tons of breadstuffs and 70,000 tons of pork products.

5. It must be a condition precedent to any supply that satisfactory arrangements are made by Germany for providing the necessary payment.

The Council recommend that the representatives of the Treasuries of the Associated Governments be given full discretion to discuss the method of payment with the German representatives and to arrange for the utilization of German credits abroad in preference to other resources; failing these the representatives should make recommendations to the Council and to their respective Treasuries.

6. The Council are of the opinion that the world's position will justify further supplies if the Supreme War Council decide that these should be continued.

IV. ORGANIZATION OF COMMISSION TO GERMANY

The Council recommend that the Commanding Generals of the Belgian, French, British, American and Italian Armies should each nominate an Officer of experience who should form a Commission to supervise the distribution of foodstuffs in Germany, acting on behalf of the Armies of the Associated Governments and of this Council and shall take instructions from and report direct to, [sic] this Council.

In the assistance of the Commission, this Council will provide it with an expert civilian staff.

Hoover Blockade Memorandum

The memorandum mentioned in Wilson's letter is not identified, but it was likely the memorandum on the blockade prepared by Hoover on January 1 and given to Wilson sometime later. The President wrote on the memorandum this approval: "To these conclusions I entirely agree. W.W." He kept it until January 13, 1919, when the Conference opened and then returned it to Hoover with the following letter.

Paris—13 January, 1919.

Mr. dear Mr. Hoover:

I place the enclosed memorandum in your hands because that is where it belongs, and I am sure that you will know what it is possible to do.

I am delighted to hear that the councils of the relief commissions are at last going smoothly and sensibly.

Cordially and sincerely yours,
[signed, Wilson's secretary]

Memorandum on Blockade

1 January. 1919.

1. In a broad sense, there is no longer any military or naval value attaching to the maintenance of the blockade of enemy territory. Its retention has political value in the right settlement of ultimate political issues but its principal incidence is now economic in character. These latter features require immediate consideration because the political values may be entirely destroyed by its present harsh action.

2. The problem of sustaining life and maintaining order in enemy territories revolves primarily around the problem of food supplies and secondarily around the gradual re-establishment of commercial life.

3. The contemplation of the provision of foodstuffs in the volumes necessary entails the provision of financial resources for the payment thereof which, under the present financial blockade situation must be drawn:

(a) internally from these territories in the form of exchange securities negotiable throughout the world, or gold;

(b) by the provision of these foodstuffs at the cost of the associated governments;

(c) by the export of commodities and the consequent liberation of
action to some degree of shipping and credit and communications.

Even the first alternative of the use of internal resources is now entirely impracticable under the effective financial blockade and in any
event can be only temporary lest the working capital of enemy countries be reduced to a point where the resumption of their economic
life and the payment by them of damage done becomes impossible.
The second alternative, of advances by Associated Governments, is
impossible to contemplate.

4. It becomes necessary, therefore, to at once consider some
modification of the present blockade measures that will establish production and exports with which to pay for food and some other imports at as early a date as possible.

The development of these processes cannot be successfully undertaken by the action of governments, but must be through the encouragement of the initiative of private commerce. This is especially
emphasized as to those countries where there is a disintegration of
government. The first step suggested is provision that we may trade
to some defined extent with surrounding Neutrals and the Western
Hemisphere.

5. Not only does this step forward in the restoration of commercial life in enemy territory imply a relaxation in absolute blockade
measures with regard to the ingress and egress of commodities, also
a relaxation to a great degree in the course of finance and credits,
but also in the movement of shipping. It has been contemplated that
this latter should be initiated by the acquirement and operation of
enemy shipping by the associated governments. It is our belief that
this step towards normality and the solution of the entire problem
cannot be obtained except through some measure of relaxation on
the movement of enemy shipping to be operated by the enemy itself,
in particular in coastwise voyage and to the Western Hemisphere. It
would appear that the immediate liberation of certain definite designated tonnage, to be used for coastwise and Transatlantic purposes,
would be the first step necessary in order to secure the solution of
the problem, and it might be made coincident with the surrender to
the Allies of a certain portion of enemy shipping for purposes of

transportation of food to liberated regions and for the return of the troops to the United States.

6. A relaxation of commodity, finance, shipping, and correspondence blockade is the only measure that will protect the situation against the evils which may arise from actual hunger. Even a partial revival of the ordinary activities of life within enemy territories will tend powerfully towards the end of Bolshevism and the stabilizing of governments.

7. It is not proposed that these measures proceed to the abandonment of blockade prior to peace but that certain agreed tonnage, agreed commodities for import and export; agreed avenues of credit operations and agreed channels of trade and communication must at once be established.

To these conclusions I entirely agree.

W. W.

[handwritten by Wilson]

Food Administration and Whitmarsh

Paris, 13th January 1919.

My dear Mr. President:

In order that there may be a complete understanding between the Food Administration in Washington and myself, I have asked Mr. Edgar Rickard, who has been Acting Food Administrator in Washington since my departure, to come to Paris for conference. In order that this may be possible, it is necessary to have the powers of the Food Administrator delegated by Executive Order during his absence.

I enclose a proposed Executive Order delegating this power to Mr. Theodore F. Whitmarsh, who has been associated with the Food Administration from its inception and is very familiar with the problems connected with European Relief. I enclose two copies of the Order and ask that one be returned to me when executed in order that I may inform the Food Administration by cable.

Faithfully yours,
Herbert Hoover

Executive Order

WHEREAS, by virtue of an executive order, dated November 16th, 1918, Edgar Rickard now exercises all powers and authority heretofore delegated to Herbert Hoover as United States Food Administrator during his absence from the United States, and

WHEREAS it is necessary that Edgar Rickard also be absent from the United States for a considerable period on matter of importance,

I HEREBY DIRECT that all such powers and authority be exercised by Theodore F. Whitmarsh during the absence of Herbert Hoover and Edgar Rickard, and that such powers and authority may be exercised in the name of Herbert Hoover, United States Food Administrator.

Brewing Ban in United States

Paris, 14 January 1919.

Dear Mr. President:

There appears to be a great deal of discussion in Washington as to the continuance of the ban on brewing. Owing to the conditions produced by the armistice, there is now no shortage of feed grains in the United States and, therefore, the prohibition of brewing under the Food Act, from a purely conservation point of view, is no longer warranted. It now becomes purely a temperance question and in this sense is, of course, entirely beyond my province to determine, as none of us can weigh the pros and cons of this situation at such a distance. May I suggest to you that you should dispatch the following telegram to the Cabinet in Washington in order that they may make a decision?

I am informed by the Food, Fuel and War Industries Administrations that there is no longer any necessity from the point of view of conservation in continuing the ban upon brewing. The problem, therefore, becomes purely one of temperance and I would be glad if the Cabinet would advise me whether, from a temperance point of view and from the legal point of view, since the powers of the government in this matter were exerted as a war conservation measure, we are any longer warranted in suppressing brewing. If the Cabinet is of the opinion that we are no longer warranted in using the war powers for this purpose, I would be glad if they would advise me that I may sign the necessary proclamations in the matter.

Faithfully yours,
Herbert Hoover

Devine's Information on Montenegro

Since 1945 Montenegro (5,333 square miles) has been one of the six republics of Yugoslavia. Prior to 1918 it was an independent nation. It lies just north of Albania on the Adriatic and has a population of a half-million people, largely Serbs. In 1914 it supported Serbia against Austria-Hungary but was occupied by the latter in 1915–1916. Freed in November 1918, it passed through a most unsettled period. French and Italian soldiers soon entered; on January 16 the Montenegrins revolted against the occupying Serbian troops, asking for protection by American troops. Hoover supplies no further information on Devine and does not mention him again.

Paris, 15 January, 1919.

My dear Mr. President:

I am obliged for your letter of the 15th with the enclosures from Mr. Devine, which I am returning. We have been in correspondence with this gentleman for sometime ourselves, and beside the fact that his information about Montenegro is far from exact, as proved by our own army and navy people on the ground, we have a very strong feeling that the solicitude he professes for Montenegro and Montenegrins is not entirely Platonic. The British Foreign Office has refused to visé his passport for France.

Faithfully yours,
[signed, Hoover's secretary]

Hoover Brewing Solution

Paris, 17 January 1919.

My dear Mr. Hoover:

The President asks me to acknowledge receipt of your letter of January 14th and to say that he has sent to the Cabinet at Washington the telegram which you have suggested in your letter regarding brewing.

> Sincerely yours,
> [signed, Wilson's secretary]
> Confidential Secretary to the President

Executive Order on Whitmarsh

> Paris, 17 January 1919.

My dear Mr. Hoover:

I beg to return herewith the executive order delegating the powers of the Food Administrator to Mr. Theodore F. Whitmarsh enclosed with your letter of January 14th, with the President's approval.

> Sincerely yours,
> [signed, Wilson's secretary]
> Confidential Secretary to the President

Unidentified Telegram

> Paris, 20 January, 1919.

My dear Hoover:

I dare say you have seen the enclosed telegram which has just come under my eye. I would like to know if you have any suggestions.

> Cordially and sincerely yours,
> *Woodrow Wilson*

Allowing Near Beer

The Prohibition movement was creating such controversy in America that the cabinet may have felt reluctant to make the decision to lift the ban on the brewing of beer as recommended by Hoover. Thus Wilson had the problem back in his lap once more. When Hoover received news of the cabinet's action, he sent the President another suggestion as a compromise solution.

Paris, 22 January 1919.

Dear Mr. President:

I understand the brewing question is referred back to you by the Cabinet, with what recommendations I do not know. It appears to me that one portion of the problem could be settled at once, that is, the brewing of non-alcoholic beers which are also closed for conservation reasons. There would appear to be no temperance question involved in this and I would like to suggest to you that the limitations on this portion of the industry at least should be lifted. I enclose herewith the necessary proclamation to effect this end, if you conclude that it is desirable to do so.

Yours faithfully,
Herbert Hoover

Proclamation

Whereas, under and by virtue of an Act of Congress entitled "An act to Provide further for the national security and defense by encouraging the production, conserving the supply, and controlling the distribution of food products and fuel" approved by the President on August 10, 1917, it is provided in Section 15 among other things as follow,

Whenever the President shall find that limitation, regulation, or prohibition of the use of foods, fruits, food materials, or feeds in the production of malt or vinous liquors for beverage purposes, or that reduction of the alcoholic content of any such malt or vinous liquor, is essential, in order to assure an adequate and continous [*sic*] supply of food, or that the national security and defense will be subserved thereby, he is authorized, from time to time, to prescribe and give public notice of the extent of the limitation, regulation, prohibition, or reduction so necessitated. Whenever such notice shall have been given and shall remain unrevoked no person shall, after a reasonable time prescribed in such notice, use any foods, fruits, food materials, or feeds in the production of malt or vinous liquors, or import any such liquors except under license issued by the President and in compliance with rules and regulations determined by him governing the production and importation of such liquors and the alcoholic content thereof.

And, whereas, on September 16, 1918 the President issued a proclamation under the aforesaid Act prohibiting the use after December 1, 1918, of all foods, fruits, food materials and feeds in the production of malt liquors including "near beer" for beverage purposes whether or not such malt liquors contained alcohol.

Now, therefore, I do hereby modify the aforesaid proclamation by excluding the production of malt liquor containing less than one-half of one per cent. of alcohol commonly known as "near beer" from the prohibition contained therein, and such prohibition is hereby modified so that after this date it shall no longer forbid the use of any food, fruit, food material or feed in the production of such "near beer".

In witness whereof I have hereunto set my hand this _____ _____ day of January in the year of our Lord Nineteen Hundred and Nineteen, and of the Independence of the United States the One Hundred and Forty Third.

By the President

Anguish over the Meat Packers

While Hoover was in Washington as wartime U.S. Food Administrator, no group caused him more anguish than the meat packers. A February 21, 1918, letter to President Wilson contains a short blunt remark, "I have no great love for the packers and they have been very difficult to deal with" (*Correspondence*, pp. 117, 156). Cattlemen trooped to Washington with complaints of huge losses on their cattle and they pointed accusatory fingers at the packers (ibid., pp. 152–53, 171). Hoover favored close regulation of the packers and curbs on their excessive wartime profits, but he opposed government operation of their plants (ibid., pp. 178, 189–91, 195–98, 215–22).

In January 1919 Senate and House committees began intensive investigations of the meat industry and reports soon reached Hoover in Paris that certain members of both chambers were attacking him for his views on the packers. In this letter he mentions senators William Borah of Idaho, James Reed of Missouri, Thomas Gore of Oklahoma, and Boies Penrose of Pennsylvania. Borah and Penrose were Republicans. Hoover states that their attacks were motivated by opposition to the hundred million dollar relief appropriation for Europe. Some solons had stated that Hoover intended to use the relief appropriation to dispose of the packers' products abroad (*Times*, Jan. 22, 1919, p. 10).

To answer these critics, Hoover asked Wilson's permission to release the lengthy and well-balanced report on the Chicago packers that he had sent to the President on September 11, 1918. The report was prefaced with the observation that "there is a growing and dangerous domination of the handling of the nation's foodstuffs"; he then presented a sophisticated review of "the underlying economics of its growth" in order to give "an objective understanding of this situation" (*Correspondence*, p. 254).

Wilson had deeply appreciated Hoover's report but felt it was unwise to make it public at that time. Finally, on January 24, 1919, he telephoned Hoover that he now approved of its release and it was accordingly given to the press on February 19.

Paris, 23 January 1919.

Dear Mr. President:

As a measure of obstruction to the passage of the hundred million dollar relief appropriation, I have been subjected to a general mud bath from Penrose, Reed, Gore and Borah, in which my principal crime seems to be in connection with the Chicago packers. The matter only interests me as a measure of obstruction and my friends in Washington think it extremely desirable that you should authorize the publication of the written opinion which I gave to you on the necessity of the legal control of the packing industry, some six or seven months ago. I would be glad to know if you can see your way to give such permission.

In reply to press inquiries, I have given the press representatives the following statement this morning:

> When asked for a statement in reply to the reported criticisms of certain Senators, Mr. Hoover said:
>
> "I apparently emerge in a new light, as the friend of the Chicago packer. The same mail brings a report from Swift & Company blaming the Food Administration for reducing their profits by ten million dollars during the last year. I don't imagine the packers would appreciate a wide circle of such friends. I

notice also I committed a crime for holding joint conferences of farmers, representatives of the forty small packers, as well as the big packers together with representatives of the Allied Governments, for the purpose of settling on a price for exports that would give the American farmer a square deal, and a distribution of orders that would protect the small packer.

"If the American farmer and the small packer feel that these arrangements are wrong it would be the greatest burden off my shoulders if I could know it quickly for the British Government particularly is anxious to be relieved from these arrangements."

All this makes it very difficult for me to secure settlement of the pressing relations with Allied Governments on our outstanding food matters. I have just yesterday proposed the enclosed contract to the British Government for the equitable winding up of their moral obligations in the matter of relations with our farmers in pork products, and already I hear that their representatives feel that this opposition in the Senate gives them some justification for delay in settling this matter. This has nothing to do with the above matter, except as it shows how difficult a path these people can provide for us.

Yours faithfully,
Herbert Hoover

Hoover Resignation

Hoover was so deeply shaken by the attacks on him in the Senate during debates on the relief appropriation bill that he decided to resign his government work and return to the mining profession. Accordingly he wrote the letter below to Wilson on January 23 and signed it. This letter is found only in the private papers of his secretary at that time, the late Lewis L. Strauss. It is not in any of the Wilson or the Hoover collections, and no mention of the planned resignation is in other letters of Hoover or Wilson. Therefore it seems reasonable to conclude that Hoover decided to weather the torrent of criticism and to remain at his post in Paris. Strauss probably had the letter ready to send to Wilson when advised to hold it. On March 10 the *Times* (p. 1) carried Hoover's statement that he would retire from European relief work in July. It is likely that passage of the relief bill by the Senate on January 24 by 54 to 18 removed some of the sting from the senators' verbal lashing and sufficiently assuaged

Hoover so as to make him reconsider his resignation resolve of January 23.

Paris, January 23 1919

Dear Mr. President:

My personality has been injected into the very bitter opposition being carried on by Senators Reed, Gore, Penrose and Barah [*sic*] in the Senate to the hundred million dollar appropriation for the relief of starvation and the prevention of anarchy in Europe, to be expended in conjunction with supplies furnished by the Allied Governments. It is an impossible conception that the personality of any one man should be allowed to retard measures of this character upon which such a mass of human life and the hope of peace depends. This work | has been | [must be][1] done for the honor of the United States and I have no wish to show so little patriotism as to embarrass you or your supporters.

You are well aware that I have approached the whole food problem of these hundreds of millions of people with great misgivings, and I have undertaken it only at your request backed by the strong representations of the French, British and Italian Governments that the Administration should be placed in my hands, not only of the American contributions but of those arising in Europe.

Four years of public service without remuneration as well as practical separation from my family leaves me but one desire and a great need, that is to return to the practice of my engineering profession. I would be glad indeed if you would accept my resignation and communicate to your friends in the Senate my earnest wish to withdraw from the entire matter, and also from the further conduct of the United States Food Administration. I could not upon any occasion fail to express my admiration to yourself and my great obligation for continuous support during these four years.

Faithfully yours,
Herbert Hoover

---

1 | has been | changed by hand to [must be].

Proclamation on Beer

Paris, 24 January, 1919.

My dear Mr. Hoover:

The President has asked me to return to you the proclamation with reference to the brewing of non-alcoholic beers which you enclosed with your letter of January 22nd and which the President has signed.

Sincerely yours,
[signed, Wilson's secretary]
Confidential Secretary to the President

Removal of Food Controls

Paris, January 24, 1919.

Dear Mr. President:

In pursuance of the policy of withdrawing license regulations covering handlers of foodstuffs, I enclose herewith a second proclamation releasing from license a considerable list of foodstuffs in which control is no longer necessary to carry out obligations or prevent extortionate prices.

I should be obliged if you would sign the proclamation and the authority to the Secretary of State attached thereto.

I should be further obliged if you would return to me either the proclamation or copy thereof when it is signed.

Faithfully yours,
[signed, Hoover's secretary]

Plans for Relief Work

Congress did not finally pass the relief bill until January 27. Therefore, in this letter Hoover was certainly referring to passage by the Senate, although he uses the word "Congress." Hoover must already have had plans formulated for structuring the organization to distribute the funds provided. Swager Sherley mentioned in this letter left Congress in March 1919, having been defeated in November 1919 for another term as a Democratic representative from Kentucky (*Times*, Mar. 12, 1919, p. 4). He did not serve in the relief organization as envisaged by Hoover.

Paris, 25 January 1919.

Dear Mr. President:

The Relief Bill having passed Congress, I desire to place for your approval the form of administration which I believe is necessary in order to comply with the law and with the American instinct in the matter.

First, I propose to set up a new organization, to be called the United States Relief Administration, and to transfer to this administration not only the $100,000,000 appropriation but also the accounting for the $5,000,000 which I have already received from your Presidential fund. I propose to establish offices for this Administration in Washington, New York, London, Paris, and the other capitals of Europe where we actually engage in work. I propose to enter into a contract between the Relief Administration and the United States Grain Corporation by which the Grain Corporation undertakes to deliver foodstuffs into various ports in Europe and to sell it at these ports to the Relief Administration.

The object of this latter matter is two-fold. First, the Grain Corporation has a large and skilled staff and working capital, out of which it can conduct these operations, thus making available the whole hundred million dollars for relief purposes and without necessary reserves of a large amount of money for working capital. Second, under the activities of the various Allied buying agencies there is a tendency to control the market in American foodstuffs abroad, and I have established agencies of the Grain Corporation in various countries in order to secure a market free from interference for our great food surpluses so that the Grain Corporation would not only be selling foodstuffs to the Relief Administration but would also be engaged in normal commercial transactions. The paralleling of the administrations to this point has the further advantage that a great deal of the feeding of Europe will be accomplished through normal commercial transaction which can be carried on by the Grain Corporation without trespassing on the capital and operations of the Relief Administration.

I also propose that the advances made by the United States Treasury to some of the minor governments in Europe under the old legislation, which advances are made primarily for the purchase of foodstuffs, such as to the Belgians, Czecho-Slovacs, Roumanians, Servians [*sic*], and so forth, should be handled by the new Relief Administration.

In the matter of personnel, I propose to appoint a commission, comprising some of the leading men of the Food Administration as the managers in the United States and I am endeavoring to secure the services of Mr. Swager Shirley [*sic*], not only to join this administrative body in the United States but also to join the Sugar Equalization Board, the Belgian Relief and the Grain Corporation. The activities of the Food Administration will quickly resolve themselves into practically the administration of these four bodies and it is my view that the Food Administration should be rapidly retired and all of these organizations will naturally dissolve some time next July.

There is one matter in connection with this proposal upon which we require some clarity of understanding. The Allies have proposed to us that our hundred million dollar appropriation should be practically placed in the Treasury of the Allied Supreme Council of Supply and Relief together with such moneys as they may contribute and the whole should be dealt with by this Council. I am legally advised that it is doubtful whether we have any right to do this and I feel strongly that from a moral and a business point of view it would be a mistake; that we should pursue the policy that we have insisted upon from the beginning, that we are prepared and will co-ordinate our American activities in relief with the activities of the European Governments but that we cannot allow them by majority to administer funds and supplies of the United States.

Under the plan that I propose we will co-ordinate the programme of foodstuffs required for any given country and the programme of finance required for this food with the programmes of the Allies. We will take our allotted share of these programmes and give execution to it through our appointed officials.

If you approve of this general plan of organization and of my appointment as Director General of the United States Relief Administration, I will have the necessary executive orders drawn to carry the Act into practical operation upon the above lines.

Faithfully yours,
Herbert Hoover

Approved
    Woodrow Wilson

Food Administration Funds

Paris, January 27, 1919.

Dear Mr. President:

I am advised by the Food Administration in Washington that they are experiencing difficulty in liquidating some of their accounts in the general endeavor to be quite prepared to close the Food Administration on the declaration of peace. These accounts cover the cost of printing a large quantity of envelopes for emergency purposes throughout the States, the employment of night watchmen (necessary owing to the inflammable character of our buildings) and some special travelling expenses and other minor accounts, all of which I understand come outside the provisions of our Congressional appropriation, and it will require $50,000 to pay these various items.

The vouchers have all been prepared and presented in accordance with Treasury regulations and I am advised could be paid from your Security and Defense appropriation of 1919. I am consequently asking your approval of our application to the Treasury for $50,000 to be transferred from your fund to the Food Administration.

The Food Administration is also having difficulty in securing the consent of the Controller of the Treasury for the payment of approximately $18,000 expended for improvements, repairs and alterations in our temporary building, and extension of the Food Administration cafeteria contracted for in the fiscal year ending June 30, 1918. The appropriation for building purposes from your fund was entirely expended and this $18,000 represents additional cost in the fiscal year ending June 30, 1918, and for which we have no appropriation.

I understand that funds are still available in the 1918 Security and Defense appropriation, subject to your order, and I would greatly appreciate your authorization for transferring $18,000 from the 1918 Security and Defense appropriation to the Food Administration.

You will no doubt be pleased to know that reduction in activities of the Food Administration will make it possible to return be-

tween two and three million dollars of the Congressional appropriation.

Faithfully yours,
Herbert Hoover

Approved and authorized:
Woodrow Wilson

Approval of Relief Bill Plan

Paris—27 January, 1919.

My dear Mr. Hoover:

The President asks me to return to you the enclosed letter of
January 25th in which you present the plan for the administration of
the recent relief bill which has been passed by Congress.

You will note that the President has indicated on your letter that
the plan suggested has his approval.

Sincerely yours,
[signed, Wilson's secretary]
Confidential Secretary to the President

Food Proclamation

Paris, 27 January, 1919.

My dear Mr. Hoover:

The President has asked me to return to you the enclosed proclamation and authorization to the Secretary of State enclosed with
your letter to him of January 24th.

Sincerely yours,
[signed, Wilson's secretary]
Confidential Secretary to the President

Relief Bill Amendments

Although the Senate approved the relief bill by a wide margin of 58
to 10 after the House passed it 292 to 43, certain senators were suc-

cessful in attaching amendments that Hoover strongly disapproved. He asked Wilson to telegraph Secretary of State Carter Glass, requesting that Glass use his influence to get these amendments removed while the bill was in conference. Glass was secretary of treasury from December 1918 to November 1919 and he had been a Democratic senator from Virginia for fifteen years when he entered the cabinet. Probably Wilson and Hoover thought his experience plus the friends he had in the upper chamber would help him influence the Senate in favor of administration bills. But he failed to mollify the opponents to the relief bill and on January 28 the measure came from conference as it had gone in; then both chambers accepted the Senate version. On January 27 Hoover sent a cable to William Glasgow of the Food Administration asking him to try to get the conference committee to see the folly in keeping the "Lodge Amendment" (Wilson Papers, Ser. B, LC MSS div.). On January 29 Hoover received a cable from Glasgow reporting on the outcome and stating that he had been advised the "bill would not have passed Senate without Lodge amendment" (ibid.).

Paris 27 January 1919

Dear Mr. President:

The Senate amended our $100,000,000 Relief Bill excluding Bulgaria, Germany, Austria-Hungary and the Mahomedan [*sic*] population of Turkey from the provinces of the Bill. These populations have to be fed if the prime objective of the action is to be secured. The Bill goes into conference and I am wondering if you could send a cablegram to Mr. Glass asking him to represent you in requesting that these exceptions should be taken out. Germany is of course excepted from the whole sense of the Bill and we do not wish to withdraw this exception.

The fact is that three of these countries have established democratic governments and are really making an honest struggle towards respectability. The men in charge of each country are men who have been against the war, and it must be desirable from a political and a humane point of view that they should be supported. The Turkish situation is one of complexity as it will be almost impossible to sort out the Christian population from the rest, and in any event we do not look for a very large expenditure of money in this direction as we have commodities ready to export and it becomes a matter of trade rather than international finance.

The Bill as passed by the House was in the form that we hoped the Senate would accede to. The large majority by which it passed the Senate and the House would seem to indicate some hope of getting it reviewed in conference without too much of a struggle.

Faithfully yours,
Herbert Hoover

Cable to Glass on Relief Funds

> On the same day that Hoover received the note below he sent a letter to the Food Administration in Washington, stating that he proposed "to put it into effect as soon as the bill finally passes Congress." Although the bill had already won House and Senate approval, it was then in a conference committee for reconciling some differences. Hoover's cable continued: "Our staff here believes we should call it American Relief Administration instead [of] either European or United States Relief Administration" (Wilson Papers, Ser. 5B, LC MSS div.).

Paris, 28 January, 1919.

My dear Mr. Hoover:

I have sent a telegram to Glass along the lines suggested in your letter of yesterday in regard to the $100,000,000 Relief Bill.

In haste, Faithfully yours,
Woodrow Wilson

Food Proclamation

Paris, February 1st, 1919

Dear Mr. President,

In pursuance of the policy of withdrawing license regulations covering handlers of foodstuffs, I enclose herewith a third proclamation releasing from license control certain additional handlers of food, where such control is no longer necessary to carry out obligations or prevent extortionate prices.

When this third proclamation is signed, license control will extend only to importers, manufacturers and distributers of fresh, canned and cured pork beef or mutton, cotton-seed and cotton-seed products and lard, importers of sugar, and manufacturers of rice, rice flour, wheat flour and wheat mill feed.

I should be obliged if you would sign the proclamation and the authority to the Secretary of State attached thereto, and if you would return to me either the proclamation or the copy when it is signed.

Faithfully yours,
[signed, Hoover's secretary]

Hoover Appropriation Request

Paris, 1 February, 1919.

Mr. Dear Mr. Hoover:

The President asks me to return to you with his approval and authorization your letter of January 27th in which you request appropriations of $50,000 and $18,000 from the funds for National Security and Defense.

Sincerely yours,
[signed, Wilson's secretary]
Confidential Secretary to the President

Blockade and Obstructionists

The President's Committee on Economic Advisers was established in early January, probably at Hoover's suggestion (*Introduction*, p. xxx, and January 1919 letter, exact date uncertain). Its first meeting on January 30 at Colonel House's office was attended by all six members and the principal matter of discussion was the blockade. They agreed to prepare a memorandum for the President that he would introduce and the Supreme War Council (the Council of Ten) would pass the following Monday. On January 31, McCormick and Hoover had a conference in McCormick's office and the next day (Sunday) the two conferred again on the blockade. On Sunday at 6:00 p.m. McCormick went to see Wilson at home and urged him to present the Supreme War Council with plans for a considerable relaxation of the embargo (McCormick Diary, pp. 36–37). On Saturday Hoover composed the following letter.

Paris, 1 February 1919.

My dear Mr. President:

Mr. McCormick will be sending to you the three resolutions which we are most anxious should be gotten through the Supreme War Council at its meeting on Monday or Tuesday. As you know, I have been advocating these points now for nearly two months and, from selfish or bureaucratic obstruction, we have as yet no results, and I see no hope of attaining any such results except through strong intervention on your part.

Our merchants are in extreme jeopardy from their surplus supplies of food, which the British now repudiate as to purchase but which they obstruct to a wider freedom of market. The French obstruct the notion of neutrals trading with Germany, although it would alleviate both the financial problem and distress. We have no justification in humanity or politics in debarring neutrals from buying all the food they wish for their own consumption now that we have ample supplies. The blockade on Mediterranean countries has no purpose whatever, except to serve detailed selfish interests. All these measures impose a much larger burden on relief than would be necessary if all these people could produce and trade where they may in food.

There is so much obstruction that I despair even getting it past the Supreme War Council unless some great world opinion is brought to bear, and I would like to have you | and |[1] advise me whether you do not think it is desirable for me to disclose the nature of these resolutions that you will propose, to the press at once, and I am sure there will be a reaction from the whole neutral world and a reaction from the United States in your support, and the very nature of this reaction will expedite acceptance of the principles.

Faithfully yours,
Herbert Hoover

---

[1] Deleted by hand.

Press Censorship by French

In answer to Hoover's letter of February 1, Wilson's comment on the censorship of the press by the French government (actually by Clemenceau) reveals a situation prevailing in Paris that alone might have justified holding the Peace Conference elsewhere, such as Lausanne or Geneva, Switzerland.

It is not clear what "papers" or documents Wilson refers to; no notation in Hoover's February 1 letter indicates an enclosure. Hoover's letter of February 4 appears to give the substance of the matter treated in these papers. But unless Hoover was speaking loosely then, the word "yesterday" implies that he had written Wilson on February 3; no letter bearing that date has been discovered.

Press censorship by the French not only excluded whatever the government deemed against the best interest of France, but also included harsh criticism of Wilson and others whenever Clemenceau and others desired to vilify them and their proposals.

Paris, 3 February, 1919.

Mr. Dear Mr. Hoover:

I dare say it would be serviceable to discuss these matters with the press as you suggest, but how can you when the French press is so carefully censored by the Government that everything is excluded which they do not wish to have published. You could probably get it in the English and the American papers but could you get publicity for it anywhere else?

I am returning the papers marked "A" and "B" herewith because your letter does not show clearly whether they are merely memoranda for my eye or whether they are papers which you wish submitted to the Supreme War Council when it meets.

Cordially and faithfully yours,
Woodrow Wilson

Clarification of Letter on Blockade

Paris, 4 February, 1919.

Dear Mr. President:

An error in the enclosure sent to you in my letter of yesterday with respect to the relaxation of blockade has, I am sorry to say, confused your mind on the matter. I enclose herewith the resolution drafted by Mr. McCormick and myself, which we are anxious to get through the Supreme War Council. It has three main purposes. FIRST. There is no right in the law of God or man that we should longer continue to starve neutrals now that we have a surplus of food. That is the object of the first part of the first resolution. SECOND. The French, by obstruction of every financial measure that we can propose to the feeding of Germany in the attempt to compel us to loan money to Germany for this purpose, have defeated every step so far for getting them the food which we have been promising for three months. The object of the second part of the first resolution and of the second resolution is to at least find some channel by which the Germans can help themselves by trade with neutrals and South America. THIRD. The object of the third resolution is to allow the people bordering on the Mediterranean to get into production and trade with all their might and by so doing not only revive their commercial life but also to a large degree supply themselves with food and other commodities and thus take a large part of the burden of relief from the back of our government.

There is no possibility that with all the restrictions on trade taken off that the old Empire of Austria could ever resurrect any military importance. At the present time, we are actually furnishing food to points in Austria at the expense of governments that could be taken care of by private individuals if they could revive their foreign credits without enemy trade restrictions, blockade and censorship, etc., on commercial transactions. Of importance also in the longer view is that the Southwestern area of Europe simply cannot be fed with any governmental resources that either the Allies or ourselves can produce over the next six months, unless they are allowed to get into the production of exportable commodities at the earliest possible moment.

I have worked consistently since arriving in Europe on the 25th day of November to secure these objects and I have to confess that although they have been accepted in principle in first one department and one government after another, they are constantly defeated by one bureaucratic and special self-interest after another of various governments, and I can assure you that the blockade against neutrals and the Southwest is being used today for purely economic ends, when its sole justification was for the protection and furtherance of military operations, which justification is now gone.

I realize that there is still some political importance in maintaining the blockade against Germany within certain limits, but it does not apply to the rest of Europe. I can see no hope of securing the removal of these restrictions except by a direct and strong intervention through yourself and mandatory orders given by the Supreme War Council.

Any reference to a given department in any government will in many cases receive a negative opinion from individuals, simply because [of] interest in the self-perpetuation of bureaucracy or special interests of government or trade in a desire to continue the use of this weapon for aims entirely apart from the war. I am confident that no action is possible except of a mandatory character from the top.

Faithfully yours,
Herbert Hoover

Proposed Resolution

To Be Presented by the President to Supreme War Council

The Supreme War Council at the present time sees no military objection to certain relaxations of economic control of the enemy and approves and recommends the following relaxations in existing export and import control.

1. Norway, Sweden, Denmark, Holland and Switzerland to be allowed to import unlimited amounts of foodstuffs and to be permitted to re-export foodstuffs to Germany subject to the control of the Associated Governments, the aggregate amount of such re-exports with other imports of foodstuffs by Germany, not to exceed the amount of foodstuffs which the Supreme War Council may, from time to time, have agreed to permit to be imported into Germany.

2. Residents of Germany to be permitted, in such manner and through such agency as may be approved by the Supreme Council of Food and Supply, to communicate with persons in foreign countries relative to the purchase of such amounts of foodstuffs as the Supreme Council may have agreed shall be imported into Germany.

3. All commodities to be allowed to be imported into or exported from South Europe and countries bordering on the Mediterranean without limit as to amount and without guarantee against re-export of imports.

Red Cross Transportation

The telegram from Secretary of War Newton Baker and Wilson's intended response, not included here, concerned the transportation of Red Cross personnel to Constantinople. Hoover did not agree with the President's reply and suggested one of his own.

Paris, 5 February, 1919.
My dear Mr. Hoover:
The President has asked me to let you see the enclosed telegram from the Secretary of War and the reply which the President expects to send, if you see no objection to it.
Will you let me know your advice in the matter?
Sincerely yours,
[signed, Wilson's secretary]
Confidential Secretary to the President

Hoover Suggestion for Baker

Judging from the following note sent by Hoover to Wilson, the telegram concerned the use of a transport for carrying Red Cross personnel from New York directly to Constantinople. Hoover was anxious to fill every transport with food for Central Europe. Therefore he immediately suggested that Red Cross personnel travel by transport to Brest, France, and hence to Constantinople on a regular passenger boat. The correspondence of February 11 finally solves the problem.

Paris, 5 February 1919.
Dear Mr. Close:
With regard to your letter of the 5th and Secretary Baker's telegram to the President which I am returning, Mr. Hoover suggests reply for the President, in accordance with the attached memorandum, which will be the means of saving a transport the long trip to Constantinople.
Faithfully yours,
[signed, Hoover's secretary]

Food for Russian Prisoners

The prisoners concerned were the Russian soldiers captured by the Germans prior to the Armistice of November 11, 1918. Some claimed that there were between two and three million such prisoners. A more accurate figure might be 1,500,000. During the war the Germans fed and clothed those able and willing to work. Others received succor by the terms of the Treaty of Brest-Litovsk of March 1918, which took Russia out of the war. All Russian soldiers in German prison camps received at least the minimum of sustenance as long as the Russians held large numbers of German soldiers. But after November 18, 1919, conditions changed rapidly. Germany no longer needed prisoners as workers in factories, and as Germany's own people experienced increasing hunger, little food was available for the Russian prisoners. Many of them left the prison camps and began a desperate trek to their homeland where their future was highly uncertain. Possibly they might join the White Russians; but probably they would become part of the Soviet army and then return as a decided threat to all Central Europe. This probability haunted Europe and was one of the main reasons prompting the letter below.

Paris, 6 February 1919.

Dear Mr. President:

The Military Council in Germany appointed to look after Russian prisoners, upon which General Harries represents us, has made an appeal to the Supreme Food Council and many other bodies for supplies for these prisoners. It appears that the British Red Cross have contributed about $2,500,000 and the American Red Cross is contributing $1,000,000, and these two organizations are prepared to furnish the necessary machinery for distribution. The total cost of the necessary food supplies, in addition to the above assistance, amounts to about $700,000 a month.

We have no American funds under the law that are available for this purpose. On the other hand, it appears that the object of taking care of these prisoners is to prevent them from going back to Russia in the middle of the winter and joining in the Bolshevik army, and therefore is solely a military purpose. Is it not, therefore, the proper duty of the American army to furnish supplies for the American contribution to this end? If you are inclined to this view, it would seem to me desirable to give some indication to General Pershing of authority for the American army to supply say one-third of the foodstuffs to be supplied, leaving two-thirds to the English and French to supply from their military stores. If the Americans took such a proportion it might be interpreted [sic] into American commodities, amounting to say 350 tons of flour per month, leaving to the other Allies a larger proportion of the commodities of non-American origin to furnish. If either the American Red Cross or the Army were to give the 350 tons of flour a month through General Harries, he could no doubt carry out the necessary distribution.

I would be glad indeed to have your views upon the matter and, if you approve my suggestion, if you would communicate it to General Pershing.

Faithfully yours,
Herbert Hoover

Objection to Food Plan

Although the letter below seems to close the matter on a negative note, Hoover continued to press for food for the Russian prisoners. On February 28 he cabled directly to Secretary of War Baker. Again he stressed the point that they must be adequately provisioned in Germany lest they return home and join the Bolshevik army. Thus he asked Baker to authorize General Pershing to advance them stores from his army supplies (Wilson papers, Ser. 5B, LC MSS div.). The sad situation was prolonged for months and never satisfactorily settled (for more, see *Russian Prisoners*).

Hoover's telegram to Baker read thus:

The provisioning of the Russian prisoners in Germany is a matter which has been determined by the allied authorities to be of the utmost importance from the point of view of preventing them joining the Bolshevik. They are therefore being retained in Germany solely for a military purpose and their suffering is indeed intense. It would seem to me that in these circumstances the food supplies which are directed for their maintenance should be supplied from the various quartermasters Stores. Under the law under which I operate I have no funds that can be used in Germany. I would strongly urge upon you authorizing General Pershing to advance the stores which are required by General Harries at Berlin for this purpose. The total [will] probably amount to above one thousand tons a month. The various Red Cross societies have exhausted funds available for this purpose and feel also that it is entirely a military measure being carried out for military purposes.

Paris, 7 February, 1919.

My dear Hoover:

It goes against every instinct of charity and prudence for me to be obliged to say so, but I do feel obliged to say that I do not think we would be justified in making this use of Army supplies, and there is no fund at my disposal which could be used for this purpose. I am afraid we shall have to rest satisfied with what the British and American Red Cross can do in this distressing and important matter.

Cordially and sincerely yours,
[signed, Wilson's secretary]

Whitlock and Paris Ambassadorship

William Graves Sharp was the American Ambassador to Paris from December 2, 1914, to April 14, 1919. Brand Whitlock had been the American Minister to Belgium since 1913. He and Hoover became well acquainted during the years that Hoover spent with the Belgian relief. Whitlock was not awarded the Paris post but in midsummer it was rumored that he was to be transferred to Rome. Soon, however, the Belgian legation was raised to ambassadorial level and on September 29, 1919, Whitlock was named the first American Ambassador to this post, which he held until early January 1922.

Paris 8 February 1919

Dear Mr. President:

I understand that Mr. Sharp is resigning his position as Ambassador in Paris. I do not wish you to think that I am proposing political appointments, but I do feel that I would be neglecting my duty if I did not mention to you the possibilities of Mr. Brand Whitlock for this position. Mr. Whitlock deserves some distinction from the American people for the very great service that he has performed, and his ability, his knowledge of the French language and people, and his intensely sympathetic character to my mind makes him the one outstanding American for this position.

Faithfully yours,
Herbert Hoover

Wilson Failure to Visit Belgium

Wilson had arrived in Paris on December 14, 1918. The day after Christmas he left for England and delivered several speeches in London and Manchester. On January 1 he sailed for Italy where he spoke to large crowds in Rome, Genoa, Milan, and Turin. Immediately thereafter he left for Paris, arriving January 7, 1919. There on January 25 he addressed the opening session of the Peace Conference. The Belgians felt chagrined that during all this period Wilson found no time to visit their war-ravaged country. Hoover naturally shared their disappointment, but it was not until June 18 and 19 that the President finally went to Belgium.

Wilson refused to visit Belgium earlier—and several other ravaged areas as well; it was his belief that before sitting down to write the peace treaty, the conference delegates should be poised with passions uninflamed. Sights of destruction wrought by the German armies might prompt them to formulate unduly harsh treaty terms for the vanquished. On June 17, when the last *i* of the treaty had been dotted, Wilson felt he could safely visit Belgium.

On the day Hoover penned the letter below, he dined with Vance McCormick who recorded, "Hoover discouraged; Allies not playing the game. Thinks he will have to play lone hand in relief. Urges tying up with Belgium in Reparation clauses and giving them priority" (McCormick Diary, p. 40). Having just returned from Belgium, Hoover had its problems foremost in his mind.

As will be seen from the President's reply of February 13 to the letter below, Wilson refused to see the Prime Minister of Belgium, even though the Belgian leader was actually then in Paris. The President stated he was to leave for the United States on February 15 and did not have sufficient time to give mature consideration to the weighty questions that the Prime Minister would likely raise.

Paris, 11 February 1919.

Dear Mr. President:

I have just returned from Brussels where I have had several conferences with the Belgian Ministry and the King. They are, of course, naturally disappointed at your inability to visit Belgium as they had been reserving a number of important matters for discussion with you at your visit. The Belgian Prime Minister asks me if it will be possible for you to make an occasion of half an hour to see him on Friday. As I will have to notify him tomorrow morning at the latest in order for him to get here in time, I am wondering if I can trouble you for an early reply.

The Belgian situation is very serious, and I feel requires some indication from you to the American Peace Mission as to their relation to Belgian problems.

Faithfully yours,
[signed, Hoover's secretary]

Proclamation on Food Controls

Paris, 11 February, 1919

My dear Mr. Hoover:

The President asks me to return to you the enclosed proclamation releasing from license control certain additional handlers of food, where such control is no longer necessary to carry out obligations or prevent extortionate prices, which the President has signed.

Sincerely yours,
Gilbert F. Close
Confidential Secretary to the President

Urgency of Near East Relief

> Arthur Curtis James was a wealthy New York merchant who had taken over the leadership of the American committee for Near East relief. The report James sent about conditions in the Near East compelled Hoover to reconsider his advice of February 5 about sending Red Cross personnel indirectly to Constantinople via Brest. Wilson's letter of February 11 was evidently the principal reason for Hoover's reappraisal of the situation.

Paris, 11 February, 1919.

My dear Mr. Hoover:

You will remember that the other day you sent me a suggested telegram to Secretary Baker with regard to the desire of the American Commission for the Relief in the Near East to secure a transport to go to Constantinople in which you suggested that the party and the provisions be sent on the transport to France and go from there in the ordinary way.

The President has just received the enclosed communication

from Mr. Arthur Curtis James, written before our message to Secretary Baker was sent. In view of the statements made in the enclosed papers the President would like to know whether the urgency of the matter is such as to change the advice which you gave him.

Sincerely yours,

Gilbert F. Close

Confidential Secretary to the President

Response on Relief Transportation

This letter obviously was written by one of Hoover's secretaries. It reveals that Hoover now felt that the slight delay entailed in the original plan could not be tolerated; he realized that conditions were so desperate in the Near East that relief workers should be sent there directly from America. Thus he had to forgo his earlier plan for the transport boat to stop first at Brest and unload food for Europe.

Paris, February 11, 1919.

Dear Mr. Close:

With reference to your letter of February 11 to Mr. Hoover, he has asked me in reply to say that in view of the fact that the necessity of getting these workers to Constantinople is deemed so urgent, it may be better to let them have the use of the transport sending the telegram to Secretary Baker as you had first drafted.

Faithfully yours,

[signed, Hoover's secretary]

Executive Order on Food Relief Bill

The executive order referred to in this letter is also the subject of Hoover's letter to Wilson on February 13. The President signed his approval on February 14 and returned the letter to Hoover immediately. On the same day Wilson returned the signed executive order for setting up the American Relief Administration.

Paris, 12 February, 1919.

Dear Mr. President:

I enclose herewith a proposed Executive Order under the recent

Food Relief Bill creating the American Relief Administration. I have not yet received from the United States the full title or date of the passage of this Food Relief Bill and it is therefore necessary to ask you to sign the order with these blank, to be filled in as soon as cable advices can be received from the United States.

I am particularly anxious that the order specifically authorize the use of the Food Administration Grain Corporation as an agency for relief because I feel certain that the use of an existing organization will eliminate the necessity of establishing a complicated machinery relating to relief only.

I should therefore be obliged if you would sign the enclosed Executive Order and return to me either the original or the duplicate.

> Faithfully yours,
> [signed, Hoover's secretary]

Proposed Financial Aid for Serbia

World War I began on June 28, 1914, when Archduke Francis Ferdinand, heir to the Austrian throne, was slain by a member of a radical group in Serajevo, a Bosnian city bordering on Serbia. The Austria-Hungarian government, suspecting Serbian complicity, made excessive demands of Serbia. When Serbia refused to accept the complete ultimatum, Austria-Hungary declared war on Serbia on July 28, 1914. In the meantime, Russia had promised to back Serbia and Germany had pledged support to Austria-Hungary.

On December 16, 1918, Hoover wrote to Wilson about the need for financial aid to the Serbian government to buy food for its destitute people. The President immediately approved Hoover's proposals. Several weeks later the Treasury Department refused to grant such aid to any government not certified by the State Department as constitutionally founded. Then Hoover had to obtain Secretary of State Lansing's seal of approval of the Serbian government which already had a recognized legation in Washington. The letter that Hoover enclosed has not been located. More than likely it was a Wilson-to-Lansing letter composed by Hoover himself and already approved verbally by the Secretary of State.

As for Serbia's ultimate fate, the Treaty of Versailles re-created an independent Kingdom of Serbs, Croats, and Slovenes that eventually became Yugoslovia.

12 February 1919

Dear Mr. President:

Under your strong recommendation of six weeks ago, the Treasury undertook to make advances to Serbia of $15,000,000 for food. After long delays caused by difficulties of communication and arrangement of the precise details required by the Treasury, the matter was apparently consummated. A new difficulty has now arisen because the State Department feels itself unable to certify that the present Serbian Government is constitutionally founded and the Treasury refuses to make advances without the necessary certification from the State Department. I do not see how we can bridge over this position without your intervention.

It does appear to me that we are in effect recognizing the Serbian Government, that we recognize their Minister in Washington and have never ceased relations from a Ministerial point of view with the Serbian Government. It appears also that the Serbian Government dissolved their Parliament at the time of their retreat and subsequently reorganized their Ministry without Parliamentary sanction, which was of course impossible to secure. I may say that the Belgian, Roumanian, and other fugitive governments are in precisely the same situation.

In the meantime, except for such amounts of food as we could spare from the appropriation from your private fund, the Serbians are now without supplies. The $100,000,000 fund was provided to take care of other governments than those which could receive direct Treasury advances. I have discussed the matter with Mr. Lansing and he informs me that if you will address the enclosed letter to him he will take the necessary steps.

Yours faithfully,
[signed, Hoover's secretary]

Criticism of Italians in Trieste

On April 15, 1915, Britain, France, and Italy signed the Pact of London. On that occasion, in order to induce Italy to enter the war on the Allied side, Italy was promised, among other things, the port of Trieste on the northeastern end of the Adriatic Sea. At the time it was the principal port of the Austro-Hungarian empire. But two-thirds of its population was Italian and this was the determining factor for the promise of the signers of the Pact of London. On November 4, 1918, Italian troops entered Trieste and the troop's activities there, as sketched in the letter below, made it impossible for Hoover to utilize the port for the many bordering people who depended on its facilities for food supplies and other ordinary commerce.

Paris, 12 February 1919.

Dear Mr. President:

The feeding of the Czecho-Slovenes, Viennese and Serbians all revolves around the use of port facilities and a single railway running out of Trieste. The Italians have taken such an attitude towards these other peoples that the operation of the railway is practically hopeless for the distance that it traverses Italian occupied territory. They have also stopped all communication through to Trieste from these territories and we are not even able to send the most commonplace telegrams with regard to food. They are apparently driving all of the other races than Italians out of Trieste and the consequence is that we have little reliable labor for discharging ships.

We have used every argument possible with the Italian authorities and there is in my view but one solution; that is, that the operation of such docks and railways as we need for feeding these interior people shall be placed under the direction of the Inter-allied Food Commission sitting at Trieste and the actual executive control vested in the American member. Their attitude on this question and many others is such that I want to protest most strongly against any further Treasury advances to the Italian Government until this matter of fearful injustice is put right. If you approve, I will ask Mr. Davis to make it a condition of further advances with the Treasury that this situation shall be straightened out to my satisfaction.

Faithfully yours,
Herbert Hoover

Visit by Belgian Prime Minister

Paris — 13, February, 1919.

My dear Mr. Hoover:

The President asks me to acknowledge your note of February 11th, and to ask if you will not be kind enough to suggest to the

Belgian Prime Minister that he take these questions up with Secretary Lansing. The President would wish to give them the most mature consideration and that is really out of the question during these last busy days before he leaves for America.

Sincerely yours,
Gilbert F. Close
Confidential Secretary to the President

Urgent Letter on Relief

The letter below to Close probably accompanied the subsequent letter of Hoover to Wilson that contained a request for appointing subdirectors for the American Relief Administration. Hoover evidently thought this matter important and wanted it concluded before the President left for America. He probably drafted his letter on February 12 and asked his secretary, Lewis Strauss, or someone else in his office, to telephone Wilson's secretary, Gilbert Close, informing him that the letter was on its way. Wilson complied and immediately approved Hoover's plan by signing the relevant letter.

Paris, 13 February 1919.

Dear Mr. Close:

Attached is the letter to the President about which I telephoned you. The matter is one which can be settled if the President will merely indicate his approval on Mr. Hoover's letter. It is very much hoped that you will be able to get this to the President's attention before he leaves, as we would like to make the transaction involved before we would have time to hear from him in the States.

Faithfully yours,
[signed, Hoover's secretary]

Procedures for ARA Matters

Paris, 13 February 1919.

Dear Mr. President:

I submitted to you yesterday an Executive Order setting up the American Relief Administration. Under this Administration I would like to have before you leave, your authority for certain procedure[s].

1st. on December 16, 1918, you cabled the Secretary of the Treasury directing him to pay at once to the U.S. Food Administration Grain Corporation Five Million Dollars from your fund for national security and defense, with which to conduct temporary relief and pay administrative expenses. This money was paid to the Grain Corporation, who have been dispensing it up to the present moment, and I would like to have your authority to transfer this sum to the new American Relief Administration, who will account for the sums already used and will use the residue of it for administrative expenses and such items as you have authorized which cannot be covered by Congressional appropriation.

2nd. I would like to have your authority to appoint subdirectors of the American Relief Administration in the United States and such points in Europe as are necessary to give effect to the administration. I propose to use for this purpose largely men formerly approved by you for appointment in the Food Administration and men drawn from the Army and Navy. So far as possible I am asking them to serve on a voluntary basis.

Faithfully yours,
Herbert Hoover

Approved:
> *Woodrow Wilson*

Executive Order Setting up ARA

On January 11, 1919, Wilson wrote Hoover to confirm his appointment as Director General of American Relief in Europe. However, the American Relief Administration and Hoover's position in it depended on the passage of the $100,000,000 European relief bill and the official signing of the act by Wilson. Congress enacted the measure in its final form on January 28, but the President was unable to sign it until he returned to Washington in late February. The day before departing for America, Wilson sent Hoover a copy of the executive order establishing the ARA in which it is called an "Act of February twenty-fourth, 1919." The executive order was written by Hoover himself (see preceding letter). Of course, since November 1918 Hoover had been engaged in European relief activity by authority of other titles he retained, especially that of American Food Administrator.

Paris, 14 February, 1919

My dear Mr. Hoover:

The President asks me to send you the enclosed executive order setting up the American Relief Administration. You will note that it has his approval.

Sincerely yours,
[signed, Wilson's secretary]
Confidential Secretary to the President

Executive Order

In pursuance of an Act entitled "An Act providing for the relief of such populations in Europe and countries contiguous thereto outside of Germany, German Austria, Hungary, Bulgaria and Turkey, as may be determined upon by the President as necessary" approved February 24, 1919, I hereby direct that the furnishing of foodstuffs and other urgent supplies and the transportation, distribution and administration thereof, provided for in said Act, shall be conducted under the direction of Herbert Hoover who is hereby appointed Director General of the American Relief Administration with full power to determine to which of the populations named in said Act the supplies shall be furnished and in what quantities, and further to arrange for reimbursement so far as possible as in said Act provided.

He is hereby authorized to establish the American Relief Administration for the purpose of carrying out the provisions of said Act and to employ such persons and incur such expenses as may be necessary for such purpose, to disburse all sums appropriated under the aforesaid Act or appoint a disbursing officer with that power; and particularly to employ the Food Administration Grain Corporation, organized under the provisions of the Food Control Act of August 10, 1917, as an agency for the purchase, transportation and distribution of foodstuffs and supplies to the populations requiring relief.

He is hereby further authorized in the carrying out of the aforesaid Act of February twenty-fourth, 1919, to contract with the Food Administration Grain Corporation or any other person or corporation, that such person or corporation shall carry stocks of food in transit to Europe, and at points in Europe, in such quantities as may be agreed upon and as are required to meet relief needs, and that there shall be paid to such person or corporation in account from the appropriation made in the aforesaid Act of February twenty-fourth, 1919, any sums which may be required for the purchase and transportation of foodstuffs and maintenance of stocks.

Woodrow Wilson

Executive Order for American Relief

> The executive order mentioned in this letter appears to be different from the one mentioned in the previous letter, because on February 14 Wilson's secretary sent two different letters to Hoover about returning "the executive order." Perhaps the secretary forgot that he had already written to Hoover. If, on the other hand, there were two executive orders for the same day, the second one has not been located.

Paris, 14 February, 1919.

My dear Mr. Hoover:

At the President's request I am returning to you the executive order with reference to the food relief bill which you enclosed with your letter of February 12th.

> Sincerely yours,
> [signed, Wilson's secretary]
> Confidential Secretary to the President

Wilson and Trieste Problem

> This brief letter, an answer to Hoover's complaint of February 12 about the Italian activity in Trieste, was written in haste because Wilson was to leave for America on February 15. Moreover, on February 14 he presented to a plenary session a draft of the commission on the League of Nations dealing with the covenant. It had been prepared under great pressure and consumed much of Wilson's time and energy. The "this" in the first line of the following letter was undoubtedly a cryptic reference to Hoover's letter of February 12 suggesting that Davis withhold Treasury advances to Italy unless Italy mended its ways regarding Trieste.

Paris, 14 February, 1919

My dear Hoover:

I think this may be a very useful piece of advice to give Mr. Davis in advising him how he is to handle this exceedingly important matter.

In great haste.

Faithfully yours,
Woodrow Wilson

Missing Enclosure

The enclosure with this letter is no longer with the Hoover papers. Whatever it concerned, Wilson viewed it as "grave and serious." Possibly the enclosure was Hoover's own February 12 letter to Wilson, which did indeed treat a most serious matter relative to Trieste. Or it may have been a memorandum or letter from a third party regarding a "serious matter" that Wilson wanted Hoover to handle.

Paris — 14 February, 1919.

My dear Mr. Hoover:

This seems to me to contain a very grave and serious matter and I would be very much obliged if you would consider it very carefully.

In haste.

Always faithfully yours,
Woodrow Wilson

Enclosure [Enclosure missing]

Hoover and Glass on Price Controls

The letter below to Wilson was written by Theodore F. Whitmarsh, acting for Hoover in Washington as head of the Food Administration. It contains verbatim Hoover's view of a cable from Carter Glass on the subject of price controls.

It is not clear whether Hoover, Whitmarsh, or Wilson received "the cablegram of Mr. Glass," Secretary of the Treasury. It would seem that the recipient was Whitmarsh who sent it on to Hoover. Then it appears that Hoover made his comments to Whitmarsh, intending that they be transmitted to Wilson who was still in Washington. Hence it properly belongs to the collection of Hoover-Wilson correspondence.

February 24, 1919

Dear Mr. President:

I have the honor to transmit the following to you at the request of Mr. Hoover:

"I have received your request for my view upon the cablegram of Mr. Glass, recommending the immediate abandonment of all control of prices by the Food Administration.

I feel that there must be some misunderstanding as to the amount and nature of the control outstanding. By the end of this month, control of all but four or five commodities will have been entirely demobilized. These four or five commodities comprise from twenty-five to thirty percent of the nation's food bill.

It is my understanding of the suggestion of the Cabinet, that Congress should undertake the compensation of all those who become losers from the alteration of Congressional or moral guarantees. In order to do this, Congress would have to make provision in advance for liquidated payment to probably fifteen million individuals in the United States. Unless this advance provision were made, there would ensue the most disastrous financial collapse in certain trades. Furthermore, taking a world view over the next four months, while some drop in prices might follow removal of control, the world situation on the few remaining commodities is such that even higher prices than the present might rule.

In order that you may see more clearly something of the situation and the difficulties, I set out below some of the circumstances surrounding the commodities which are under some measure of control.

Firstly, as to wheat; I would be obliged if you would consult Mr. Barnes who will inform you how impossible it is to reach the loser by any form of direct payment to the producer, in the event of abandonment of the Congressional guarantee. Furthermore, the farmer who raises wheat would be subject, more acutely than in the case of any other commodity, to the present "world control" of wheat which covers 80 percent of the

world export and which "world control" could make any price
at will. We would thus have to fix some price at any event. In
view of the spread of famine in India, the demand in Europe,
the total supplies, etc., I am convinced that in a free market, the
price would not be appreciably changed from the present level,
but there can be no free prices before next harvest and any relaxation in our control would simply mean a gift to the "international wheat control." All this is, of course, aside from the technical difficulties of compensating the farmer.

Secondly, as to sugar; the price of this commodity is being
retained even now at ten and eleven cents retail and has been
prevented from advancing during the war to twenty-five or
thirty cents a pound by various measures adopted by the Food
Administration. The price today ranges from fourteen to twenty
cents per pound in the blockaded countries. We have the cheap-
est sugar in the world today, with the exception of a few small
countries producing a surplus of sugar, and who at the same
time, restrain exportation. The present stabilization is based not
only on a moral guarantee to our beet and Louisiana cane producers, but also on a binding contract between the United
States and Cuba for the purchase of two-thirds of the Cuban
crop. Any change would require either; (A) the consent of the
Cuban Government to cancel this contract, or; (B) a direct appropriation by Congress to meet the losses on reduction of the
Cuban price. This would imply the abandonment of the moral
guarantee given to the beet and Louisiana sugar producers. If
the contract fixing the Cuban price were rescinded and stabilization withdrawn, it is possible that during the next two or three
months of restricted shipping and blockaded trade outlet, there
might be a drop of one or even two cents a pound in the value
of raw sugar, but thereafter, to all appearances, there would develop a world shortage. It is extremely unlikely that a drop in
raw sugar price would ever be reflected to the consumer in the
face of the speculation and profiteering that would ensue and
much higher prices would probably maintain later in the year.

Thirdly, cottonseed and rice products were placed under
control to restrain profiteering and high prices and are now subject to the uncertainties of domination of foreign buying agen-

cies and blockade and are still subject to some degree to moral assurance to the producers until next summer. The prices of cottonseed and rice products bear a very small relation to the cost of living and the great proportion of these products remaining in the United States should go for export.

To sum up, it seems to me impossible even by Congressional appropriation, to reach the many millions of farmers, manufacturers, and tradesmen who would be losers by the abandonment of the control of wheat and sugar, and a period of speculation and possibly even higher prices would follow. As to the cottonseed and rice production, these can be terminated at once if advisable and you consider it justifiable. The resulting losses would be local.

I recognise that the tide of criticism is now turning from that of the producer who has felt that prices were unduly restrained, to that of the consumer who feels prices are unduly maintained in these few commodities. I feel deeply the necessity of lowering food prices for the consumer and of freeing the distributive trade from all control as not only a necessity for the United States, but as a movement towards fundamental stability of the world. The unemployed in the United States give more emphasis to this, but I feel that in pressure to secure these desirable results, we cannot justly disregard the other factors which enter into the demobilization of our war measures, lest the evils we create are greater than those we remedy. Hoover.

I have the honor to remain, Always faithfully yours,

> *Theodore F. Whitmarsh*
> Acting for Herbert Hoover,
> United States Food Administrator

Gift of Wilson War Address

Hoover had been in London when Wilson delivered his war message to Congress on April 2, 1917. On April 4 the Senate adopted a war resolution by a vote of 82 to 6 and the House did the same April 6 by a 373-to-50 vote. Within hours Wilson signed the proclamation that "a state of war exists" between the United States and Germany. Until the very end Hoover had hoped that America could be saved from entry into the armed conflict. However, he was so impressed with Wilson's address that on April 3, 1917, he cabled him a long and warm message of congratulations. Nearly a year later the President sent Hoover a bound copy of the address; it was the day after Wilson reached Paris from Washington. His four-week absence from the Peace Conference was regrettable and his return ushered in a critical period for those engaged in drawing up the treaty.

Paris, 15 March, 1919.

My dear Mr. Hoover:

I am taking the liberty of sending you herewith a package containing a bound copy of President Wilson's address to the American Congress in April, 1917 which I am sending you at the request of Mr. Charles W. McAlpin, Hotel McAlpin, New York City. Mr. McAlpin was for many years Secretary of Princeton University and is an intimate friend of the President's.

Sincerely yours,
[signed, Wilson's secretary]
Confidential Secretary to the President

Thanks for Copy of Address

March 17, 1919.

Dear Mr. Close:

I thank you for your letter of March 15th, and for the handsome volume which accompanied it. I am also writing to Mr. McAlpin.

Faithfully yours,
Herbert Hoover

Letters from Georges and Boysen

Paris, 17 March, 1919.

My dear Mr. Hoover:

I am sending you herewith letters from Mr. Georges and Mr. Fran D. L. Boysen.

Sincerely yours,
[signed, Wilson's secretary]
Confidential Secretary to the President

Releasing Packers from License

Paris, March 18, 1919.

My dear Mr. President:

I enclose herewith draft of Proclamation releasing the meat packers from license.

As you are aware the stabilization of the price came to an end on March 1st, and there appears to be no reason why the same policy could not now be followed in this case as has already been adopted with respect to practically all the other food trades.

I should be greatly obliged if you would sign the Proclamation and return to me either the original or enclosed copy.

Faithfully yours,

[signed, Hoover's secretary]

Approval of Releasing Packers

Paris, 19 March, 1919.

My dear Mr. Hoover:

The President has asked me to send you the enclosed proclamation releasing the meat packers from license which you forwarded with your letter of March 14th. You will note that the President has signed the proclamation and I am forwarding a copy of it to the White House at Washington for their record.

Sincerely yours,

[signed, Wilson's secretary]

Confidential Secretary to the President

Letter from Hollis

Paris, 19 March 1919.

My dear Mr. Hoover:

I am sending you herewith a communication from Mr. P. Hollis of Hardstone, England, for such consideration as may be deemed proper.

Sincerely yours,

[signed, Wilson's secretary]

Confidential Secretary to the President

Houston on Wheat Crop

Paris, 19 March 1919.

Dear Mr. President

I understand that Secretary Houston is cabling you recommending a plan for the handling of the next wheat crop. I hope that you will take occasion to consult me before coming to a decision on the matter, as it necessarily involves the present situation.

Faithfully yours,
Herbert Hoover

Army Goods for Europeans

On March 17, 1919, Hoover addressed a letter to Judge Edwin B. Parker, chairman of the United States Liquidation Commission, and explained to him the feasibility of relieving the army of its surplus supply of clothing and food rations for the benefit of such countries as Poland, Rumania, and Greater Siberia.

It can be presumed that Parker answered affirmatively, for Hoover wrote to Wilson on March 22 for approval of the project. The President gave this approval by sending a letter to Parker. This letter, written March 22 and sent March 24, emphasized that the plan would not only serve a humanitarian purpose but also help dispose of much unsalable army material. It is likely that Hoover wrote this letter for the President, as he often did in similar cases. It was sent to Parker on March 24 with only one word changed from the March 22 version.

Paris, 22 March 1919.

My dear Mr. President:

The need for clothing in the various liberated regions of Europe is almost beyond description. The large surplus supplies of Army clothing have been placed in the hands of the United States Liquidation Board, of which Judge Parker is Chairman, to be sold. The Liquidation Board has large powers in the matter and are entirely sympathetic towards realizing the material on fair terms and extending credit for its payment. In order to get a rapid execution, it is necessary for someone to take responsibilities in the determination of prices and values. I am perfectly willing to take my share of these responsibilities. In order for the Board to take action in this direction, they desire to have from you an indication that you are in agreement with this policy, and we have jointly drafted the attached letter, which, if you could see your way to address Judge Parker, would put the matter in motion.

> Yours faithfully,
> [signed, Hoover's secretary]

Hoover Retirement, Barnes Appointment

> Paris, 25 March 1919.

My dear Mr. President:

The determination of the method of administration of the 1919 wheat crop requires an early decision. I have the feeling that with the completion of this harvest year the great call for relief work in Europe will have been completed and before this time the Food Administration will have ceased legally to exist, except so far as it is necessary to carry on outstanding contracts in the 1918 wheat crop and in connection with sugar purchases. I believe that the completion of the harvest year, therefore, offers a proper opportunity for me to retire after five years of public service.

The handling of the 1919 wheat crops, however, is a matter of extreme importance and I am convinced that the world demand for wheat would be such that if it is capably carried out there need not necessarily be a single dollar lost to the government. The only reason why, on present prospects, any loss should be incurred, would be amateur handling of a matter of extreme technical and financial complexity or, alternatively, of deliberate desire of the government to subsidize the price of flour for economic reasons. The addition of this latter function would, in any event, be one that could only be carried out by the very highest experience and skill.

I am convinced that the only man in the nation today who is capable of carrying through this difficult operation is Mr. Julius Barnes, who, as you know, has had charge of this work for the last two years. He has, directly and indirectly, handled nearly two billions of dollars of money, has not cost the government a penny of loss, and there has never been even a suggestion of either incapacity or of bad faith in his work. His recent announcement that he felt that he would retire with the harvest year has brought a storm of protest throughout the nation, both from the farming community and the trades, as they feel that his administration has been not only capable but just, as between the conflicting interests concerned. I have also received urgent telegrams from many different quarters, including even Senators, urging that he should be continued as a matter of national importance. Mr. Barnes is, I believe, nominally a Republican, but his principal politics consist of great personal devotion to yourself. I have inquired of him by cable whether he would be willing to continue for another year to direct this matter and I believe he could be induced to accept it but with one reservation, that is, that he should be placed directly under yourself, without the intervention of any other government department. He is that type of man who requires a considerable latitude of action, but, of course, would accept entirely your direction.

In order to carry out the guarantee in the light of the new legislation, it will be necessary to make some legal changes in the present United States Food Administration Grain Corporation to adapt it to the legislation. I would suggest that these changes should be made some time in June, that a complete statement be made of its operations, prepared up to July 1st as marking the end of its Food Administration association and that the name be changed to the United States Wheat Corporation. Under these plans, Mr. Barnes, as President of the corporation, would become at that date directly responsible to you instead of to myself as Chairman.

As the whole problem is one of our greatest national liquidation problems, I believe that the same direct association with yourself that I have enjoyed is of the utmost importance.

Faithfully yours,
Herbert Hoover

Gibson as Minister to Czechoslovakia

Paris, 25 March 1919.

My dear Mr. President:

I understand that Mr. Hugh Gibson, who is now attached to me as diplomatic advisor in Europe, has been suggested to you as Minister to Czecho-Slovakia. I would like to place before you how extremely serviceable it would be in the handling of one of our most difficult food situations if the man appointed were possessed of his background of experience connected with this work.

Mr. Gibson was, as you know, First Secretary in Belgium during the occupation and has been a First Secretary of Embassy up to the time that I arrived in Europe when, at my request, he was attached to me for negotiations with the governments comprising the old Austrian Empire, with whom he has been in close contact ever since.

I cannot speak too highly of his abilities nor do I feel it would be amiss to mention that he has been in the diplomatic service for ten or fifteen years and has reached that point where either he will need promotion or, as the result of his high abilities, he will be attracted from the service. I have known him under the most difficult of circumstances and he has never failed in a representation of the United States in the way that all of us would desire, both as to ability, courage and accomplishment in the diplomatic service. To my knowledge, he has been one of your most ardent and constant supporters.

> Yours faithfully,
> [signed, Hoover's secretary]

Telegram from Andrews

> Paris, 26 March, 1919.

My dear Mr. Hoover:

I am taking the liberty of referring to you for consideration the enclosed telegram which the President has received from Mr. E. C. Andrews of the Merchants Exchange in St. Louis.

> Sincerely yours,
> [signed, Wilson's secretary]
> Confidential Secretary to the President

Relief and Shipping Board Tonnage

Vance McCormick, a member of the Supreme Economic Council (McCormick Diary, March 22, p. 56), wrote that he and Hoover went together to the Hotel Crillon hoping to see Wilson on a matter they believed called for his immediate personal attention. It was in the late afternoon and the President was tied up with a long session of the League of Nations committee. So the pair camped in an outer room and saw him when he came out. McCormick records that "Hoover got his approval of strong cables to Shipping Board and Treasury Department concerning great need of ships for immediate supply of food, for Europe. Predicted no food here June unless gets 500,000 tons of shipping immediately."

As the following letter shows, the cables did not produce the hoped-for results. However on April 9 Hoover wrote Wilson of success in getting the needed shipping.

27 March 1919

My dear Mr. President:

I have received the attached telegram from Mr. Hurley in response to my request for 500,000 tons of food loaded in the month of April and in response to your direction to him and the War Department that he should find this tonnage. Mr. Hurley states that he will not find more than 300,000 tons.

In arriving at 500,000 tons, I took the theoretical necessity of the various peoples under relief, which amounted to 800,000 tons, and I reduced each single item to the lowest point that I thought was possible, and arrived at 620,000 tons but knowing the acuteness of Mr. Hurley's position I reduced it on block to 500,000 tons. I wish to say that I simply cannot take the responsibility for this situation unless this tonnage is provided as we have requested. Every country that we have under relief is rumbling with social explosion. All the people in these countries are under drastic food regimes and to make a cut in the amount of 60% of their practical necessities can mean only a total collapse.

Faithfully yours,
Herbert Hoover

Hoover and Relations with Bolshevists

In this letter of March 28, 1919, Hoover addresses himself to the subject of Bolshevism and the posture the United States should assume in the face of its advances in Russia and its threats to other European countries. When the Bolsheviks seized power in November

1917 they openly expressed their conviction that "proletarian" revolution in Russia could not succeed unless promptly followed by similar revolutions in the capitalist countries of the West. The failure of such an event in Germany after the Armistice of November 1918 was a bitter disappointment to the Russian Bolsheviks. In this setting, the Communist International—the Comintern, or Third International— was founded in Moscow, and just days before Hoover's letter of March 28, 1919, it issued a manifesto calling on workers in other countries to overthrow capitalism. For months prior to this manifesto the Soviet government had been fomenting revolutions by sending money and revolutionary agents into eastern European countries.

It is against this background that the letter must be read with its indictment of Communism and its advice to Wilson on the proper response to make if the Soviets should resort to armed force to spread their doctrines. Hoover also indicated what action would be appropriate should Communist revolution erupt from native forces within a particular country. The letter also offered detailed suggestions for providing food for starving Russian people.

In his *Ordeal* (p. 117) Hoover states that his letter of March 28 was written in response to Wilson's request on March 26 for "a memorandum on my information and opinion on the Soviet problem." The letters written about Russia on April 3, 9, 21, and 23 and Hoover's anti-Bolshevist statement of April 25 were directly related to this memorandum.

28 March, 1919.

Dear Mr. President:

As the result of Bolshevik economic conceptions, the people of Russia are dying of hunger and disease at the rate of some hundreds of thousands monthly in a country that formerly supplied food to a large part of the world.

I feel it is my duty to lay before you in just as few words as possible my views as to the American relation to Bolshevism and its manifestations. These views at least have the merit of being an analysis of information and thought gleaned from my own experience and the independent sources which I now have over the whole of Europe, through our widespread relief organization.

It simply cannot be denied that this swinging of the social pendulum from the tyranny of the extreme right to the tyranny of the reactionaries in Eastern and Central Europe for generations before the war, and the suffering of their common people is but a commonplace to every social student. This situation was thrown into bold relief by the war and the breakdown of these reactionary tyrannies. After fighting actually stopped on the various fronts and famine which followed has further silhouetted the gulf between the lower and the upper classes. The poor were starved and driven mad in the presence of extravagance and waste.

It is to be noticed that the Bolshevik ascendency or even their strong attempts so far are confined to areas of former reactionary tyranny. Their courses represent the most unnatural violence of a mass of ignorant humanity, who themselves have learned in grief of tyranny and violence over generations. Our people, who enjoy so great liberty and general comfort, cannot fail to sympathize to some degree with these blind gropings for better social conditions. If former revolutions in ignorant masses are any guide, the pendulum will yet swing back to some moderate position when bitter experience has taught the economic and social follies of present obsessions. No greater fortune can come to the world than that those foolish ideas should have an opportunity somewhere of bankrupting themselves.

It is not necessary for any American to debate the utter foolishness of these economic tenets. We must all agree that our processes of production and distribution, the outgrowth of a hundred generations, in the stimulation to individual initiative, the large equality of opportunity and infinite knowledge of mind and body, while not perfect, come about as near perfection as is possible from the mixture of avarice, ambition, altruism, intelligence, ignorance and education, of which the human animal is today composed. The Bolshevik's land of illusion is that he can perfect these human qualities by destroying the basic processes of production and distribution instead of devoting himself to securing a better application of the collective surplus.

Politically, the Bolsheviki most certainly represent a minority in every country where they are in control, and as such they constitute a tyranny that is the negation of democracy, for democracy, as I see it, must rest on the execution of the will of the majority expressed by free and unterrified suffrage. As a tyranny, the Bolshevik has resorted to terror, bloodshed and murder to a degree long since abandoned even amongst reactionary tyrannies. He has even to a greater degree relied upon criminal instinct to support his doctrines than even autocracy did. By enveloping into his doctrine the cry of the helpless and the downtrodden, he has embraced a large degree of emotionalism and has thereby given an impulse to his propaganda comparable only to the impulse of large spiritual movements. This propaganda, however, in my view will stir other populations only in ratio to their proportions of the suffering and ignorant and criminal. I feel myself, therefore, that the political danger of spread of Bolshevism of propaganda is a direct factor of the social and political development of the population which they attempt to imprognate [*sic*]. Where the gulf between the middle classes and the lower classes is large, and where the lower classes have been kept in ignorance and distress, this propaganda will be fatal and do violence to normal democratic development. For these reasons, I have no fear of it in the United States, and my fears as to other countries would be gauged by the above criticism. It is possible that the Soviet type of government might take hold in some other countries as a primitive form of democracy, but its virulence will be tempered by their previous degree of political subversion.

There remains in my mind one more point to be examined, that is, as to whether the Bolshevik centers now stirred up by great emotional hopes will not undertake large military crusades in an attempt to impose their doctrines on other defenseless people. This is a point on which my mind is divided with the evidence at hand, and it seems to me that the whole treatment of the problem must revolve on the determination of this one question. If this spirit is inherent in their doctrine, it appears to me that we must disregard all other questions and be prepared to fight, for exactly the same reasons that we entered the European War against Germany. If this is not the case, then it appears to me that from an American point of view we should not involve ourselves in what may be a ten year military entanglement in Europe. The American people cannot say that we are going to insist that any given population must work out its internal social problems according to our particular conception of democracy. In any event, I have the most serious doubt that outside forces entering upon such an enterprise can do other than infinite harm, for any great wave of emotion must ferment and spread under repression. In the swing of the social pendulum from the extreme left back toward the right, it will find the point of stabilization based on racial instincts that could never be established by outside intervention.

I think we have also to contemplate what would actually happen if we undertook military intervention in, say, a case like Hungary. We should probably be involved in years of police duty and our first act would probably in the nature of things make us a party to re-establishing the reactionary classes in their economic domination over the lower classes. This is against our fundamental national spirit, and I doubt whether our soldiers under these conditions could resist infection with Bolshevik ideas. It also requires consideration as to whether or not our people at home, on gradual enlightenment as to the social wrongs of the lower classes in these countries, would stand for our providing power by which such reactionaries held their position, and we would perchance be thrown into an attempt as governors to work out some social reorganization of these countries. We thus become a mandatory with a vengeance. We become, in fact, one of four mandatories, each with a different political and social outlook, for it would necessarily be a joint Allied undertaking. Furthermore in our present engagements with France, England and Italy we become a junior in this partnership of four. It is therefore inevitable that in these matters, where our views and principles are at variance with the European Allies, we would find ourselves subordinated and even committed to policies against our convictions.

In all these lights I have the following suggestions:

First: We cannot even remotely recognize this murderous tyranny without stimulating actionist radicalism in every country in Europe and without transgressing on every National ideal of our own.

Second: That some Neutral of International reputation for probity and ability should be allowed to create a second Belgian Relief Commission for Russia, to give him diplomatic, financial and transportation support; that he should open negotiations with the Allied Governments on the ground of desire to enter upon the humane work of saving life, and ask the conditions upon which ships carrying food and other necessaries will be allowed to pass. He should be told that we will raise no obstruction and would even help in his humanitarian task if he gets assurances that the Bolsheviki will cease all militant action across certain defined boundaries and cease their subsidizing of disturbances abroad; under these conditions that he could raise money, ships and food, either from inside or outside Russia; that he might even demand that Germany help pay for this. This plan does not involve any recognition of relationship by the Allies of the Bolshevik murderers now in control any more than England recognizes Germany in its deals with the Belgian Relief. It would appear to me that such a proposal would at least give a period of rest along the frontiers of Europe and would give some hope of stabilization. Time can thus be taken to determine whether or not this whole system is a world danger, and whether the Russian people will not themselves swing back to moderation and themselves bankrupt these ideas. This plan, if successful, would save an immensity of helpless human life and would save our country from further entanglements which today threaten to pull us from our National ideals.

Third: I feel strongly the time has arrived for you again to reassert your spiritual leadership of democracy in the world as opposed to tyrannies of all kinds. Could you not take an early opportunity to analyse, as only you can, Bolshevism from its political, economic, humane and its criminal points of view, and, while yielding its aspirations, sympathetically to show its utter foolishness as a basis of economic development; show its true social ends; rap your own reactionaries for their destruction of social betterment and thereby their stimulation of Bolshevism; point, however, to the steady progress of real democracy, in these roads of social betterment, I believe you would again align the hearts of the suffering for orderly progress against anarchy, not alone in Russia but in every allied country.

If the militant features of Bolshevism were drawn in colors with their true parallel with Prussianism as an attempt at world domination that we do not stand for, it would check the fears that today haunt all men's minds.

Faithfully yours,
[signed, Hoover's secretary]

Barnes and 1919 Wheat Crop

This letter should be read in conjunction with Hoover's letter of March 25 concerning his retirement and successor. Recall also that Hoover wrote a letter of resignation as early as January 23, although he probably did not mail it. Hoover actually stayed on the job for some time longer. On June 23, five days before Wilson left for the States, Hoover informed the President orally that he wanted to retire on July 1. But the next day he wrote Wilson that he had changed his mind and he now thought it more feasible to remain as head of the Food Administration until he returned home. Six weeks later, August 2, he cabled Wilson in Washington a long and discouraging message on the food situation. He reminded Wilson of the oral resignation and asked that it be considered effective as of that date (See also the letters for June 24 and August 2).

Paris, 28 March, 1919.

My dear Hoover:

If ever a man has earned the right to retire from great responsibilities, you have earned it by the admirable way in which you have done the work, the very burdensome and difficult work, which has fallen to you in this great war, and yet I experience a pang in thinking of your retirement.

I won't discuss that right now. I will instead turn to the suggestion you make about the handling of the 1919 wheat crop. I am quite ready to subscribe to your judgment of Mr. Julius Barnes and to concur in your plan for putting him at the head of the work which lies before us, and if you will be kind enough to make me a brief memorandum of just what steps are necessary and when they should be taken, I would be very much obliged to you indeed.

With warmest regards, Faithfully yours,

Woodrow Wilson

Houston Telegram on Wheat Crop

The telegram referred to in Wilson's letter was from David F. Houston, Secretary of Agriculture. Wilson wanted to receive assurances that Hoover's project for handling the 1919 food crop under the guidance of Julius Barnes did not conflict with any plan of Houston's; hence this short letter of inquiry about Houston's views. Hoover's letter of March 31 assured the President that there was perfect agreement between the two. In that letter Hoover enclosed a draft of a telegram for Wilson to send to Houston conveying the same assurance.

Paris, 29 March, 1919.

My dear Hoover:

When I wrote you yesterday, I had not seen this telegram from Houston. There was some mixup about it, and it had not come under my eye. Do the suggestions contained in your letter of the other day, which I answered yesterday, in your judgment take care of the exigencies mentioned by Houston?

You see I have not been able to study the matter at all.

Cordially and faithfully yours,
Woodrow Wilson

Telegram against Hoover Retirement

Paris, 29 March, 1919.

My dear Mr. Hoover:

Here is a telegram which you ought to "read, ponder, and inwardly digest". It certainly is a high tribute to you and one to which I entirely subscribe.

Cordially and faithfully yours,
Woodrow Wilson

Enclosure

Pullmann Washn

Woodrow Wilson, President of the
United States, Paris

We see by the Associated Press reports that Herbert C. Hoover, United States Food Administrator has announced his intention to resign his post. We would respectfully urge that if it is possible to be done that Mr. Hoover be induced to reconsider this for the following reasons:

FIRST. That no other living man has at his instant command the facts and conditions of the worlds [*sic*] food supply as has Mr. Hoover.

SECOND. He can market and distribute our coming crop without any loss in dollars and cents to the billion dollar revolving fund appropriated to handle this crop.

THIRD. In doing this he will establish and open up to the citizens of our country markets that will be worth more billions to us in future years.

FOURTH. He has the respect and confidence of the producers and business men of our country as no other man could have without the knowledge and training he has gained through his work during the past four years.

FIFTH. He has a personal acquaintance with the Food Administration of the other peoples of the world and knows their individual conditions and problems and therefore would be in closer touch with them than it would be possible for a new man without this knowledge.

SIXTH. He has a most intimate knowledge and insight into the thoughts and minds of the peoples of the war torn and starving countries of the world through his most valuable work of past four years and therefore his retention as Food Administrator would do much to combat Bolshevikism and Anarchy and bring the people to a sober and sane state of mind and advance the cause of Democracy and Good Government throughout the world.

> *A. A. Elmore*
> President of the Joint Organization
> of the Farmers Union and State Grange
> of the States of Washington, Oregon and Idaho

Hoover Comments on Two Telegrams

Paris, 31 March 1919

Dear Mr. President:

Mr. Houston's telegram is exactly in line with my own recommendations which you approved, i.e., that Mr. Barnes and the present organization be continued.

My minor amendment is that the Grain Corporation needs some simple legal reorganization to bring it in line with the new act, and in these matters we are preparing the necessary executive order to make the arrangements effective.

I am obliged for the copy of the complimentary telegram you received from the combined farmers associations of the Northwest.

I enclose draft telegrams to Mr. Houston and to the Farmers Associations which I suggest would be in order for you to dispatch.

Faithfully yours,

[signed, Hoover's secretary]

Keeping Food from Hungarians

The Causey who wrote the telegram that Hoover reproduced here was Lt. Colonel William B. Causey, who had recently (March 18, 1919) been appointed president of the inter-Allied commission representing the communications section of the Supreme Economic Council with headquarters at Trieste.

The French were holding up the food because Hungary had recently been taken over by the Communist leader Béla Kun.

31 March 1919

My dear Mr. President:

Our food trains for Hungary from Trieste and our other arrangements, which were proceeding for the supply of foodstuffs from certain surplus districts in Jugo-Slavia, have been stopped by various authorities in that region. I have the following telegram this morning.

Food train for Hungary still held at Zagrab by order of Commanding General French Army, Belgrade. Serbians released this train last night so far as they were concerned. Demand was made on the French to release this train this morning. No reply has been received. Direct telephone communication Trieste to Budapest this afternoon reports everything quiet, and urgent request made for delivery of food which has been purchased from American Relief Administration. Can you bring pressure to bear on French to release food train now held at Zagrab? Causey.

This food and more has been paid for by the Hungarians and is their property. This raises the whole question as to whether or not in the present situation the provisioning of Hungary should proceed, and it involves political issues which are beyond myself and my colleagues to determine. My own view is that this provisioning of Hungary should go on, so long as no excesses are committed by the Government of the day, and it is my belief that if the feeding of Hungary were put on this basis and dissociated from all political interest except the one requirement, it would do more than anything else to hold this situation in check.

We have a clear proof of the value of feeding in the maintenance of order in the case of German-Austria where any action of the Bolshevik element is, on statement of their own leaders, being withheld until harvest, because of their dependence upon us for their daily supply of food. I am confident that the only thing today that prevents German-Austria from falling into a complete state of anarchy is this daily arrival of 1000 to 1500 tons of food, together with the steady arrival of coal which our staff have arranged from Czecho-Slovakia and Germany.

I regret to have to add to your burdens, but this is a problem that can be determined by no one short of the four heads of government.

> Yours faithfully,
> [signed, Hoover's secretary]

Approval of Hoover Telegrams

> The telegrams referred to here were composed by Hoover and sent to Wilson in the letter of March 31: one to Secretary of Agriculture Houston, and the other to the association of farmers who had urged Wilson to induce Hoover not to retire as Food Administrator.

Paris, 1 April, 1919.

My dear Hoover:
Thank you for your letter and for the suggested telegrams. I am sending them both today.

> Cordially and faithfully yours,
> [signed, Wilson secretary]

Letter from Taylor

> Alonzo Taylor was with Hoover in Washington during the early days of the Food Administration. He also served in the restoration of Eu-

rope after the Armistice. His principal function was to travel to various countries to determine their food needs. In the letter sent to Hoover from Trieste on March 29, he refers to Károlyi, the President of Hungary since late October of 1918. The Vix in this letter was a French colonel and Chief of the French Missions. On March 20 Vix informed the Hungarians of the new borders that the treaty drafters had set for their country, putting substantial areas of prewar Hungary under the jurisdiction of neighboring states. Taylor considered this announcement premature since the resentment it created forced the Károlyi government from power and opened the door to a Communist regime under Béla Kun. During his 133-day rule of Hungary this Lenin-trained Hungarian caused Hoover great anguish.

Hoover's relief agent in Hungary, Colonel T. T. C. Gregory, also sent a report from Trieste on March 29. In it he urged the use of food and military power to bring down the Béla Kun government. Gregory's report apparently was not referred to Wilson as was Taylor's letter; but it is included here because it is an example of the type of information Hoover was receiving and how such information shaped his views on conditions in various continental countries.

Paris, 2 April, 1919

Dear Mr. President:

I am enclosing herewith a copy of a letter which I believe you will find well worth reading. It is from Dr. Alonzo Taylor, a man I am sure is known to you, and whom I believe to be one of the most able American observers.

Faithfully yours,
[signed, Hoover's secretary]

Taylor Letter (HIS)

Triest [*sic*], Saturday, March 29, 1919.

Dear Mr. Hoover:

Arrived here with Gregory. Unless otherwise instructed, I plan to return to Belgrade with Gregory, just as soon as we have instructions from you on Hungary, to try and put through interstate trades so necessary for the relief of this area. No less than 200,000 tons can be moved from Baranya and Banat into Roumania, Austria and Hungary if we can arrange for compensation.

The Hungarian situation assumes each day more the appearance of a well-organized communistic coup d'etat, but still with nationalistic character. Vix and Karolyi are now conducting public controversy, since Vix declares he was misunderstood by Karolyi. But even if the supposed ultimatum on the boundaries were withdrawn, Karolyi cannot be returned to power. The change in government is irreversible.

Those of us who have been in this country are convinced that an error was made in announcing the decision on Hungarian boundaries in advance of announcements of other disputed boundaries and in advance of the presence of the delegates from the defeated countries in Paris. The isolated and premature announcement by Vix was the provoking moment that threw the present government off the handle and allowed the waiting Communists group to seize the government. Whether by a mistake from Paris or a blunder by Vix, the Karolyi government has fallen. Bela Kuhn [sic] is in, Bolshevism has advanced a step, the Allies have lost an outpost, the commerce and relief of central and southern Europe have suffered an injury and return to military operations may have been made inevitable. A crucial point in the program of relief of central and southern Europe was the return by Hungary to Roumania of locomotives and tanks. Whether under the present circumstances these can be obtained, seems at present unfortunately more than doubtful, unless seized by military force.

I am convinced that American and British could have secured from Karolyi the necessary locomotives and tank cars, to be operated by your organization, without prejudice to ultimate title. To assume that the present definition of the Hungarian-Roumanian boundary constituted an advantage to Roumania is incorrect. What Roumania needed was reorganization of transport and reestablishment of commercial relations, not an announcement of boundaries prior to the signing of preliminary peace.

Believe me to be, Very truly yours,
Taylor

Gregory Telegram (LC)

Trieste, March 29th, 1919.

For Hoover.

Just returned Belgrade. Have been Prague, Vienna, Budapest, Bucharest. Take up internal questions and those affecting territory

accupied [*sic*] by adjoining states where most questions arise. Satisfactory understanding with most governments and acquainted them
plan, purpose of the Commission, incidentally settled numerous state
and inter-state matters; started many internal trades. With communication started, with transportation situation settled by you, with
arrangement for coal to move on Danube, with food moving inland,
and with delegates arriving Trieste, felt that your constructive work
of the Economic Council carried out hereby. This Commission was
beginning show above ground, and was really going [to] carry those
people along until harvest and withstand Bolshevists. On our return
to Belgrade from Bucharest received information for first time that
Entente had ordered Hungarians back 160 Kilometers on Roumanian
front, two days out from Budapest. Government, of course, was unable to withstand pressure strong Nationalist party, and Karoly [*sic*]
is informed resignation permitted Communists, who have been constantly in communication with Lenine [*sic*] to combine with Socialists and take government. The Communists have cleverly taken advantage of strong popular nationalistic spirit, prevalent in Hungary
and which opposes further partition, and called on Lenine [*sic*] to
help Bolshevist troops to drive back invader. This policy of Entente,
which is either stupid in conception or execution, has aroused popular indignation, that has been cleverly capitalized to the extent of
provoking an appeal for support for Russian Bolshevistic troops. Now
the question is what to do about it. The object must be necessarily
to keep Hungary quiet, and keep Russian Bolshevist [ ]¹ troops.
French and Italians are not considered prejudiced, disinterested, but
there is still hope. Trust in Americans and British. Your policy, forcing in the food which we have already sold, is directly in line with
my efforts done here without your advice, and is of distinct tactical
advantage with regard to further dealings with the Hungarians. Admiral Troubridge at Belgrade, in command of Danube, is competent
and is in situation [?] well and is in full accord with constructive
policy which we are pursuing. I believe that Troubridge, Taylor and
I, representing you, can do more than any one else towards helping
this situation. Budapest is completely out of fats and, ostensibly dealing with fats and coals, we could size up situation and advise quickly
regarding policy. Peasants are not taking to this Government rapidly
and have ejected representative, who came to list their property for

the Government. All property of banks and Commercial houses have been already systematically listed, showing Communists organization was well prepared. Lenine [*sic*] now has required further assurance from Government as to the certainty of completing Communistic control, and unless Entente make strong showing with British or American troops, or both, country will lose faith in Allies and feel that its only hope lies with Bolshevistic Russia. I do not know how quickly Russian army can move, but with present coal and transport situation it is bound to be slow, and now is our time to get food and troops in, so that the Socialists and those opposed to Bolshevist movement will have something to hang on to. If this is not acted on quickly it is going to waste much money and work later. America should determine at once whether they are going to get in or get out. Food and military support must now go together. If difinite [*sic*] boundary has not been established, Hungarians should be so advised at once and they should [ ]² indication of exact nature and condition of boundary at present occupied.

GREGORY.

---

¹ Apparent omission.
² Ibid.

Clemenceau and Hungarian Blockade

In a letter to Wilson on March 31, 1919, Hoover protested against the French for holding up a trainload of food at Zagreb, a city in the north of present-day Yugoslavia about 100 kilometers from the Hungarian border. Wilson reports on the action that he and Clemenceau had taken to have the train released. The Hungarians were most impressed by this evidence of the Americans' integrity in keeping their promise (*Ordeal*, p. 134).

Paris, 2 April, 1919.

My dear Hoover:

I gave Mr. Clemenceau a copy of the telegram you quote in your letter of the 31st of March about the holding of the food train at Zagreb. He assured me that on the afternoon of the same day, that is yesterday, he had sent a telegram directing its release.

In haste, Faithfully yours,
Woodrow Wilson

Use of Danzig for Food

This letter is directly related to the sending of Polish and Allied troops to maintain order in the area of the former Russian Empire that later became part of the re-created nation of Poland. If a sea route to that area were chosen, the port of Danzig would be the most suitable place for debarkation. But this was fraught with peril. Poland was demanding the port, since it was Poland's only outlet to the sea. Germany replied with equal insistence that, since 95 percent of the city was of German stock, the principle of self-determination would be flagrantly violated if Polish demands were met; and, furthermore, sending Polish troops into Danzig as part of the Allied army could touch off dangerous demonstrations there and in surrounding areas that were ethnically somewhat more Polish.

Hoover's principal concern was to bring food to people in that area. For this purpose Danzig was vital; hence the anxiety that motivated his letter to President Wilson.

General Tasker H. Bliss, mentioned in the letter, favored Hoover's overall plan of fighting Bolshevism with food rather than bullets. He was one of the five plenipotentiaries on the American delegation to the Peace Conference.

In his *Memoirs* (vol. 1, p. 349) Hoover implies that Wilson had called him for a conference on the Bavarian question and that the letter of April 2 (Apr. 3 in *Memoirs*) was his written reply. This conference is confirmed by Hoover's April 1 letter to General Pershing stating, "I am having an interview with the President on Thursday"—which was April 3 (Hoover Calendar, HPL). The President was ill at the time and deeply disappointed with the attitude of Allies, particularly the French. His general disgust engendered the thought of abandoning the Peace Conference and returning home. On April 7 he actually called for the *George Washington* to be readied for such a return (*Ordeal*, pp. 198–202).

Paris, 2 April 1919.

My dear Mr. President:

I have been for many days filled with the greatest anxiety over the feeding of Poland, due to the proposed transportation of troops through Dantzig [*sic*], the absorption of the railway facilities, and the conviction on the part of all of our staff that bloodshed and disturbances will break out, probably requiring considerable military occupation. It is not alone the attitude of the German Government, but the local feeling is so high that I do not conceive that these troops can be taken through without trouble from the local people.

I have not hitherto said anything about it as I assumed that it was the only course to be pursued. I had of course made up my mind that there must be a longer or shorter break in the food supply and that the Allies were taking the account of the balance of starving populations versus more soldiers in their calculations. I learn however today from General Bliss that the Germans show a disposition to transport these troops overland direct from France. I cannot urge upon you too strongly the importance of taking this action leaving the port of Dantzig [sic] alone to the food people until its fate has been settled by peace negotiations. These proposed military plans for Dantzig [sic], together with the military actions taken at Budapest and other instances through Europe, make the whole problem of trying to maintain stability by food completely discouraging.

Faithfully yours,

[signed, Hoover's secretary]

Supplying Bavaria via Switzerland

France was determined to reduce the potency of Germany to engage in any future military action. Therefore, the French delegates to the Peace Conference were happy to see the German state truncated by annexing substantial numbers of its people to Poland and Czechoslovakia. France also wished to promote Separatist movements within the borders of shrunken Germany. To this end France proposed alleviating the Bavarians with food sent through Switzerland and distributed under the French flag. Wilson asked Hoover for his views on this plan and Hoover replied on April 3.

Paris, 2 April, 1919.

My Dear Hoover:

I promised Mr. Clemenceau that I would ask you if it were feasible to send food directly to Bavaria through Switzerland without subtracting from the total supply for Germany or increasing the proportionaly [sic] supply due to Bavaria. Is this feasible?

Cordially and faithfully yours,
Woodrow Wilson

Hoover's Nansen Letter to Wilson

This letter was signed by Fridtjof Nansen, a well-known Polar explorer from Norway, but its real authorship has been claimed by Hoover (*Memoirs*, vol. 1, pp. 413–16). For a fuller understanding of the proposal discussed, it is necessary to reread Hoover's March 28 letter to Wilson in which Hoover warned the President that any use of outside military force against the Soviets would do "infinite harm." As a substitute he proposed that a person from a neutral country be authorized to perform in Russia what he himself had done in Belgium with food and clothing. The person he had in mind was Nansen, who since 1905 had taken an active part in international affairs and humanitarian causes. In 1917 he came to Washington seeking food for his country and in this enterprise he had met Hoover. In 1919 he spent some time in Paris. Vance McCormick, chairman of the War Trade Board and a member of the Supreme Economic Council, writes in his diary of March 18: "Had conference with Dr. Nansen, who called to discuss Russia. The Russians in Paris trying to get him to head international movement to help Russia get arms and munitions to down Bolshevism. He talks sensibly; wants more concrete information" (McCormick Diary, pp. 54–55). McCormick dined again with Nansen at the Ritz on March 21 (ibid., p. 55); and at a luncheon on March 29 attended by a small group of men the two men met again. McCormick jotted this note in his diary (p. 59): "Dr. Nansen and I discussed Russia. Hope he will agree to go in for a survey. I believe he is the man to start a satisfactory neutral relief to aid Russia without recognizing Bolshevist Government."

In his *Memoirs* (vol. 1, pp. 414–15) Hoover writes that he had telegraphed to Nansen in Norway—presumably sometime between March 30 and April 2—and that Nansen was reluctant to come to Paris to discuss the Russian venture. This reluctance may have been due to the fact that (according to McCormick) he had just been in Paris. In any event, he did come on April 2 and 3 and signed the letter to President Wilson that Hoover had prepared.

On April 3 Hoover had an interview with Wilson and undoubtedly the Nansen mission was discussed. The outcome of this plan is explained in subsequent letters of April 9, April 23, and May 17.

Actually the plan for economic relief for Russia seems to have been a joint product of Hoover and McCormick. On March 4, the two had dined with Oscar Straus, Paris representative of the League to Enforce Peace; Sergei D. Sazonov (Sasinoff), high-ranking Russian diplomat; and Russian Ambassador Boris Bakhmetev. In his diary for March 4 (p. 48) McCormick writes, ". . . proposed my scheme for economic relief of Russia by joint Allied and neutral action, distributed under proper military protection. Straus had arranged the dinner to discuss this as I had broached it when Hoover and I lunched with him several days ago."

As early as June 13, 1918, both Lansing and Colonel House had suggested to Wilson that he send Hoover himself to Russia on a food mission. Hoover was enthusiastic about such a plan that was designed partly to prevent the Allies from taking military action in Russia, but apparently Wilson was reluctant to take Hoover away from his work as Food Administrator (*Intimate Papers*, vol. 3, pp. 409–10; *Life and Letters*, vol. 8, p. 210; *Memoirs*, vol. 1, p. 266).

Paris, April 3, 1919

My dear Mr. President:

The present food situation in Russia, where hundreds of thousands of people are dying monthly from sheer starvation and disease, is one of the problems now uppermost in all men's minds. As it appears that no solution of this food and disease question has so far been reached in any direction, I would like to make a suggestion from a neutral point of view for the alleviation of this gigantic misery, on purely humanitarian grounds.

It would appear to me possible to organize a purely humanitarian Commission for the provisioning of Russia, the foodstuffs and medical supplies to be paid for perhaps to some considerable extent by Russia itself, the justice of distribution to be guaranteed by such a Commission, the membership of the Commission to be comprised of Norwegian, Swedish, and possibly Dutch, Danish and Swiss nationalities. It does not appear that the existing authorities in Russia would refuse the intervention of such a Commission of wholly nonpolitical order, devoted solely to the humanitarian purpose of saving life. If thus organized upon the lines of the Belgian Relief Commission, it would raise no question of political recognition or negotiations between the Allies with the existing authorities in Russia.

I recognize keenly the large political issues involved, and I would be glad to know under what conditions you would approve such an enterprise and whether such Commission could look for actual support in finance, shipping and food and medical supplies from the United States Government.

I am addressing a similar note to Messrs. Orlando, Clemenceau and Lloyd-George.

Believe me, my dear Mr. President,

> Yours most respectfully,
> *Fridtjof Nansen*

Objection to French Swiss Plan

This letter was written in response to Wilson's inquiry of April 2. As Hoover suggests, France was suspected of trying to weaken Germany by fostering Separatist movements there; one means would be to send food into Bavaria through Switzerland and have it distributed under the French flag. Hoover informs Wilson that this method of feeding Germany was not feasible and he intimates that it would be against the spirit of the Brussels Agreement of March 14, 1919, which lifted the blockade on German northern and eastern ports and allowed food to be brought in at these points.

Paris, April 6, 1919.

Dear Mr. President:

With respect to feeding Bavaria through Switzerland, this is totally infeasible in any volume worth considering both from a transportation, food and financial point of view.

For your confidential consideration, the whole of this question has been repeatedly agitated up by the French Minister at Berne, who is constantly endeavoring to create a separatist spirit in Bavaria and who wishes to send a few carloads of food into Bavaria under the French flag. The pressure from this quarter became so great in this particular about ten days ago that it was raised before the Council of Four Ministers of Foreign Affairs, and I gathered Mr. Lansing and Mr. Balfour were against this encouragement toward separatist movement from the rest of Germany, and its moral violation of the Brussels agreement.

Foodstuffs are moving into the ports of Germany as rapidly as we can secure transportation and the large industrial centers in the North are in far more acute distress than Bavaria. While we are insistent that some portion of shipments should be made to Bavaria, I myself consider it fundamental that we should get some American food at the earliest possible moment into the larger centers of the North and West.

As quickly as the first German passenger ship left the German harbors, and before any of the financial arrangements were completed, I diverted several cargoes intended for other quarters into German harbors, anticipating by about two weeks the settlement of financial questions. I was able to do this by virtue of the reserve of some two or three millions of dollars, which I had from the fund you supplied me with, and you would, I believe, be extremely pleased with the reaction created in Germany by this act, which is evidenced by the German press. The question of food to Germany from the United States has become a byword in Germany due to the three months [sic] delay arising from our difficulties in negotiations with the Allies, and its realization without quibbling over detailed arrangements which created a certain amount of confidence by the people that we are good for our undertaking. I may add, however, that the situation in Germany is extremely dangerous and that I am not at all sure that our food supplies have not arrived sixty days too late. In any event, it is a neck and neck race as to whether food will maintain stability as against the other forces that have grown out of hunger in the meantime.

Faithfully yours,
[signed, Hoover's secretary]

Barnes' Handling of Wheat Crop

Paris, April 8, 1919.

Dear Mr. President:

I now hear from Mr. Barnes that he will accept the formal invitation of yourself to undertake the administration of the Government guaranty of the 1919 crop and, in order to advance the matter a step further, I have prepared the attached draft telegram, which, if you could use your way to dispatch, will procure the necessary response from Mr. Barnes.

You will recollect that his staff is composed of volunteers of considerable substances and at a great deal of sacrifice and I have taken the liberty of attaching to this telegram a direct appreciation of their services as I feel that it may help Mr. Barnes in securing their continuation in service for a further period.

Faithfully yours,
[signed, Hoover's secretary]

Shipping Board and Hoover's Needs

This letter and the telegram quoted in it seem directly related to the complaint Hoover made to Wilson in his communique of March 27.

Paris, April 8, 1919.

Dear Mr. President:

I take pleasure in quoting herewith telegram received from our Washington office indicating that after all the Shipping Board will find the tonnage over which I have been in such distress for April loadings:

"Shipping Board furnishing tonnage more freely. Rickard Barnes conference today developed fact that Hurley had not informed other members of your urgent cables, had not consulted with them before replying and they were not aware of receipt of President's cable and what full [*sic*]. Board only learned these facts few days ago. Stevens now states tonnage available by diversion from commercial assignment and we feel board now intends provide your necessities."

Faithfully yours,
Herbert Hoover

Allies' Views of Nansen Mission

The opinions of the Allies on the mission of Nansen possibly were solicited by Hoover at the April 7 meeting of the Supreme Economic Council. Besides Hoover, Cecil, Clémentel, and Crespi were there as representatives of Great Britain, France, and Italy, respectively.

Paris, 9 April 1919

Dear Mr. President:

I have had a very brief discussion of Dr. Nansen's proposition for relief of Russia with Lord Robert Cecil, M. Clemental [*sic*], and Signor Crespi. My understanding of their views is as follows:

(a) They express themselves as in agreement in principle with the proposals.

(b) They point out that the finance of this relief must be settled. The only immediate method is for the Russian authorities to pay from their own resources.

(c) The shipping required must be found. Possibly neutral governments could be persuaded by Dr. Nansen to undertake the transport as their interest in the project is of large moral and political order. In any event, proposals should not go forward unless the Associated Governments are prepared to make the necessary sacrifice of shipping as a last resort.

(d) The exact boundaries of Bolshevik Russia would need be determined, if fighting is to be stopped.

To save time, I have amended the proposed reply to Dr. Nansen, which was handed me so as to include these points and I am transmitting this note to each of the above gentlemen, and no doubt if I do not correctly express their views they will notify their Premiers.

Faithfully yours,
Herbert Hoover

Allies' Reply to Nansen Proposal

This letter of April 9, 1919, was the reply of the Big Four to the proposal that Nansen (i.e., Hoover) made to them on April 3. Hoover claimed that he himself drafted this reply for the four. (*Memoirs*, vol. 1, p. 416; *Ordeal*, p. 121). Others have claimed that it was written jointly by Gordon Auchincloss, House's secretary at the Peace Conference, and David H. Miller, special assistant to the State Department, with minor revisions by William Bullitt, who was also in the State Department as chief of the Division of Current Intelligence Summaries (*Bullitt*, pp. 87–89; *Politics, Diplomacy*, pp. 478–81). On April 11 the *Times* (p. 6) mentioned the Nansen mission in reporting a statement from Hoover that the Norwegian patriot should head a food commission to Russia. On April 13 the *Times* (p. 1) quoted Hoover as stating that the Russian bourgeoisie might be wiped out by famine. These accounts do not prove that Hoover wrote the Allied reply but they suggest that he may have been working closely with Auchincloss and others who had a hand in the matter.

Considerable public sentiment was against giving any aid to Russia while it was still under a Communist regime, or making any kind of gesture that might be taken as recognition of a Soviet government. Clemenceau reflected the sentiment of the French people and of his Chamber of Deputies by refusing to sign the Big Four reply for several days; when he did so on April 16 it was with great reluctance.

Thus it was not until April 17 that Nansen was able to dispatch a message to Lenin. It contained quotations from Nansen's (i.e., Hoover's) original proposal of April 3 and from the reply of the Big Four. Hoover states that he arranged to have the message radioed to Lenin from the Eiffel Tower radio station. The French apparently never sent it, so Hoover directed his representative at The Hague to transmit it from the Dutch radio station. Lenin radioed his reply on May 14 via the Denmark radio station (*Memoirs*, vol. 1, pp. 417–18; *Ordeal*, pp. 122–23). (See introduction to letter of May 16, 1919, for Lenin's reply and the final outcome of the Nansen mission.)

Paris, 9 April, 1919

Dear Sir:

The misery and suffering in Russia described in your letter of April 3rd appeals to the sympathies of all peoples. It is shocking to humanity that millions of men, women and children lack the food and the necessities which make life endurable.

The Governments and peoples whom we represent would be glad to cooperate, without thought of political, military or financial advantage, in any proposal which would relieve this situation in Russia. It seems to us that such a Commission as you propose would offer a practical means of achieving the beneficent results you have in view, and could not, either in its conception or its operation, be considered as having any other aim than the "humanitarian purpose of saving life."

There are great difficulties to be overcome, political difficulties, owing to the existing situation in Russia, and difficulties of supply and transport. But if the existing local governments of Russia are as willing as the governments and peoples whom we represent to see succor and relief given to the stricken peoples of Russia, no political obstacle will remain. There will remain, however, the difficulties of supply, finance and transport which we have mentioned, and also the problem of distribution in Russia itself. The problem of supply we can ourselves hope to solve, in connection with the advice and co-operation of such a Commission as you propose. The problem of finance would seem to us to fall upon the Russian authorities. The problem of transport of supplies to Russia we can hope to meet with the assistance of your own and other Neutral Governments whose interest should be as great as our own and whose losses have been far less. The problems of transport in Russia and of distribution can be solved only by the people of Russia themselves, with the assis-tance, advice and supervision of your Commission.

Subject to such supervision, the problem of distribution should be solely under the control of the people of Russia themselves. The people in each locality should be given, as under the regime of the Belgian Relief Commission, the fullest opportunity to advise your Commission upon the methods and the personnel by which their community is to be relieved. In no other circumstances could it be believed that the purpose of this Relief was humanitarian, and not political, under no other conditions could it be certain that the hun-gry would be fed.

That such a course would involve cessation of all hostilities within definitive lines in the territory of Russia is obvious. And the cessation of hostilities would, necessarily, involve a complete suspen-sion of the transfer of troops and military material of all sorts to and within Russian territory. Indeed, relief to Russia which did not mean a return to a state of peace would be futile, and would be impossible to consider.

Under such conditions as we have outlined, we believe that your plan could be successfully carried into effect, and we should be pre-pared to give it our full support.

V. E. Orlando
D. Lloyd George
Woodrow Wilson
G. Clemenceau

Getting Important Letters to Wilson

Paris, 9 April, 1919.

My dear Mr. Hoover:

In order that we may be sure to get to the President immediately such important communications as cannot properly wait to go through the regular course of mail here, I am writing at the President's suggestion to ask if you will not be kind enough to have noted on the envelopes containing such communications the following words:

" From Mr. Herbert Hoover.
For the President's immediate
attention."

For the President's convenience, we want to make sure that only the most urgent and important mail should go directly to his desk, all other communications taking the usual course.

Sincerely yours,
[signed, Wilson's secretary]
Confidential Secretary to the President

Approval of Wilson Plan

Paris, April 9, 1919.

Dear Mr. Close:

Many thanks for your letter of the 9th, and note your suggestion, which I think is a very good one. It will be followed in the future.

Faithfully yours,
Herbert Hoover

Allied Shipping for Russian Relief

Paris, April 9, 1919.

My dear Mr. President:

The most difficult point in relief of Russia is shipping. On this, in case neutral tonnage proves deficient, I feel you must take some pledge from the three Premiers to make sacrifices to this end, particularly Mr. Lloyd George. The deficiencies of shipping for France, Italy, Belgium and the General Relief (after deducting available German tonnage) in food and coal seem to me to be a burden upon the United States and United Kingdom as being the two Governments with surplus shipping over their own food and supply import needs. This burden ought to fall upon each in proportion to their available mercantile tonnage. I enclose a recent statement showing that today we are furnishing 31% of our ships to these purposes and the British 18%. If they tood [took?] 31% of the burden the Russian relief would be solved. If you could get Mr. Lloyd George to agree that we and they should carry these deficiency [sic] (i.e., France, Italy, Belgium and Relief) in proportion to our resources in shipping, this problem for Russia would be solved.

Faithfully yours,
[signed, Hoover's secretary]

U.S. Commission Membership

While President Wilson was in Paris for the peace negotiations, the question arose whether the United States should be permanently associated with the many commissions and committees being created. The following letter of advice—apparently unsolicited—was penned by Hoover at his Paris headquarters on April 11, 1919. Wilson responded on April 15, saying he was "very much impressed by your objection to the United States continuing to supply members to the various commissions . . . and am ready to say at once that I agree with you."

Hoover's letter suggests that his four months' experience of dealing with the victor nations had made him skeptical of their methods and means. The letter also shows that as of mid-April he was a strong supporter of the League of Nations; but he thought its usefulness would be adversely affected if the United States continued to participate in the various commissions (established to assist in the drafting of the peace treaty) if they were perpetuated after the treaty was signed.

In February 1920 this April 11, 1919, letter was published in American newspapers. This touched off a debate in the Senate and Senator William E. Borah, the isolationist Republican from Idaho, had the letter inserted in the Congressional Record—undoubtedly as part of the arsenal for use against United States involvement in the League. Hoover denounced the publication of his letter (*Times*, Mar. 17, 1920, p. 1; Mar. 18, 1920, pp. 1, 3).

Paris, 11 April 1919

Dear Mr. President:

Your economic group has had before it the question of whether the United States should continue membership in the various commissions set up under the peace treaty. I should like to lay before you my own views on this subject.

I feel strongly that any continuation of the United States in such an Allied relationship can only lead to vast difficulty and would militate against the efficiency of the League of Nations. My reasons are as follows:

I. These commissions are primarily to secure the enforcement of reparation and other conditions imposed upon the Central Empires. As the United States is not calling for any form of reparation that requires continued enforcement, our presence on these commissions would appear to be for one of the following purposes.

(*a*) To give moral and political support to the Allied Governments in measures generally for their benefit. It cannot be conceived that in the prostrate condition of the enemy that the Allies will require any physical assistance to the enforcement of their demands. In this event, the United States will be lending itself to the political and financial interests of other governments during peace, a situation that must be entirely repulsive to our national interests, traditions and ideals.

(*b*) Another objective might be that we should remain in these commissions with a view to securing justice and moderation in the demands of the Allies against the Central Empires. We would thus be thrust into the repulsive position of the defender of our late enemy, in order to secure what we would conceive to be constructive and statesmanlike rehabilitation in Europe. Our experience during the last three months has shown us bitterly that we thus subject ourselves to complaint and attack from the Allied Governments and such a continued relationship should only breed the most acute international friction.

II. If our experience in the last four months counts for anything, the practical result always is that the Allied Governments, knowing our disposition, necessarily ask for more than they expect to get, and that we find ourselves psychologically and, in fact, politically on the side of the enemy in these negotiations, and in a constant desire to find practical working formula we are frequently forced to abandon some measure of what we consider sane statesmanship. The continuation of this relationship will bind us for a long period of years to a succession of compromises fundamentally at variance with our national convictions. I am not attempting to dispute the righteousness of any Allied demand, but merely to set up the fact that our viewpoint is so essentially different. One other practical result of our experience already is that the Americans who sit on such commissions, if they don't acquiesce and assist in enforcing any propositions from various government officials, become immediately and personally subject to attack as being inimical to their interests and with the powerful engines of propaganda which they employ in Europe and our own country no such man can endure for long. These governments, if they were faced with the sole responsibility for their actions, would not attempt the measures which they seek under our protection. Therefore, for all reasons, I do not see that we can effect any real justice in these matters.

III. If we continue to sit in the enforcement of this peace, we will be in effect participating in an armed alliance in Europe, where every change in the political wind will affect the action of these commissions. We will be obliged to participate in all European questions and we will be firmly tied definitely to one side, unless we precipitate a break and lend ourselves to the charge that we have been traitors to the "common cause."

IV. This whole matter has a very practical relationship to the League of Nations. If we can bring to an early end our whole relationship to these political combinations in Europe, which grew up before and during the war and can lend our strength to the League of Nations, that body will gain a stability and importance which it could not otherwise attain. As the Central Empires and Russia will not be for some years admitted to the League, and if we continue in what is in effect an armed alliance in Europe dominating these empires, the League will become simply a few neutrals gyrating around this armed alliance. It will tend to drive the Central Empires and

Russia into an independent League. If, on the other hand, we can again secure our independence, we can make of the League that strong and independent Court of Appeal that will have authority.

V. I am convinced that there has grown up since the Armistice the policy, perhaps unconscious but nevertheless effective, of dragging the United States into every political and economic question in Europe and constantly endeavoring to secure pledges of economic and political support from us in return for our agreeing to matters which we consider for their common good, where we have no interest, and constantly using us as a stalking horse economically and politically, solely in the interests of internal political groups within the Allied governments. These objectives and interests may be perfectly justified from their point of view, but it forces us into violations of our every instinct and into situations that our own people will never stand. For instance, I don't see how we can remain in these enforcement commissions unless we participate in the military enforcement with its enormous cost and risk, and the tendency will always be to exact the political objectives with the military strength of the United States as a background.

VI. I have the feeling that revolution in Europe is by no means over. The social wrongs in these countries are far from solution and the tempest must blow itself out, probably with enormous violence. Our people are not prepared for us to undertake the military policy of Europe while it boils out its social wrongs. I have no doubt that if we could undertake to police the world and had the wisdom of statesmanship to see its gradual social evolution, that we would be making a great contribution to civilization, but I am certain that the American people are not prepared for any such a measure and I am also sure that if we remain in Europe with military force, tied in an alliance which we have never undertaken, we should be forced into this storm of repression of revolution, and forced in under terms of co-ordination with other people that would make our independence of action wholly impossible.

VII. It grows upon me daily that the United States is the one great moral reserve in the world today and that we cannot maintain that independence of action through which this reserve is to be maintained if we allow ourselves to be dragged into detailed European entanglements over a period of years. In my view, if the Allies cannot be brought to adopt peace on the basis of the 14 points, we should retire from Europe lock, stock and barrel, and we should lend to the whole world our economic and moral strength, or the world will swim in a sea of misery and disaster worse than the dark ages. If they cannot be brought to accept peace on this basis, our national honor is at stake and we should have to make peace independently and retire. I know of nothing in letter or spirit of any statement of your own, or in the 14 points, that directly or indirectly ties the United States to carry on this war through the phase of enforcement or the multitudinous demands and intrigues of a great number of other governments and their officials. It does appear to me that your conception of the League of Nations was with view to the provision of a dominant Court, where these difficulties could be thrashed out and if we sit as one of the prosecutors, the Court will have no judge.

Faithfully yours,
Herbert Hoover

Appeal of Latvian Government

Paris 11 April 1919.
My dear Mr. Hoover:

I am enclosing herewith a communication from Mr. J. Tschakste, President of the Lettish Delegation.

Sincerely yours,
Gilbert F. Close
Confidential Secretary to the President.

Enclosure

Paris, April 11, 1919.
Your Excellency:

In the name of the Provisional Lettish Government, the Lettish Delegation has the honor to call your attention to the following facts:

M. K. Ulmanis, Prime Minister of Latvia, announced in a telegram sent from Libau April 2d and received in Paris April 7th, that the Provisional Lettish Government has forwarded by Col. Tallents, of the Supreme Economic Council, and by Mr. Grant Watson, Representative of the British Government at Libau, a request to the Allied Powers that 3000 tons of flour, over and above the monthly shipments, be sent to Libau without delay. Riga cannot be taken because the Provisional Lettish Government has not enough flour to nourish the population of this city. The captured towns Sloka (Scholck), Tukums, Mitau, Windau, Kuldiga (Goldingen), Saldus (Frauenburg) and many rural districts are without food. At Libau the weekly ration has been reduced to 1200 grams per head, and the reserves will soon be exhausted. The immediate shipment of 3000 tons is necessary to avoid the natural consequences, that is famine.

At Riga conditions are terrible. The population is awaiting its deliverance and food. But the Lettish Army lacks arms, uniforms and shoes. The Provisional Lettish Government has forwarded through Major Keenan a request for equipment for 4000 men. The Lettish mobilization is affected although the population is enthusiastic and volunteering in large numbers.

Terror reigns in the regions occupied by the Bolshevists. Peters, the Moscow executioner, has arrived at Riga and is killing 200 to 300 people a day without trial. A large number of hostages taken at Mitan [Mitau] has perished. The Bolshevists are forcing even the women to serve in the Red Army.

In many regions the Lettish people are revolting against the Asiatic tyranny and are driving out the Bolshevists. At Sesswegen, in Livonia, the peasants have driven out the Bolshevist detachments and arrested the leaders. All these revolts should be supported by the armed force of the Provisional Lettish Government.

In the name of the Provisional Lettish Government, the Lettish Delegation has the honor to request the Allied Powers to send supplies to Latvia without delay, food, arms, munitions and equipment for the Lettish national troops.

Very sincerely, etc.

J. Tschakste

President of the Council of State of Latvia

President of the Lettish Delegation

Hoover Reply to Latvian Head

The distraught Tschakste apparently wrote an identical letter to Hoover who immediately sent a reply. Whatever may have been the exact contents of Hoover's letter, he had been sending food to the Latvian people since early April (*Memoirs*, vol. 1, p. 372). Although Hoover seems to have personally written nearly all his letters to Wilson, the following one was written by Lewis L. Strauss, his longtime secretary.

Paris, April 12th, 1919

Dear Mr. Close:

In reply to your letter of the 11th, enclosing a communication from Mr. J. Tschakste, President of the Lettish Delegation, you may be interested in a copy of a letter which was sent this gentleman on receipt of a communication identical in text to that sent to the President.

Faithfully yours,
[signed, Hoover's secretary]

Report on American Relief Work

The report mentioned in this letter was seven typed single-spaced pages. It showed that $111,280,000 of supplies were distributed by the United States, Great Britain, France, and Italy during March 1919. Recipient countries were Poland, Finland, the Baltic States, Czechoslovakia, German-Austria, Greater Serbia, Rumania, Turkey, Armenia, Belgium, northern France, and Bulgaria. Exact figures for Bulgaria and for Russian prisoners in Germany and Russian refugees were not given. America gave over 270,000 tons, the other nations 74,000 tons. About 42,000 tons came from unknown sources.

Paris, 14 April 1919.

Dear Mr. President:

I hope that you will have time to at least glance over the attached report, which will show what the Americans are doing in the Relief.

Faithfully yours,
Herbert Hoover

Approval of Telegram to Barnes

> The cable referred to here appears to have been composed by Hoover and intended for Julius Barnes whom Hoover had suggested as the man best equipped for handling the distribution of the 1919 wheat harvest (see letters of March 25, 1919, and April 8, 1919).

14 April, 1919

My dear Mr. Hoover:

I have been very glad to sign the enclosed cable and hope you will have it dispatched.

Cordially and faithfully yours,
[signed, Wilson's secretary]

Wilson Response to Taylor Letter

> The Taylor letter referred to here was received by Hoover on March 29 and sent to Wilson on April 2.

Paris, April 15, 1919.

My dear Mr. Hoover:

The President asks me to thank you for your letter of April 2nd, enclosing a copy of the letter addressed to you by Doctor Alonzo Taylor, and to say that the President has read it with the greatest interest. I am returning Doctor Taylor's letter.

Sincerely yours,
[signed, Wilson's secretary]
Confidential Secretary to the President.

Wilson Approval for Hoover's Commission Views

Paris, 15 April, 1919.

My dear Mr. Hoover:

I am very much impressed by your objection to the United States continuing to supply members to the various commissions which are to be set up under the Peace Treaty and am ready to say at once that I agree with you.

I am afraid that we cannot escape membership on the Financial Commission on Reparation because that commission will undoubtedly need an umpire, and I am afraid we must take the necessary risks in that matter. But with regard to most of the others, you may be sure I shall fight shy.

With warm appreciation of your letter,

Cordially and sincerely yours,
Woodrow Wilson

Vienna and Budapest Peace Missions

The enclosed letter mentioned below was probably the second letter of April 15 in which Hoover suggests methods of feeding the Hungarians under the Communist government of Béla Kun. Archibald C. Coolidge was a special assistant to the State Department who was dispatched on a prolonged mission to Vienna to gather information of food conditions in that region. Professor Philip Marshall Brown, the second-ranking member of the Coolidge mission, was in Vienna through the 133 days of Kun's rule. James A. Logan was on the Supreme Council of Supply and Relief and an executive officer of the American Relief Administration in Paris. Captain T. T. C. Gregory, a lawyer, had long been associated with Hoover, who soon after arriving in Europe sent him to Vienna as chief of a food and relief mission. Colonel W. B. Causey, a prewar railroad man, was a Hoover assistant in charge of operation of the railroads in countries dependent on Adriatic ports. (Causey is quoted in Hoover's second letter of March 31).

Paris, 15 April 1919.

Dear Mr. President:

With respect to the enclosed letter, which represents a matter of extreme urgency and upon which hangs a great deal of life and suffering, I have the benefit of a consultation with Professor Coolidge and Mr. Brown, representing the American Peace Missions in Vienna and Budapest, respectively, together with Colonels Logan, Causey and Gregory of my staff. The latter three, except one, are not soldiers, but are in fact civilians of distinction and I rely greatly on their combined judgment. I may add as to the Hungarian situation that we are maintaining a thin line of food to show that we stick to our engagements.

The following telegram we have received may be of interest to you.

Trains of food recently held up by the French arrived yesterday Budapest. Created most favorable feeling for Americans as demonstrating their integrity in carrying out their engagements, more particularly among the Anti-Bolshevik labor element in Budapest.

Faithfully yours,
Herbert Hoover

Food and the Hungarian Government

Paris, 15 April 1919.

Dear Mr. President:

I regret the necessity to trouble you to secure the approval of the three premiers to a short statement that I desire to make to the Hungarian Government by way of premise to the completion of certain negotiations with them vital to the relief of Central Europe.

The position is that just prior to the fall of the Hungarian Government I had been made by the Council of Ten the mandatory for the operation of the railways of the old Austrian Empire so far as it related to the movement of vital supplies and I had established a railway control there. In accordance with this, we had arranged a quota of rolling stock under our control from each of these States, together with the regular operation of our 80 food trains. The participation by Hungary in this matter is vital as they control the majority of certain types of cars and locomotives which we wish to use and the operation of our trains over certain Hungarian railways is vital. My representatives have now reopened the matter with the Hungarian Government and find that they are prepared to accede to all the points that we desire to secure, amongst them the handing over to us of a large number of tank cars which are necessary to the distribution of lubricating and other oils from Roumania in exchange for foodstuffs from the Banat and to enable us to maintain railway service generally.

On the other hand, if we put Hungary on precisely the same

food basis as the other states, we shall lose our control of the situation in the surrounding states. We have ample indication that the restraining influence that we hold on the overturn of these governments is effective but if the disturbing elements in Austria, Czecho-Slovakia, Jugo-Slavia, etc., consider that they will be as secure as to food supplies after disturbance as before, our present potentiality to maintain the status quo of order is lost. Furthermore, there are no doubt difficulties in the minds of some of the Allied Governments about the recognition of the Hungarian Government. Therefore, in order to avoid these various pitfalls, I propose to complete the negotiations with the Hungarian Government as to transportation and supply of food with the preliminary announcement on the following lines:

> The proposed economic arrangement with the Food Administration as to railway transportation and food supplies for Hungary is provisional and purely humanitarian and has no relationship to the settlement of any political questions.

> That the Associated Governments do not at present intend to accord the same consideration to Hungary as they are according to liberated countries and German Austria today. To these latter countries they are sending a constantly increasing flow of food supplies for the purchase of which the Allied Governments are voluntarily providing the necessary finances. So far as Hungary is concerned, the Associated Governments will for the present only advance food supplies for such services and funds as may be acceptable to the Food Administration on behalf of the Associated Governments.

The matter is of urgent character and it is impossible for anyone to agree [on] the political issue involved except yourself and the three premiers. Any amount of discussion between the members of the bodies in which I sit cannot possibly result in other than a reference to yourself in the end. All of the economic and practical issues involved have long since been settled by our various Inter-Allied arrangements.

Faithfully yours,
Herbert Hoover

Approval of Hoover Plan for Hungary

[Note handwritten by Wilson]

[ca. April 15, 1919]

My dear Hoover
*The Four this morning approved the enclosed plan and I beg
that you will proceed with it.*

W.W.

Reply to Hoover Relief Report

Paris, 16 April, 1919.

My dear Hoover:
The report you have been kind enough to send me showing
what the Americans are doing in Relief, is a most extraordinary and
striking document. I did not need to have it proved to me that the
tasks were immense and various, but this gives me a most striking
conspectus of the whole thing.

Cordially and faithfully yours,
Woodrow Wilson

Request for Advice on Redfield Letter

William C. Redfield was Secretary of Commerce. The substance of
his letter is revealed in Hoover's reply of April 18.

Paris, 16 April, 1919.

My dear Hoover:
I would be very much obliged if you would read the enclosed
letter from Secretary Redfield and let me know your judgment as to
what reply I should make.

Cordially and faithfully yours,
Woodrow Wilson

Hoover Reply to Redfield Letter

18 April 1919.

Dear Mr. President:

I have received from you Mr. Redfield's letter with regard to the price of wheat.

This problem divides itself into two distinct stages. The first is with regard to the balance of the 1918 harvest year, that is until the new harvest is available in quantity, say September 1st, 1919; the second is the 1919 harvest year.

Mr. Redfield's proposition is, I understand, that wheat should be allowed to take its normal course in the market, that is at its "world price."

With regard to the first stage, that is, up to the 1st of July, the "world price" is probably $3.00 or $4.00 per bushel as we are now plunged into an effective world shortage by inability to send enough tonnage to the Argentine and Australia to secure supplies from that qaurter [sic], and if the control of prices were removed in the United States and if all buyers were allowed to enter that market, the price will go to extremely high levels. We have, in fact, a shortage of thirty million bushels of wheat to supply the demands on us to July 1st. And this, after refusing to make further supplies to Neutrals (in order to force them to the Southern Hemisphere).

You will perhaps recollect that six weeks ago, when Mr. Redfield and his associates demanded that we remove the price control on wheat, pork and cottonseed products, I and my entire staff protested that this was fraught with extreme danger in view of the world situation and the speculative activities that would follow, and that prices would rise. The control of pork products was removed and the price of hogs has ascended from $17.50 to $21.00, and although I have not purchased any pork products for Relief purposes or for Germany since the control was removed, and [sic] I am sure an even worse situation would arise if we removed the fixed price on wheat.

As to the harvest of 1919, as Mr. Redfield points out, there can be only one seller of wheat in the United States, and there will probably be a continuation of consolidated buying abroad. There can, therefore, be no natural flow of supply and demand on which to base any "world price" of wheat. One might approach the problem in two or three ways—none very effective. A guess might be made at the world supplies and the probable world demand. To present appearances the world supply of wheat next harvest will be again insufficient to take care of the world demand assuming always that Europe does not fall into complete anarchy and is able by its products to pay for its bread. Even on this assumption of a shortage, it is impossible to tell what the price should be. In the hands of speculators a shortage of 5% might mean $3.50 wheat as in 1917. In the hands of Government it might mean $1. or $4. depending upon the predilections of the controllers. Another factor that enters into the price of wheat and which has been much overlooked is the factor of currency inflation. Wheat is practically the only commodity under price control today in the United States, and yet all prices are very high and, in fact, although I have not calculated it accurately, I think that it is probable that the ten or twelve principal staples would prove on investigation to be higher on comparative levels to wheat itself. It would not appear, therefore, that the price of wheat can be influencing the price level of other commodities so much as depreciated currency and world shortage. Another method by which the problem might be approached is to make an economic determination from time to time as to what the price level is of any some ten other principal food staples and adjust the price of wheat downward to such level, should they indicate a level below the guaranteed price. Such a procedure would be based on the assumption that there is a free flow of supply and demand in the other staples and as the world controls of these other staples have been largely liquidated this might be possible. On the other hand, the technical difficulties of adjusting the price of wheat downward to the consumer and yet maintain it at the guaranteed price for the producer will require the utmost ingenuity, with the assumption of a uniform high integrity on the part of some hundreds of thousands of people. The wheat of the United States physically cannot come all into the market in one day and placed in the possession of the Government and be resold on the next day at a lower price, but it must naturally flow into the market every day for the whole 365 days, and as near as I can recollect there are about 44,000 wheat buyers in the United States. Each of these buyers would need become a Government agent paying the guaranteed price and reselling at some lower price with a great bureaucracy of watchmen against fraud. A great number of methods have been suggested for handling this technical problem, but none of which have yet appealed to me.

There is another broad problem involved that even assuming the guaranteed price of wheat is higher next year than the world price or the economic price would indicate that it should be, two factors enter into it from a public point of view. The first is that out of probably 1,100,000,000 bushels we shall want to export 800,000,-000 bushels. If we take a dollar off the entire crop, it will cost the Government a billion one hundred million dollars and of this money we shall have conferred upon the rest of the world five hundred million and I doubt whether the rest of the world would give thanks.

The price of flour on the guaranteed price of wheat should be about $11.00 a barrel wholesale, Atlantic seaboard. The pre-War average price was approximately $5. to $6.00, but if we are to maintain our present wage level and present increased railway rates a reduction in the price of wheat so as to absorb the entire one hundred million dollars would probably not reduce the price of flour below $8.50 a barrel, and at the consumption of the American public this would be a saving to the United States consumer of approximately $350,000,000 at a cost to the Government of $1,100,000,000.

To sum up this very confused and problematical statement, I would say that the same policy would need be pursued with regard to next year's wheat that has been pursued in regard to all food emergencies, and that is a consultation between yourself and those whom you can best depend upon for advice from time to time and an adjustment from time to time based on the economic, political and social outlook without any pledges to a definite course of policy.

Yours faithfully,
[signed, Hoover's secretary]

Hoover Memorandum on Bolshevism

It is difficult to identify the memorandum referred to in Hoover's letter. Possibly it was the elaborate anti-Bolshevist statement prepared for the press and dated April 25 (see Hoover's second letter of that date). But judging from the opening sentence, it more likely was a digest of that statement, with Hoover's stronger remarks deleted (see Wilson's letter for April 23).

The first sentence also states that it was intended for "the American people," suggesting that Hoover hoped it would be printed in American newspapers and thus help silence critics in the Senate and a substantial element of the American public that viewed Hoover's sponsorship of the Nansen mission as evidence of a softness toward Communism. In addition it would blunt the attack in the French and British press that he was pro-Bolshevist.

Mayer wrote that on April 18 Hoover "gave out an intemperate statement" on "the tyranny, cruelty, and incapacity of the Soviet regime" and that House and Wilson silenced him on April 19, arguing that such words would defeat any hope that the Nansen mission might be accepted by the Russian leaders (*Politics, Diplomacy,* pp. 481–82). If true, Hoover's letter of April 21 and his long statement of April 25 are difficult to explain. It is also unclear what Mayer means by "gave out" a statement, for there is no evidence that any statement by Hoover on Bolshevism was ever published in the contemporary American or British press. If publicly released, it surely would have been picked up by foreign correspondents in Paris.

On the other hand, the first sentence in Hoover's April 21 letter suggests that the enclosed memorandum was a mollified version of *some* previous statement. It does not clear up the mystery of the April 25 statement which is replete with the most severe observations on the Bolshevist movement. It does, however, lead to the conclusion that the memorandum was the brief statement on the purpose of the Nansen mission that Wilson returned to Hoover with his approval on April 23.

As for Hoover's remark that he had in mind another statement for "an entirely separate early occasion," it would appear that the long statement on Bolshevism of April 25 represents a fulfillment of this intention.

Paris, April 21, 1919.

My dear Mr. President:

I enclose you herewith memorandum containing the points which I desire to present to the American people, eliminating the whole of my very strong opinions on the whole Bolshevist movement. I do not wish to involve anyone in these latter views, and I think I could satisfy my own conscience by taking an entirely separate early occasion when there is no national or allied question involved to give expression to what I think of the purely social currents that are developing in Europe and their relations to the United States.

Yours faithfully,
[signed, Hoover's secretary]

British Memorandum on German Situation

The note mentioned in Wilson's letter was a report sent to the President by an important British official urging that Hoover increase the volume of food for Germany to help prevent the overtake of the country by the Bolshevists. The note also advocated a reorganization of the Ebert ministry in Germany so as to accommodate Communists (Sparticists) in the government, and it presented methods whereby the Germans could be pressed to accept the peace treaty (*Memoirs*, vol. 1, p. 350; *Ordeal*, p. 176).

Freidrich Ebert (1871–1925), chairman of the Social Democratic Party, had helped guide Germany during the critical period from October 1918 to February 1919 when at Weimar he was elected president of the provisionary government. He held this post in the Weimar government till 1925. Philip Scheidemann, also a Social Democrat, was at the same time chosen the first chancellor of the new government.

The terms "majority Socialist" and "independent Socialist" can be traced back to 1916 when a split developed in the Social Democratic Party. From the perspective of the conservative right, the former represented the "parlor pinks" while the latter were "near reds." Further to the left stood the Sparticists or "radical Communists."

Hoover was sophisticated enough not to be frightened by the word "socialism." In his elaborate statement of April 25 (see below for Hoover's press statement on Bolshevism, April 25, 1919) he observes that "the Social Democratic party in Germany is probably more conservative than the present government of England."

21 April 1919.

Dear Mr. President:

I enclose you, herewith, memorandum on the note which you handed me today with regard to the situation in Germany. I have put it in the form of a memorandum in case you with [wish?] to hand it to one of your colleagues for their edification.

Faithfully yours,
[signed, Hoover's secretary]

Memorandum

21 April 1919.

With regard to the attached memorandum we consider it an extremely able analysis of present state of affairs in Germany. We are not entirely clear as to the method of procedure to avoid a complete Bolshevist government.

We agree that unless something constructive is done at once we shall be ultimately faced with either Bolshevism or Military occupation, or both. Of the intermediate courses proposed in this document, we would certainly agree that any combination of Soviet and Assembly Government that would maintain order and enable the construction of peace would be infinitely preferable.

We do think, however, that the proposed formula to Ebert would be dangerous. It strikes us that the party with whom to open such a suggestion are the Independent Socialists, as these are not Bolshevists in the ordinary sense of the word, and probably come nearer representing the yearnings of the German people at the present time. Ebert, of course, is a Majority Socialist and has two complexions; in the first place, he is a Majority Socialist himself and has a Majority Socialist cabinet under him, and second, as President he could probably summon an Independent Socialist cabinet. If negotiations with Ebert would result in the establishment of such a cabinet there is a possibility of Germany being saved from chaos. It does appear to us, however, that it would be impossible to settle an agreement with the Independent Socialists in advance that they would accept any given treaty of peace. What is desirable is that in the event of the Schiedeman [*sic*] Government (which seems almost certain) refusing to sign the treaty, that Ebert should be guided to create an Independent Socialist cabinet. Whether these gentlemen will be any more inclined to sign the treaty than the former, of course, we do not know, but certainly they stand a better chance of preserving order in Germany today than the Schiedeman [*sic*] cabinet.

We cannot fail to again mention what we consider is one of the absolute fundamentals to constructively handle this situation. You and all of us have proposed, fought and plead for the last three months that the blockade on Germany should be taken off, that these people should be allowed to return to production not only to save themselves from starvation and misery but that there should be awakened in them some resolution for continued National life. The situation in Germany today is to a large degree one of complete abandonment of hope. The people have simply lain down under the threat of Bolshevism in front and the demands of the Allies behind. The people are simply in a state of moral collapse and there is no resurrection from this except through the restoration of the normal processes of economic life and hope. We have for the last month held that it is now too late to save the situation. We do think, however, that it is worth one more great effort to bring the Allied countries to realize that all the bars on exports and imports should be taken down without attempts to special national benefits; that the Germans should be given an assurance that a certain amount of ships and working capital will be left in their hands with which to re-start the national machine.

We feel also from an American point of view that the refusal of the Allies to accept these primary considerations during the last three months leaves them with the total responsibility for what is now impending.

We do not believe that the acceptance of any possible treaty is very probable under present conditions, and we feel certain that the hope of reparation is gradually being extinguished by the continued use of the noose. We do not believe the blockade was ever an effective instrument to force peace; it is effective, however, to force Bolshevism.

Thanks for Memorandum

22 April, 1919.

My dear Hoover:

Thank you warmly for your letter of yesterday enclosing your memorandum on the situation in Germany apropos of the British memorandum which I handed you. It will be very serviceable to me indeed.

Cordially and faithfully yours,
Woodrow Wilson

Passports for Wives of Hoover Workers

Paris, 22 April 1919.

My dear Mr. President:

Some difficulties have arisen in my staff owing to the very proper ruling prohibiting wives of members of the Peace Mission from coming to Europe, and I am about to lose some of my best men if this ruling is applied to us as well. A good many of my helpers have been away from the States for as much as two years and now have the opportunity of going home and joining their families. Unless I can get their wives over, I shall lose their services at the most critical period.

It does not appear to me that men who are engaged on food work, whether they be Army officers or otherwise, fall in quite the same class as others. When Army officers, they are no longer compelled to live in mess and therefore their wives are no interference. I will need to hold them here until late August or September, at which time the transport of the Army home will have been largely completed and there will no longer be any shortage of passenger space in that direction. Of course, there is no difficulty about transportation in coming this way.

I would indeed be glad if you could see your way to give a hint to the State Department that they should issue passports on my request for the wives of men on my own staff. I dislike very much to bother you over a trivial detail of this kind, but I understand the whole matter has been referred to you for decision. I have a little personal interest in this as well, as I have seen comparatively little of my own family in five years and would like to have them over myself. Of course, I could not think of doing so unless the members of my staff had the same privilege.

Faithfully yours,
Herbert Hoover

Approval of Statement on Nansen

Hoover's memorandum on the general purposes of the Nansen mission to Russia and the procedures to be followed in distributing food to that country were enclosed in this letter. Hoover had sent it to the President on April 21 stating that the memorandum contained information he wanted communicated to the American people, many of whom were strongly opposed to any gesture of recognition or goodwill toward the Bolshevik government. On April 25 the *Times* carried a front-page report of Hoover's memorandum.

The day after Wilson wrote this letter, Nansen called on Vance McCormick and discussed the mission. He remarked that "he had not yet been able to get his message through to Lenine [*sic*]," wrote McCormick (Diary, p. 74), adding, "I rather hope it will be delayed as things are moving pretty fast with Kolchak government and I think further thought should be given to recognizing Omsk government. Every plan in Russia, however, a gamble."

The naval Russian officer Aleksandr Kolchak was leader of the "White Russians" after a military coup d'état at Omsk on November 18, 1918. His armies were moving successfully against the Bolshevik forces in April and many Allied leaders were urging recognition of his regime as the legitimate government of Russia. On May 2, McCormick thought "Nansen's relief expedition a mistake . . . as it might be necessary to recognize Omsk government" (McCormick Diary, p. 80). But Omsk fell to the Red Army on November 14, 1919. In early 1920 Kolchak's armies had completely collapsed and he was executed by the Bolsheviks on February 7, 1920.

Paris, 23 April, 1919.

My dear Hoover:

I think the enclosed is all right and I hope you will feel at liberty to give it out.

In unavoidable haste, Cordially and faithfully yours,
Woodrow Wilson

Enclosure

21 April 1919.

The favorable reply of the Associated Governments to the proposals of Doctor Nansen that a neutral commission should be allowed to undertake the feeding of the people of the principal cities in Russia, is based on three conceptions:

First, that in giving permission to a Neutral commission to undertake the humanitarian work, it in no way comprises any negotiations between the Allies and the government of Russia, nor does it imply any approval of their methods of government. The situation in this particular is very much akin to the Belgian Relief Commission, through which the Allied Governments did not make a recognition of the German Government of Belgium.

Second, that there shall be complete justice in distribution to all classes, regardless of all distinctions, and the guarantees of a strong neutral commission that this will be the case.

The third conception is that the Bolsheviki are to keep themselves within a certain circumscribed area, ceasing all military action and attempts at invasions.

The primary reasons for this action are purely humanitarian. Hundreds of thousands of people are dying monthly from starvation, and beyond even this it is the wish of the world that fighting and the killing of men should cease. Other reasons have been also brought to bear. The newly born democracies of Siberia, Kuban, Finland, Esthonia, Lettlant, Livonia, Poland, Ruthenia, Roumania, Armenia, Servia, Bulgaria, and Austria, and other nationalities which surround Bolshevik Russia must have a breathing spell to build up some stability. There is little hope of setting any orderly government in these places, and of getting their people back to production unless they can raise food and necessities for next year, unless they can be relieved of the constant threat of Bolshevist invasion and the necessity to keep armies in being out of resources founded on misery.

Again the brunt of this famine in Russia is being thrown by the Bolshevik upon the skilled workmen who refuse to accept their doctrine, upon the merchants, the storekeepers, and professional classes, and unless food is put into Russia all these classes will be dead before next harvest.

Wilson Approval of Passports for Wives

Acute commentators have remarked that Hoover's letter of April 22 and the following answer of Wilson are significant in revealing the unique relationship existing between the two men. Because of this relationship, Hoover frequently felt confident enough to ask the President for favors that others might judge bold or importunate. Moreover, Wilson appears seldom to have denied Hoover the favors he asked. Here it is noteworthy that other members of the American delegation at Paris were not permitted to bring their wives with them. Wilson's relaxation of the prohibition for Hoover's staff prompted many protests and undoubtedly made Hoover an object of some jealousy and hostility within a wide circle of Americans in Paris.

Paris, 25 April, 1919.

My dear Hoover:

I think the case you make out for the wives of your associates is an unanswerable one. Your associates are after all not in any proper sense part of the staff of the Peace Mission. Their job is all but permanent, if one looks both backward and forward, and they may be said to be feeding Europe. I am perfectly willing that you should say to the Secretary of State that I shall make no objection.

Cordially and faithfully yours,
Woodrow Wilson

Shipping Needs for Relief Programs

On March 22 Hoover had obtained Wilson's permission to send a "strong" telegram to Edward N. Hurley, chairman of the Shipping Board, on the subject of more tonnage for relief programs. On March 27 he registered a complaint with the President about Hurley's response that he could supply only 300,000 and not the 500,000 tons requested. One month later Hoover wrote Wilson another letter containing a tale of woe over Hurley's failure to supply needed shipping.

Paris, April 25, 1919

My dear Mr. President:

I am extremely sorry to trouble you with any matter of lesser import than those with which you are faced.

You will recollect having sent a direction to Mr. Hurley to furnish the Relief Administration with 500,000 tons of shipping for loading in the month of April, this being a minimum on which I believed we could hold the tide of starvation during the month of May, when these cargoes would arrive. I regret to inform you that up to the present moment we have been furnished shipping for actual loading and dispatch from the United States of less than 220,000 tons since

April 1st. This comes on top of the failure of the Shipping Board to keep its promises to give us 350,000 tons of loading in March, in which month we received only 200,000 tons. We are at present in the midst of a positive famine of supplies, and I am only able to eke out during the present month by borrowing from other governments as against future replacements on an extremely expensive basis.

I feel that I have at least the right to inform you of my total inability to carry out the obligation that has been placed upon me in this situation. I have no desire to desert the post, but it does not seem to me fair that I should be given this responsibility and given assurances that would enable its execution, and then to be faced with this constant failure. When you consider that the American mercantile fleet delivered into Europe during the last days of the war nearly one million tons of commodities per month and that the Army is now delievering [sic] only 100,000 tons per month of supplies, and when you consider the very considerable increase in our fleet, I think you will appreciate that I am not asking for the impossible. We have in effect asked that in the month of April,—our most trying month,—that we should have one-third of our fleet withdrawn from commercial trades in order to save Europe.

Incidentally, I hear that Mr. Hurley is about to assign ships for loading of coal to Italy, in order to enlarge employment of our coal miners. I would like to point out that if the same rates are charged on coal to Italy that are charged on food to starving populations, it will cost from $35 to $40 a ton to deliver this coal in Italy, out of which some $4 or $5 will be the purchase price of the coal on the Atlantic seaboard and from this amount the American miner will receive less than $2.00 a ton. The Italian credits are absolutely worthless and therefore in order to give $2.00 worth of employment in the United States, our Government is about to expend $35. The British have taken the obligation, and are performing their obligation, to furnish Italy with coal. It would occur to me that it is better to stem the tide of starvation in Europe and to devote the waste of $33 on sending a ton of coal to Italy to the employment of workmen at shoveling sand on the beach.

Yours faithfully,
Herbert Hoover

Hoover Views on Bolshevism

The following statement seems to have been written for immediate release to the press, but it was probably never printed in American or British newspapers; indeed, it appears never to have been given out to the press. Mayer has claimed that Wilson prevented Hoover from delivering a similar statement on April 19 (see Hoover Memorandum on Bolshevism). In the light of information offered by Mayer, the date of April 25 on the following "press statement" is perplexing. Perhaps this was a new statement or it may have been the one Hoover wrote on April 19 with the intention of publishing it on April 25; possibly it was the statement Hoover promised to write in his April 21 letter.

Also perplexing are the pencil markings in the right-hand margins of the original. Who made them, when they were made, and whether they indicate approval or disapproval is unknown.

Views on Bolshevism—Press Statement

25 April 1919

Mr. Hoover was asked to make a statement upon the progress of Bolshevism in Europe. He said:

Of course, the prime objective of the United States in undertaking the fight against famine in Europe is to save the lives of starving people.

The secondary object, however, and of hardly less importance, was to defeat Anarchy, which is the handmaiden of Hunger. The United States Food Administration in Europe therefore necessarily has to take into account all of the political and social currents that are in motion in each country where it operates. We have a considerable staff of specialists constantly engaged in study of the social situation as well as food needs. In fact, the agents of the Food Administration are in some countries the only Americans there. While no foodstuffs have been sent into Bolshevik Russia, we have had numerous reports from reliable agents as to that situation.

Practically the whole territory involved in the war from the old western front is in state of political and social revolution—330,000,-000 people. Only Serbia and perhaps Roumania may escape political revolution but social revolution will touch even them. Out of four great States, eighteen new States have already emerged. In none of them is there visible scarcely a single political leader of six months ago.

These are not merely political revolutions, as a reaction from failure of their politicians in war, they are infinitely deeper seated. The misery and suffering that has followed the war has silhouetted the enormous gulf between the upper and lower classes, the poor are starving and driven mad in the presence of extravagance while the middle classes are still living comfortably. Practically all of these governments were tyrannies of the extreme reactionary type, and the political and economic suffering of the common people for scores of years before the war was a commonplace to every social student. The basis of these revolutions while superficially political, is basically economic. Populations engulfed in starvation and misery are easily misled by all those who cry out in the phrases of humanity, liberty, freedom and equality, and become easy victims of political patent medicines. Confidence in the old leaders is gone and in fact the demands of misery, already trained and armed for violence, gives [sic] no time or opportunity for even sanity to evolve constructive reform. The swing of the social pendulum under this impulse is in each locality roughly proportioned to the amount of social grief.

Bolshevism is a theory or practice of Socialism by which economic equality is to be obtained by destruction of the organization and processes of production and distribution that all men may restart the race level and then be held level during the race. Its method of execution is to create a mass of town industrial and other committees called soviets. These committees are to be in majority common laborers with these committees piling one on another with a pinnacle of a so called proletariat dictator at the top. If we use the terms Communist and Committee we divest Bolshevik and Soviet of their mysterious romance. The term socialist is meaningless from a political point of view. For instance, the Social Democratic party in Germany is probably more conservative than the present government of England. There are all degrees of political socialism in Europe from the type satisfied with a government control of utilities under private ownership to the type who, like the Russians, believes the railway trains should be operated independently by a committee of the train crew and all forms of government advocated carry out the ideas ad-

vanced ranging from normal legislative bodies to the executive bureaucracies to a mass of communist committees, each enacting daily
decrees and appointing myriads of commissioners to carry them out.
The Communists in Russia represent the extreme left in this swing
of the social pendulum from the extreme right of reactionary tyranny
and it is to be noticed that up to this time the tendency of the Communist ideas, or even the strong attempts to put them in action, are
confined to the areas of the greatest reactionary tyranny. Their
courses represent the not unnatural violence of a mass of ignorant
humanity, who themselves have learned in grief and tyranny and
violence over generations and who are trained by war in the arts of
killing. Our people who enjoy so great liberty and general comfort
cannot fail to sympathize to some degree with these blind gropings
for better social conditions. If former revolutions in ignorant masses
are any guide, the pendulum will yet swing back to some moderate
position when bitter experience has taught the economic and social
follies of the present obsessions. No greater fortune can come to the
rest of the world than that the ideas of Communism and its handmaiden Socialism should have an opportunity somewhere of bankrupting themselves. This bankruptcy is already in process. It is hardly necessary for any American to debate the utter foolishness of these
economic tenets. The vast majority of our people will agree that our
processes of production and distribution, the outgrowth of a hundred
generations in their stimulation to individual initiative, the large
equality of opportunity, the infinite ramifications of training and differences in body and mind, while not perfect comes about as near
perfection as is possible from the mixture of avarice, ambition, altruism, intelligence, ignorance and education of which the human animal is as yet composed. The communist land of illusion is that he can
perfect these human qualities by destroying the basic organization
and processes of production and distribution instead of the ideal of
democracy that devotion should be given to the stimulation of production and distribution and to securing a better application of the
collective profits arising therefrom. The mixture of theorists, dreamers and murderers that have conducted the Communist's Governments in Russia for eighteen months have now themselves to some
degree realized the infinite calamity they have brought on their people and are themselves floundering around endeavoring to restore

those normal processes of production and distribution. Russia was formerly not only a well-fed country but exported as much food as did the United States and yet her people are dying today in thousands from starvation for no other reason in the world than the fool idea that the organization of productive industry can be destroyed and the populations still live. One item in a recent and reliable report shows what this means. At the fall of the Kerensky Government there were under operation in Russia 34,000 miles of railways equipped with 15,000 operating locomotives and 500,000 operating cars. Today under 12,000 miles of railway, 4,000 locomotives and under 150,000 cars are in operation. In the year prior [to] the Communist Government, 400 locomotives were repaired and in the last twelve months only 80. A statement by one of the Communist Ministers at Moscow on March 4th states that his department holds six million bushels of grain which will spoil because he cannot move them and yet the people of Moscow are dying of starvation. He complains that the peasants are spinning their own cotton and flax and using the balance for fuel because they do not wish to accept the current money in payment. In fact, with unlimited printing the ruble has depreciated from a value of 50¢ to less than 2¢ and it is little wonder. He complains of the hoarding of food by the peasants and that many of the local Soviets hide their surpluses. The Bolshevists have now abandoned their plans for nationalizing the land because they find the land will not be planted for a remuneration in phrases like the "common good." They have abandoned the notion that banks and financial institutions can be abolished and have themselves instituted a series of saving banks because they find the people had no object in working if they could not save their wages. They are themselves offering enormous wages to skilled workmen because they found skilled men would not do more than common laborers. For common laborers [*sic*] wage they are offering fantastic salaries in rubles for engineers and directors of works in a frantic endeavor to again secure competent organization against their overwhelming idleness. They have tried to abolish the shop soviets and to get discipline into work, and have now ordered that the railways shall no longer be run by the working men but be taken over by a Central Administration and have enacted dire penalties for failure to labor. A part of this great mental revolution is due to an endeavor on the part of their theorists and idealists to correct the horrible calamity in which they stand and in part due to the desire of the criminal classes who, having gotten possession of property, are anxious to re-establish property rights. Politically they have always represented a minority in any country where they have established control. They have set it up frankly as a tyranny of the so-called Proletariat and have rested its political strength on the organization of working men and policing by criminals. Today they are endeavoring to establish some kind of franchise and have granted five votes to the working man to one vote to the farmers. As a tyranny they constitute the negation of democracy, for democracy must rest on the execution of the law of the majority expressed by free and unterrified suffrage. As a tyranny they have resorted to terror, bloodshed, murder to a degree long since abandoned even amongst reactionaty [sic] tyrannies. They have summoned the help of the criminal classes to support their doctrines even more than the autocracy under which they suffered. By enveloping in their doctrines the cry of the helpless and the down-trodden, they have embraced a great degree of emotionalism and thereby given an impulse to their propaganda comparable only to the impulse of large spiritual movements. This propaganda travels in a starving and suffering population, who have lost confidence in her leaders and in God, more rapidly than the bubonic plague. It has won further impetus that it has in these populations one constant impulse in the utter distress and disillusionment with regard to their political leaders. It offers the panacea of daily decrees from town and trade committees as giving an immediate political expression to the yearnings of suffering people. The political danger of the spread of Communism by pure propaganda is a direct factor of the social and political development of the population which they attempt to infect and their degree of misery. Where the economic gulf between classes is broad and where the masses have been kept in ignorance and thrown into distress, this propaganda will be fatal and will do violence to progressive democratic development. For these reasons I have no fear of it in the United States beyond the abilities of the police and my fears as to other countries would be gauged by the above standards. There is one reservation on this and this is that Communism offers opportunity to the criminal classes to perpetrate murder, theft, robbery in all of the fine phrases of humanity and embraces along with these the hairbrain [*sic*] and foolish dreamers. There is one other factor of importance to the world in this communistic movement; that is the question as to whether or not these centers now stirred by great suffering and by great emotional hopes will not undertake large military crusades in an attempt to impose their doctrines on other defenseless people. How far this impulse is likely to go is as yet difficult to determine. If these forces are inherent in the situation, it would appear that the world must disregard all other questions and be prepared to fight for exactly the same reasons that it entered in the war against Germany. Domination and tyranny can no more be tolerated in the name of Communism than in the name of Autocracy. We will soon have a test as to how far this is the case for the Communists of Russia have been offered food supplies for their starving millions if they will keep within their own boundaries and cease these invasions. If they will keep at home, then it would appear to me that from an American point of view we should not involve ourselves in what may be a ten year military engagement in Europe for it is not up to us to say that we are going to insist that any given population must work out its internal social problems according to our conception of democracy. I have the most serious doubts that outside forces entering upon such an enterprise can do other than infinite harm for any great wave of emotion will only ferment and spread under repression. In the swing of the social pendulum it is bound to swing from the extreme left back towards the right and it will find the point of stabilization based on racial instincts that could never be established by outside intervention. That swing to all appearances has already started in Russia and Communism from that center now has the character of a prairie fire for the burning and destructors are on the edges with some slight evidence of the new growth in the center. It may be that the new growth will come up invigorated into a great Russia, but prairie fires are poor methods of cultivation. I do not feel that the revolution has spent itself in other centers of Europe. The social pendulum has yet to swing further to the left than it has so far gone because constructive social effort has lagged behind the insistent and impatient demands of the people in many of the new States. None of them have, however, such a denseness of ignorance and such impressionism as the Russian people. With food, peace and employment the others may be able to work out their social salvations without violence. The probabilities are that social solutions in Central Europe will be attained with infinitely less violence and destruction, not only because of the greater intelligence and education of the people, but also because there is better distribution of the land and more intelligence by the farmers. In all of the States and Central Europe, the rock upon which Communism is breaking today is the farmer. The prompt boycotting of food supplies from the farmers to Munich has broken that distance. On the other hand the large land holdings and the treatment which the agricultural classes received in Hungary make it a more fertile field for Communists reactions until the land is decided. The problem is a town problem and at the moment the job is to get these people fed that they do not go entirely mad. The problem immediately after Peace will be to secure them employment at the earliest moment that they may return to the normal impulses of life. All central Europe and Eastern Europe must have financial assistance to reestablish broken currencies, to find raw material, to rehabilitate production. If they have wise statesmen who go to the root of social wrongs, who sincerely move to correct the inequalities of life and the division of profits from production and distribution, Europe may pull through without a cataclysm. The chances of accomplishing all of these things are about fifty fifty.

Recognition of Independence of Finland

Finland had been part of the Swedish kingdom since early in the fourteenth century. In 1808 the Russian Emperor Alexander I invaded the country and annexed it to Russia; however, Finland was allowed a great measure of autonomy until late in the nineteenth century when the Soviets began to curtail its liberty considerably. In January 1918 the Soviets felt constrained to accord recognition to the free government in Finland while retaining 40,000 Russian troops within its borders. This situation engendered a "White" and "Red" war. Hostilities ended in May when the Russian troops were compelled to leave Finland.

For months Hoover had pleaded with Wilson to bring before the Council of Foreign Ministers the recognition of a free Finnish

142 / Two Peacemakers in Paris

state. In April 1919 he importuned the President to carry this question to the Big Four, whereupon Wilson asked for the usual memorandum. Hoover prepared one and sent it to him on April 26, 1919. The President read the memorandum at the April 29 meeting and then announced his endorsement of Hoover's proposal. Lloyd George expressed some doubts and asked for more time to consider. Clemenceau replied that he would have to consult his foreign minister, Pichon. Orlando was not present. On April 30 the Big Three agreed to send the plan to the Council of Foreign Ministers. In the meantime Wilson suggested that Hoover speak directly to Clemenceau who, as in all dealings with the Director of Relief, was most considerate. Without delay the foreign ministers agreed to the recognition of Finland. It was announced formally on May 3 and soon thereafter Hoover had food on its way to the Finnish people (*F.R., P.C.*, vol. 4, p. 662, and vol. 5, pp. 119, 316; *Memoirs*, vol. 1, pp. 363–67; *Ordeal*, pp. 123–26).

Paris, April 26, 1919

My dear Mr. President,

I am wondering if there is not some method by which the recognition of the full independence of Finland could be expedited. They have now had a general election; they have created a responsible Ministry; this Ministry is of liberal character. There are many reasons why this matter should be undertaken, and at once.

1. The United States has always had a great sentiment for the suffering of the Finnish people and their struggle of over a century to gain independence.

2. By lack of recognition they are absolutely isolated, from a commercial point of view, from the rest of the world. They are unable to market their products except by the sufferance of special arrangements with Governments at every step. They have ships without flags, and have no right to sail the seas. They are totally unable to establish credits, although they have a great deal of resource, as no bank can loan money to a country of unrecognised Government. They are isolated by censorship. Their citizens are not allowed to move as their passports do not run.

3. The most pressing problem is their food supply. In January last the Finns were actually starving in hundreds. Order in the country was preserved by sheer military repression. By one measure and

another, and altogether out of Finnish resources, without the cost of a dollar to us, we have for the last three months fed Finland. Order has been restored. The populations are rapidly recovering nutritional conditions. They have begun to take hope of the future. They have prepared large quantities of materials for export. All through these operations they have shown the most sturdy independence, and have asked for nothing but the facilities to make their own solutions. Their resources are now practically exhausted. Unless they can have immediate recognition, so that they can create further commercial credits and can sell their products, they are either doomed or we must support them on charity.

If ever there was a case for helping a people who are making a sturdy fight to get on a basis of liberal democracy, and are asking no charity of the world whatever, this is the case. I am convinced from our reports that unless Finland is recognised within a very short time that the present Government cannot survive the difficulties with which it is faced. One instance would show the utter paralysis under which they are suffering. Their banks have deposits of upwards of ten millions of dollars in the United States, but, so long as their Government is unrecognised, our American banks must refuse to honour the drafts of the Finnish banks, as they can secure no legal assurance that the control and ownership of these banks is the same as that which existed at the time the deposits were made. It is purely a technical question, but it, amongst numerous other instances of this character, threatens absolutely to destroy the Finnish Government.

Nor do I see why any half-measures need to be taken in this matter. They have gone through every cycle that the world could demand in political evolution, to the point of an independent people, and I feel that they would long since have been recognised had it not been for the terrible cloud of other questions that surrounds the world, I realize that there are a lot of people who consider that General Mannerheim casts a sinister shadow over the present Government, but the very fact that under this same shadow Finland has established democratic institutions should be enough of an answer.

Faithfully yours,
Herbert Hoover

Reparation in Kind for Belgians

Paris, April 29, 1919.

My dear Mr. President:

The Belgians inform me that some phases of the reparation terms are likely to come before you today. In the capacity to which you have appointed me, that is, as sort of friend and guardian to the Belgians, I would like to emphasize one phrase of this matter, in respect to "reparation in kind," as applying to animals.

The Belgians have lost two-thirds of their horses and over one-half of their cattle. Except for a certain breed of horses, of which the Germans removed to Germany all of the stallions and mares, there are scarcely any of these animals which could be identified as stolen property. I assume that there would be no question about actual identifiable animals, but there is also a very large question of a very large replacement in kind of a certain number of other animals. The Germans today have over two-thirds of their original herd of animals. They lived during the war by stealing horses and cattle from their neighbors, to the preservation of their own herds. It would require three or four years to breed up enough dairy cattle to support the children of Belgium without the importation of condensed milk, and it would require four or five years to secure enough draft horses to carry on the commerce of the country. I understand that the Belgians are now asking for a certain minimum restitution as low as 10% of their claim of total animal losses.

The French authorities have told the Belgians that you were personally opposing this reparation in kind. I do not, of course, know the arguments against it, but I would like to bring before you the actual facts of the situation, which may not have been known to you, before you form a judgment in the matter.

Yours faithfully,
[signed, Hoover's secretary]

Objection to Davis Views on Belgium

> Norman Davis was a member of the American Council of Six established in early January to help coordinate the various activities of the United States at the Peace Conference and to give advice to the

President. Hoover recommended its establishment and the six members who were immediately approved by Wilson. Davis had served in the war administration at Washington in several capacities. In Paris he represented the United States Treasury and at the same time was on Wilson's staff which negotiated questions of finance and reparations. He was also on the Supreme Economic Council.

The "draft letter" written by Hoover and enclosed in his communique was evidently accepted by Wilson and immediately dispatched to Davis.

Paris, 2 May 1919.

My dear Mr. President:

The letter addressed to you by Mr. Davis at the request of the Secretary of the Treasury has been called to my attention. The proposal of the Treasury is apparently to stop all advances to Belgium for foodstuffs, and they are asking for your approval for the withdrawal of a credit authorized by you to Belgium, of which there is an unexhausted balance of $22,250,000.

I, of course, do not know all of the Treasury's reasons, but the statement made that it is because of the completion of the operations of the Relief Commission does not meet the point. In an endeavor to secure the gradual development of the various relieved countries from the nursery stage of relief, I had insisted that the Belgians should take over their entire relief measures and thrust the responsibility up to them as from the first of May, with the full anticipation that they would continue to draw from the United States Treasury such sums as were needed for their foodstuffs. Under the proposal of the Treasury, the Belgians will be out of foodstuffs within sixty days, and I do not think we have any more right to withdraw credits from Belgium for food, than we would from England, France, Italy, or any of these countries, without proper and ample notice. More especially is this the case in the rather delicate situation in Belgium and in connection with the peace negotiations at the present time.

With the retirement of the Relief Commission we had arranged for the reduction of the Belgian food programme from approximately $20,000,000 a month to $15,000,000 a month. Since that time, I have been able to sell some accumulated Belgian stocks to the Germans, with the intention of re-investing the realized sums in foodstuffs, and if the Treasury could see their way to grant to Belgium the balance of the authorized credit, that is $22,250,000, I think we could establish a situation by which their food supply would be taken care of until the end of August. I do earnestly recommend that the Treasury should take this course, and if you approve I enclose a draft letter which I would suggest should be addressed to Mr. Davis. I simply do not see how Belgium is to be fed otherwise.

Faithfully yours,
Herbert Hoover

Enclosure

2 May 1919

Dear Mr. Davis:

In connection with your letter of the first of May, I enclose herewith copy of a letter which I have received from Mr. Hoover, and it does seem to me that we cannot end the food supplies to Belgium in this summary manner. I earnestly suggest to the consideration of the Secretary of the Treasury that he should continue advances to the Belgian Government for food purchases until the exhaustion of the balance of the $40,000,000 credit, which I approved.

Faithfully yours,
[President Wilson]

Heath Telegram on Food Prices

This note from Wilson's secretary enclosing a long telegram from a group of American housewives, aroused over rising food costs, represents one of the many domestic problems that plagued Wilson while he was handling international problems in Paris. Hoover answered Close on May 20 (see below for letter of that date).

Paris, 3 May, 1919.

My dear Mr. Hoover:

The President asks me to send you the enclosed telegram from Mrs. Julian Heath, President of the National Housewives League of the United States. He would be obliged for your advice concerning the matter about which Mrs. Heath writes.

Sincerely yours,
Gilbert F. Close
Confidential Secretary to the President

Telegram

May 5, 1919.

President Wilson, Paris.

The Housewives of Seventy percent of the Consumers of this country, the remaining thirty percent being farmers wives, thru the National Housewives League of the United States appeal to you for immediate Legislative action at the coming session of Congress to reduce the cost of living which thru present prices of bread, meat and corn has become unbearable.

This situation more than anything else is the cause of the discontent of labor. Will you not use your unlimited power for good to put bread into the mouths of our people. Give us back our five cent loaf and help suffering humanity now staggering under the cruel yoke of prohibitive prices of the bare necessities of life. You have more personal influence than any other person in the world today. Will you not use it to repay the average American citizen for the great sacrifice made during the trying years of the war to secure peaceful living conditions in our home life? If this is not attained we personally will get small comfort out of the international victory you have made. The strong feel a moral obligation for the protection of the weak and the rich for the redemption of the poor.

Rome was lavish in the days of yore in gifts of grain to the common people. Distinguished citizens such as Augustus and Julius Caesar were accustomed to make donations of food sucffs [sic] to the multitude on occasions of great public rejoicings and thanksgiving. How different has been the treatment of the consumer in this country since the achievement of the great victory.

Prices of food have steadily increased ever since the armistice and are daily going higher. The pre-war price of bacon was thirty cents and it has now risen to seventy cents. Pre-war lard thirteen cents now forty cents; pre-war pork seventeen dollars now fifty-two dollars; pre-war wheat ninety cents now two dollars and twenty cents and pre-war corn sixty cents now dollar sixty. Current statistics show that we have the greatest stocks of wheat, meats, fats, hogs and cattle that were ever known in the history of the country—yet they are withheld from the people, except at prices none but the rich can pay. Everything follows wheat. Reduce wheat to a maximum of dollar twenty-five to the people paying the farmer the difference between that price and the surrendered price out of the fund provided for handling the 1919 crop and everything else will go. It is open talk that the ambition of the Food Administration Grain Corporation is to save the Government from any loss on its guarantee of the 1919 crop. The American consumers pay cash, the foreign governments pay with credits furnished by this country. They have to pay the price or get no credits. The American consumer is taxed double, first to furnish the Government credits and again by the enormous prices those credits have produced is [*sic*] a land of plenty, but prices have been so inflated by artificial interference with the natural course of prices by government agencies that American plenty is beyond the reach of the American people who are now strained to the point of breaking.

The idea of feeding Europe is fine, but what about the seventy-seven million American consumers? Where do they come in? Legislation should be enacted immediately to restrict the export of foodstuffs and provisions until the people are first supplied at a fair living price and to that end we call on you as a friend of the American people to act. When the war was on we suffered hardship without a murmur. Now that it is over we demand prices at which we can live. The daily press has frequently noted in editorials and otherwise that one of the dangers ahead of us is the unrest developing because of the ever-increasing high prices. It is disputed by none that the interests are making ever-increasing and abnormally high profits through what I believe to be illegal methods. The packers of this nation are forcing a corner on provisions notwithstanding the fact that our warehouses are filled to the bursting point.

Wont [*sic*] you authorize forthwith importations of Argentine and Canadian wheats which are selling at a discount under American wheat, so that cheaper bread can be secured for the American consumer. Your attitude and immediate favorable reply will decide the costs to the ultimate consumers of America whose backing will support you in prosecuting these necessary measures.

Wont [*sic*] you restore to us our five cent bread. We as women who bear the brunt of the suffering in providing nourishing food for our families appeal to you to enact Legislation prohibiting the export from this country by the interests of our national birthright to plenty and the blessings of the fruits of our lands [*sic*] products. Why is it not just to limit the export of food stuffs, thus holding for domestic consumption a sufficient proportion of our products to make prices reasonable and bring them from their now unattainable levels. We pay so much for food that we are forced to take inferior quality and to deprive our families of the necessities of life lest they starve. Will you consider this question before the next session of Congress and recommend effective legislative action to the desired end.

Mrs. Julian Heath
President National Housewives
League of the United States
175 West 88 Street, New York

Esthonia, Latvia, Lithuania

> The Baltic states presented great problems. For centuries they had been the victims of oppression by Germans, Poles, or Russians; yet somehow they had preserved their ethnic identity. During World War I they were invaded by the Germans, who annexed them under the Treaty of Brest-Litovsk forced on the defeated Russians in March 1918. Soon after November the Bolsheviks were again threatening, so the German armies were allowed to remain as the lesser of two evils; order would at least be maintained until the Allies could decide on the future of the three states. But Hoover was not satisfied with the conduct of the German troops in these areas, and their presence did not prevent the Communists from some successful invasions in sectors of these countries.
>
> On the day that Hoover wrote the following letter, he appeared before the Council of Foreign Ministers and elaborated on the subject of the letter. His exposé sparked a long discussion in the committee, and their conclusion was only partially satisfactory to Hoover. In consequence he felt compelled to call Wilson's attention once more to his letter of May 9. The President answered on May 21 (*F.R,. P.C.*, vol. 4, pp. 688–95; *Ordeal*, pp. 126–34).

Paris, 9 May 1919.

My dear Mr. President:

I feel the time has come when it is necessary to take some more definite action with regard to the situation in the three Baltic States of Esthonia, Latvia, and Lithuania. I enclose herewith a sketch map showing approximately the ethnological boundaries and at the same time the present military status.

The food conditions in these states are simply terrible. From a shipping, finance and food point of view, we could overcome them if some kind of order could be established. We are gradually extending our distribution along the coastal fringe of the non-Bolshevik area, but even in such areas the hinterland is in a state of chaos due to Bolshevik invasions, with the resultant arson and slaughter. About one-half of the coast area is held by the Bolshevik, or is in such a state of anarchy as to make it impossible to send in ships. At Riga, for instance, the Red Army withdrew some days ago, leaving the town in the hands of a starving mob, as a result of which some twenty thousand bourgeois women and children have been driven onto an island in the bay, and the results are beyond all description.

From a relief point of view, the situation is hopeless for all except a few coastal towns, unless we can have some sort of order and protection. The Germans, of course, occupy Lithuania, and some instructions must be given them to cease interfering with the development of the government there, for some order must be established to succeed the German occupation.

The population in none of these states is Bolshevik. In many places they are putting up a good fight to try and establish their independence of the Moscow tyranny. They insist if they were given military supplies they require no other help to establish their boundaries and to maintain order, and our people concur in this opinion.

The problem seems to me as follows:—

(a) To place enough naval strength (not large) in each of the ports to protect the relief of all the coastal towns;

(b) To furnish military supplies to the established governments so as to enable them to maintain order in the interior and to defend their borders.

Sheerly [sic] as a matter of preserving life, it does appear to me worth while to give them this support. All this requires collective action by the Allies, and a definition of policies.

The situation is one that is so appealing from every human point of view, that I am wondering whether or not it would be possible for yourself and the Premiers to set aside a short period, when the British and American naval authorities, who are familiar with this situation, could appear, together with myself on the side, in the hope that some definite political and relief policy could be arrived at.

Faithfully yours,
[signed, Hoover's secretary]

Barnes as New Wheat Director

Paris, 13 May 1919.

My dear Mr. President:
You will please find herewith an Executive Order prepared after lengthy correspondence between ourselves and Mr. Barnes, so as to give effect to the new law and the appointment of Mr. Barnes as Wheat Director next year.

I would be very glad if you would see your way to sign and return it to us in order that we may cable over to them that they may at once initiate the new administration.

Faithfully yours,
[signed, Hoover's secretary]

Blockade to Force Treaty Signing

On May 7, 1919, on being presented with a copy of the full treaty that was to be handed to the Germans that day, Hoover experienced profound misgivings. "I was greatly disturbed. In it hate and revenge ran through the political and economic passages. . . . Conditions were set upon which Europe could never be rebuilt or peace come to mankind" (*Memoirs*, vol. 1, p. 461). One week later, after Marshall Foch had proposed that the food blockade be reimposed to compel the Germans to comply, Hoover was provoked to write the following letter to President Wilson. Then on May 15 Hoover, Davis, Baruch, and McCormick went to see Wilson at 2 p.m. to speak about the problem. Hoover urged that food should not be withheld even if Germany refused to sign the treaty; he repeated the arguments of his letter on May 14. The President replied that he had told his three colleagues the previous day that he preferred military occupation to the blockade. He also freely revealed his general problems with the other three; Wilson called them "mad men, particularly Clemenceau." This conversation, which also touched upon Yugoslavia and Italy, lasted for an hour and a quarter (McCormick Diary, pp. 86–87).

Paris, 14 May 1919.

Dear Mr. President:

The principal objects for which I have been asking for an interview have been:

First, that I might express to you my strong view that we should not be led into joining with the Allies in a food blockade against Germany as a method of forcing peace. The margins on which the German people must live from now until next harvest are so small that any cessation of the stream of food, even for a short time, will bring the most wholesale loss of life. It might be that the imposition of a blockade would be effectual in securing the German signature to the peace. I seriously doubt that it would consider a peace obtained upon such a device as the starving of women and children as being binding upon the German people. If the Germans did resist, it is my impression that it would throw Germany into complete chaos and military occupation would need to follow in order to save Europe.

My second point is that I am placed in a serious embarrassment by the threat of a blockade, because we have a constant stream of nearly one hundred million dollars worth of food in motion towards Germany. With all the effort they make, they are scarcely able to keep pace with their gold and security payments with the actual arrivals in Germany, so that the total risk of this vast current of foodstuffs is now falling on my shoulders. If the current were stopped, it would mean we would have to pile up large amounts of foodstuffs in Europe, a large part of which is not of the type at present salable to the Allied countries. For instance, we are shipping rye, which the Allies do not eat, and types of fats of which the Allies have ample supply. We would have to face very great loss and seriously jeopardise the financial stability of the Food Administration. I have been willing to take the risk, in the feeling that without it peace and stability will not be secured, but I seriously doubt whether I have any right to involve you in the ensuing difficulties if I were to continue without your approval after I knew the gate to Germany would probably be closed.

My third point is that it is my belief that Germany cannot pay for her foodstuffs through until next harvest with any liquid resources she can secure. Under the new Wheat Act I believe we could sell Germany breadstuffs on credit. This would probably involve acrimonious feeling in the United States for a time, of which I am prepared to stand my full share should it come to this issue. Any proposal of this kind should be contingent upon the Allies doing their share and securities being given in priority (except Belgium) to reparation.

Faithfully yours,
[signed, Hoover's secretary]

Credits to Serbia and Others

> This communique is only a draft of a letter from Hoover to Wilson. Since there is no response from the President on the matter discussed, it is possible that the letter was not sent.

Draft

May 15, 1919

My dear Mr. President:

With regard to the proposed reduction of the credits to Serbia, Czecho-Slovakia, and Roumania, would you be so kind as to introduce into your approval of these reduction[s] the phrase to the effect that such reduction should not encroach upon the $25,000,000 credits set aside for foodstuffs for Roumania, the $45,000,000 credits set aside likewise for Czecho-Slovakia, and the $20,000,000 set aside for Serbia, without the approval of Mr. Hoover?

I fully realize the difficulties to the Treasury, but not only are these credits absolutely vital for the feeding of these people, but they have been agreed upon with the Treasury, and the food is actually purchased and a large part of it is in motion toward Europe.

I may mention that I have made such re-arrangements in Belgian finance as to enable a reduction of $20,000,000 credits for food previously established, for French account, and similarly a reduction of $5,000,000 in Serbian accounts.

Yours faithfully,
[signed, Hoover's secretary]

Executive Order for Barnes Appointment

Paris 15 May 1919

My dear Mr. Hoover:

I am returning herewith the Executive Order giving effect to the new law regarding food products and fuel and the appointment of Mr. Barnes as Wheat Director for next year, which was enclosed with your letter of May 13th to the President. You will note that he has signed it.

I am taking the liberty of holding the duplicate of the Executive Order for the President's files.

Sincerely yours,
Gilbert F. Close
Confidential Secretary to the President

Bolshevik Reply on Nansen Mission

The French were reluctant to accept any proposal that would aid the Russian government, even the indirect aid that would come from the Nansen food mission, for they clung to the hope that anti-Bolshevist forces fighting in Russia would prevail. Thus Clemenceau delayed signing the Allied acceptance of Nansen's proposal until April 17; immediately, Hoover arranged to have it sent from the Eiffel radio station. When no reply was received for ten days Hoover surmised that the French had not sent it. He then arranged to have it sent by Dutch radio station, and on May 3 the Russians acknowledged reception through this station. On May 7 a full reply was sent through the Swedish station and picked up by the Dutch. On May 14 Hoover received a copy of the reply in Paris. It carried a warm acceptance of the proferred relief and paid homage to the humanitarian motive behind it, but it also bitterly attacked the evils of capitalism and brought an adamant refusal to cease fighting—one of the Allies' conditions for the Nansen mission.

Nonetheless, Nansen sent these words to the Big Four: "Please tell Hoover that I intend to meet Lenin's delegates perhaps Stockholm but shall be glad hear Hoover's opinion soon as possible" (*P.R.*, *P.C.*, *1919 Russia*, p. 115). On May 16, a meeting was held by the committee originally appointed to advise the Supreme Council on the Nansen mission. Hoover was present and it was agreed that he should inform the Norwegian leader that "until the whole matter has been given further consideration by the Governments here we consider it extremely inadvisable to arrange any meeting with Bolshevik representatives." That terminated the whole idea of the Nansen mission, although in his May 16 letter to Wilson, Hoover mentions that the Bolsheviks were willing to have Nansen go ahead with his food mission while they opened up the question of peace directly with the Allies. Hoover does not indicate whether or not he was inclined to probe this possibility further.

In July 1921 a famine compelled the Communist leaders to beg aid from Hoover, now in Washington as Secretary of Commerce, and plans were arranged to send and distribute considerable American food for the next eighteen months. On July 10, 1923, the Russian government sent an elaborately designed scroll of thanks to Hoover and the American people. It is on display at the Hoover Presidential Library in West Branch, Iowa (*Memoirs*, vol. 2, pp. 23–26). A translation of the scroll is given below following the Hoover letter.

Paris, 16 May 1919.

Dear Mr. President:

You will please find enclosed herewith copy of the reply of the Bolshevik Government to Doctor Nansen's proposal. One has to read it with a certain sense of elimination. Approaching it from this point of view, they do not accept the conditions laid down by the four national Chiefs, but in turn propose that Doctor Nansen should go ahead with his food work and that on the political side they should open up peace negotiations direct with the Allied and Associated Governments.

For what it may be worth, I will be addressing you in the course of the day a memorandum as to my views on the whole Russian situation.

Faithfully yours,
[signed, Hoover's secretary]

Message of Thanks

RESOLUTION OF THE SOVIET OF
PEOPLES COMMISSARS

In the trying hour of a great and overwhelming disaster, the people of the United States, represented by the A.R.A., responded to the needs of the population, already exhausted by intervention and blockade, in the famine stricken parts of Russia and Federated Republics.

Unselfishly, the A.R.A. came to the aid of the people and organized on a broad scale the supply and distribution of food products and other articles of prime necessity.

Due to the enormous and entirely disinterested efforts of the A.R.A., millions of people of all ages were saved from death, and entire districts and even cities were saved from the horrible catastrophe which threatened them.

Now when the famine is over and the colossal work of the A.R.A. comes to a close, the Soviet of Peoples Commissars, in the name of the millions of people saved and in the name of all the working people of Soviet Russia and the Federated Republics counts it a duty to express before the whole world its deepest thanks to this organization, to its leader, Herbert Hoover, to its representative in Russia, Colonel Haskell, and to all its workers, and to declare that the people inhabiting the Union of Soviet Socialist Republics will never forget the help given them by the American people, through the A.R.A., seeing in it a pledge of the future friendship of the two nations.

L. Kamenev,
Acting President of the Council of
Peoples Commissars.
N. Gorbunov,
Chief of the Administrative Dept. of
the Council of Peoples Commissars.
L. Fotieva,
Secretary of the Council of Peoples
Commissars.

Moscow, Kremlin,
July 10, 1923.

Relief Measures, December to May

The report, referred to below, reveals that from December 1, 1918, to May 1, 1919, food given to European countries totaled 591,843 metric tons. By far the greatest amount went to Germany and German-Austria.

17 May 1919.

My dear Mr. President:

You may be interested in a summary of the relief measures that have been effected from December 1st to May 1st.

Faithfully yours,
Herbert Hoover

Hoover Plan to Restore Europe

No letter exists prior to May 17 in which the plan mentioned in this short note might have been enclosed. Nor does there appear to be any subsequent letter containing a discussion of the plan. Possibly Hoover and Wilson discussed it in one of their private conversations. What the plan embodied involves some uncertainty. However on June 7 Hoover gave a long statement to the press containing his proposal for America's part in the future rehabilitation of Europe; it is presented here on the reasonable presumption that it was the plan Hoover sent to Wilson sometime prior to May 17. Its release to the press on June 7 provides adequate proof that Wilson had endorsed it.

Paris, 17 May, 1919.

My dear Hoover:

Thank you for sending me your suggestions with regard to a plan for the financial rehabilitation of Europe. I shall read it with the greatest interest.

Cordially and faithfully yours,
Woodrow Wilson

Press Statement

Financial Requirements of Europe

7 June 1919

Mr. Hoover was asked by the Associated Press for a statement of the financial requirements of Europe from the United States next year. He said:

Any statement is premised upon Peace and return of Europe to work. I don't take it we will finance any more wars in Europe either directly or indirectly, nor do I take it that we will provide finance to enable people to live without work or to work part time, such as is going on all over Europe today. The excuse for this sort of economic delirium tremens will be over with peace.

The amount of credits from the United States to Europe during the twelve months after peace revolves around their inability to pay for:

(a) Raw material, machinery and tools
(b) Food
(c) Currency re-organization
(d) Interest payments on money borrowed from our government

The volume of the financial assistance needed and the solution for it, varies with the situation in each State. The neutral states are in a flourishing condition and need cause no concern. Roumania, Greater Serbia, Bulgaria, Arabia, Turkey (except for Armenia), Portugal, Greece and Hungary, will be practically self-supporting in food and, in fact, some of them should be able even to export food, and with their other commodities they can export they can pretty well provide for all their necessities, except perhaps, in some cases, railway reconstruction material and agricultural implements and currency reorganization. These States represent nearly one-third the population of Europe.

Poland and the Baltic States will produce almost enough bread grains and vegetables for their own people, but they will be short of meats and fats. If they secure resources for currency reorganization and some working capital for raw material imports so as to get exports going, they should with economy be self-supporting within a very few months. Czecho-Slovakia, Belgium and Finland have a larger import food problem, for they always require both breadstuffs, meat and fats, throughout the year to supplement their own production. These people are already moving energetically to get their industries moving, even under the terrible difficulties presented by the armistice situation. They must have working capital to reorganize their currencies, to provide raw material and to carry their food problem for a while. The economic problems of most of these States are simple compared to the larger European nations and the world will be astonished with their recovery if they have peace. There will be great poverty among individuals who have suffered most directly from the war and these individuals will comprise a proper scene for the charitable work for many years, but it will be individual, not national, as has been the case this winter.

The condition of Germany and German-Austria can have no intelligent discussion until Peace is signed. Out of the total of 70,000,-000 Germans in these two states, some 25 or 30 million lived before the war by trade, by import of raw material and exports in exchange for food and other necessities, and these cannot be supported on the land. How they will pay indemnity and at the same time secure credits for raw materials and food imports is a problem for the new Commission whose duty it will be to secure the maximum reparation. If they do not get raw material and food they will never be able to pay indemnities. In any event, one possibility that must not be overlooked is that 10 to 12 million of this population may emigrate eastward or overseas under the economic pressure which will be their fate at the best.

The Great Allies have, of course, an uphill load to pull in the resurrection of industry and their economic life. France has the smallest need of food imports of the three, Great Britain can feed herself largely from her colonies, but both will need financial help in the provision of credits for raw material, and Italy will require not only assistance in raw material but in the provision of food supplies. They will want relief from payment of interest on the debts they owe our Treasury for some period.

Altogether, the dominant problem in the rehabilitation of Europe is one wholly of credits with which to buy overseas and, if such finance can be provided, Europe should be on a self-supporting basis within another year. Whether the United States will undertake a third stage in our intervention in Europe must be for Congress to decide. The first stage has been to end the war, the second to feed the people until peace and harvest, and the third may be to give our financial assistance to bring back economic life. In my own personal view, the largest part of the credits required from the United States should be provided by private credits and we should, except for certain limited purposes, stop the lending of money by our Government. Credits next year are required for business operations, and when Governments are engaged in business they always overspend, and the years to come must be years of economy, not of extravagance.

Moreover, such credits breed political difficulties. I feel that something like half a billion dollars' assistance from the American Government may be needed to join with the other Allies in the reorganization of the currencies of the new States and to take care of some particularly acute and otherwise insolvable situations.

On the other hand, much larger sums will be required from private credit for raw material and food, and in order to secure that these private credits to Governments or especially to individuals should be established, our Government would probably need to consider some further measures of encouragement in this direction. The credit of private individuals and firms of even the most wrecked of States in Europe is still worth something, and what is needed most is to re-establish confidence in such credits; and in this matter the Government could, by different devices, lend its assistance with comparatively little risk. In any event, some solution will have to be found or we will again be faced with starvation in some parts of Europe on a lesser scale next Spring when the forthcoming harvest is exhausted.

We may have some further political revolutions in Europe, because the social pendulum has not reached the point of stability in some spots, but, in my view, the great danger of red terror and destruction by Bolshevism and Anarchy has greatly mitigated and will have actually passed in most countries on the signing of peace.

If we undertake to give credits, we should undertake it in a definite and organized manner. We should have a consolidated and organized control of the assistance that we give in such a way that it should be used only if economy in imports is maintained, that definite rehabilitation of industry is undertaken, that people return to work, that orderly government is preserved, that fighting is stopped and that disarmament is undertaken, that no discrimination is made against the United States in favor of other countries. If these things are done, the matter is of nothing like such enormous figures as we have been handling during the war, and generally I look upon the third stage of our intervention in the assistance of Europe as infinitely less difficult and less expensive than the two previous stages in our intervention.

If those things are not done, Europe will starve in spite of all we can do. The surplus of our productivity could not support a

Europe of today's idleness if every man of us worked fifteen hours daily.

On Copy of Bolshevik Reply to Nansen

In his May 16 letter to Wilson, Hoover promised to send "in the course of the day a memorandum as to my views on the whole Russian situation." In the following letter, the President thanks him for this promise. Actually, five weeks passed before Hoover sent such a memorandum (see letter of June 21).

Paris, 17 May, 1919.

My dear Hoover:
Thank you for sending me the copy of the reply of the Bolshevik Government to Dr. Nansen's proposals and also for your promise to let me have a comprehensive memorandum of your own views about the Russian situation.

Cordially and faithfully yours,
Woodrow Wilson

Thanks for May 9 Baltic Letter

Paris, 19 May, 1919.

My dear Hoover:
Thank you for the letter about the Balkan [Baltic?] Provinces. It will help me in a matter about which I haven't been able to think definitely enough.

Faithfully yours,
[signed, Wilson's secretary]

Thanks for Report on Relief

Paris, 20 May, 1919.

My dear Mr. Hoover:
The President asks me to thank you for your note of May 17th

enclosing a summary of the relief measures that have been effected from December 1st to May 1st.

> Sincerely yours,
> *Gilbert F. Close*
> Confidential Secretary to the President

Answer to Heath on Food Prices

Paris, 20 May 1919.

My dear Close:

I am returning the telegram from Mrs. Julian Heath herewith. In the matter of the five cent loaf, one can theorize to his heart's content. Mrs. Heath overlooks the fact that there is twice as much currency in circulation today as before the war, with its consequent depreciation in purchasing power as against pre-war standards.

Her admonition to the President to emulate such "distinguished citizens as Augustus and Julius Caesar" is, of course, amusing. You might call her attention to the fact that these gifts of grain to the idle populace of Ancient Rome date the commencement of the decline of that population and are the early prototype of modern "chomage" in demoralized Austria and Germany.

I do not see any harm in her request that this whole question be considered before the next session of Congress. I can picture it as a fruitful topic for debate.

> Faithfully yours,
> [signed, Hoover's secretary]

Proxies and U.S. Equalization Board

Paris, May 20, 1919.

My dear Mr. President:

I enclose herewithin a proxy required in order that the shares of stock in the United States Equilization [*sic*] Board, Inc., standing in the name of the United States of America may be voted at the annual meeting to be held June 2nd.

I should be greatly obliged if you could see your way clear to sign these proxies and return them to me.

Faithfully yours,

[signed, Hoover's secretary]

Reply to Hoover on Baltics

Paris, 21 May, 1919.

My dear Hoover:

I read with deep interest and concern your letter of the ninth of May about the situation in the | Balkan | [Baltic][1] Provinces, and yesterday had an opportunity to read it to the other members of the "Council of Four." Mr. Lloyd George suggested that I request you to have a conference with Admiral Hope, or anyone else who represents the British Admiralty here, in order to ascertain whether it was feasible from a naval point of view to carry out the programme you suggest. If the programme were adopted, it would, I suppose, necessarily be the British Navy that executed it, and we would very much appreciate a memorandum from you as to the result of your conference with the British Admiralty.

Cordially and sincerely yours,

Woodrow Wilson

---

[1] | Balkan | changed by hand to [Baltic].

Additional Information on Baltics

The "enclosed report" mentioned in Hoover's letter was a recommendation made by the Council of Foreign Ministers at their meeting on May 9, not on May 13 as Hoover states (*Memoirs*, vol. 1, p. 374; cf. *F.R.*, *P.C.*, vol. 4, pp. 678, 693). It provided for appointment of an Allied committee to report on the best means of keeping order in the Baltic States and supplying the population with food. Hoover was a member of this committee. The delay that followed prompted Hoover to take action on his own. He sent food into Riga by trains, wagons, handcarts, and ships. Admiral William S. Benson sent a destroyer into the harbor of Riga in Latvia; although the Germans were fighting in the suburbs, American doughboys were able to distribute the food. When the Germans prevailed over the Communists, a "white terror" followed compelling Hoover to protest. Eventually order was established (*Memoirs*, vol. 1, pp. 374–76).

Paris, 21 May 1919.

Dear Mr. President:

Since addressing you on the ninth day of May, with respect to the situation in the Baltic States, the matter came up before the Council of Ministers of Foreign Affairs and they appointed a committee comprising representatives of the Army, Navy and food organizations of each of the four governments. This committee has made the enclosed report to the Council of Five. No action has as yet been taken upon it.

With regard to the possible contribution of $12,500,000 from the United States for these purposes, I may say that this entire amount will be covered by our food programme and it will not, therefore, be necessary for the United States Treasury to consider the matter. It is a question of agreeing [to] the policy and of securing that the other Governments do their share in the provision of other materials required in these states.

Faithfully yours,
[signed, Hoover's secretary]

Approval of Hoover on Proxies

Paris, 21 May, 1919.

My dear Mr. Hoover:

At the President's request I am returning herewith the proxies that are required in order that shares of stock in the United States Equalization Board, standing in the name of the United States of America may be voted at the annual meeting to be held June 2nd. You will note that the President has signed both the original and the duplicate.

Sincerely yours,
Gilbert F. Close
Confidential Secretary of the President

Letter from J. S. Talbot

Hoover does not speak of J. S. Talbot in any of his works. If he took action on the matter treated in the letter from Wilson, no such evidence is in the Hoover-Wilson correspondence.

Paris, 28 May, 1919.

My dear Mr. Hoover:

I am sending you herewith a letter from Mr. J. S. Talbot for such consideration as may be deemed proper.

Sincerely yours,
[signed, Wilson's secretary]
Confidential Secretary to the President

Releasing Cotton Controls

May 29, 1919.

My Dear Mr. President:

I submit herewith for your consideration a proclamation, releasing from license under the Food Control Act all handlers of cotton seed products in the United States. This proclamation is in accord with the general policy of releasing industries as quickly as normal conditions can be restored. I should be obliged if you can see your way clear to sign this proclamation and return it to me, so that I may take the proper steps to have it recorded with the State Department.

Faithfully yours,
[signed, Hoover's secretary]

Letter for Hoover Consideration

The following letter that Wilson sent to Hoover has not been identified and apparently no subsequent correspondence dealt with the matter it treated.

Paris, 30 May, 1919.

My dear Mr. Hoover:

I am sending you herewith a letter for such consideration as may be deemed proper.

Sincerely yours,
[signed, Wilson's secretary]
Confidential Secretary to the President

Executive Order on Cotton Products

Paris 31 May 1919

My dear Mr. Hoover:

The President has asked me to return to you the enclosed proclamation releasing from license under the Food Control Act, all handlers of cotton seed products in the United States, in accordance with your note to him of May 29th.

I am retaining the carbon copy of the proclamation for our files.

Sincerely yours,
Gilbert F. Close
Confidential Secretary to the President

Reported Mistreatment of Polish Jews

Paris, 2 June 1919.

My dear Mr. President:

As you are perhaps aware, there is a great agitation in the United States over the mistreatment of Jews in Poland. This agitation has been founded to some extent on misinformation. A good deal of the news that comes to the United States from Poland filters through German or Bolshevik sources. On the other hand, there has been wrong-doing and a proper illumination of it will not only act as a deterrent but will give the Polish Government an opportunity to prove its good faith.

The continuation of this agitation is likely to do the future of Poland in American estimation a great deal of harm, and I do believe that regardless of the temporary obsessions of the Polish Government for territorial aggrandizement, it must be a fundamental principle with us that we must support the Polish Republic. Therefore, in order to meet the question, I have suggested to Mr. Paderewski that he should ask you to appoint an independent committee to reinvestigate these matters, and the Polish Government should undertake to deal out justice on any conclusions they might come to. I, of course, do not know whether you would be inclined to appoint such a commission, or not, but if so I should like to suggest that there should be on such a commission of at least four or five, at least two prominent American Jews of the broad character of Mr. Oscar Straus and Mr. Henry Morgenthau.

It might quite well be that there has been wrong-doing along the Bolshevik edge of Poland, but, on the other hand, a section of Jews in Poland have shown no support whatever to the Polish Government, and, if such a commission were wisely selected, it might not only act as a deterrent to outrages on Jews but it might also act in an advisory capacity to the Jewish community in Poland, that they should support this growing democracy as being their ultimate salvation from the tyrannies they have endured. The Polish Government is generally meeting a great deal of difficulty from the Jews in the fact that they are peculiarly subject to Bolshevik influence because of the total misery in which they have been left by the last two hundred years of mistreatment and they have also been stimulated to make trouble by the Germans, because during the war the Germans played strongly upon the past sufferings of the Jewish population as against the Poles, and many of them are rather pro-German.

This country needs moderation and good counsel on both sides of this problem.

Yours faithfully,
[signed, Hoover's secretary]

Reply to Hoover on Polish Jews

Wilson accepted Hoover's suggestion in the June 2 letter to appoint a commission to investigate the reported mistreatment of Jews in Poland. One of his appointees was Henry Morgenthau, an American

Jew who had been ambassador to Turkey from 1913 to 1916. In his *Memoirs* (vol. 1, p. 358) Hoover states that the commission did "fine service by exposing falsity and creating a generally more wholesome atmosphere."

Paris, 3 June, 1919.

My dear Hoover:

I have received the request of Mr. Paderewski to which you refer in your letter of the second, and I am going to try to act upon it, for I have the deepest interest, as you have, in assisting Poland in every way and, amongst other things, in this troublesome question of the treatment of the Jewish people.

Cordially and faithfully yours,
Woodrow Wilson

Hoover Views on Peace Treaty

On May 14 Hoover wrote Wilson of his objections to the use of a blockade to force Germany to sign the treaty. The next day Hoover and three other Americans spoke personally with the President on this point and on certain other features of the treaty. Because of considerable dissatisfaction with this final product of the Peace Conference, Wilson called a meeting on June 3 with a large group of Americans. Hoover stated that concessions should be made to get Germany to sign (McCormick Diary, p. 96). His remarks "irritated the President, and he made sharp replies" (*Memoirs*, vol. 1, p. 464). For instance, when Hoover urged that justice demanded the alteration of the Saar and the Silesian terms, Wilson bluntly replied, "I do not see any essential injustice in the Saar Basin terms" (*World Settlement*, vol. 3, p. 502).

Hoover continued to be dissatisfied with the treaty and the blockade. On June 14 he and McCormick—who thought the treaty would work—lunched with Bliss and Baruch. The discussion became heated with Hoover threatening to resign if the blockade were imposed (McCormick Diary, p. 102).

Ten days before, on June 4, at the request of Secretary of State Robert Lansing, Hoover had drawn up a detailed memorandum on the whole German question. Lansing forwarded a copy to Wilson. Sometime thereafter the President summoned Hoover for a discussion of this memorandum and the treaty in general. The two met on June 17 (Hoover Calendar, HPL) and possibly on this occasion

Hoover exposed some fundamental defects in the treaty. Years later Hoover confessed that he "had, perhaps, used over-vigorous words" and Wilson "flashed angrily at these expressions as being personal accusations against him" (*Memoirs*, vol. 1, p. 466).

Hoover stated that he never again saw Wilson while he was President except for a formal goodbye when Wilson left Paris for home a few weeks later. But at 10:30 on June 17, Hoover was with Wilson and a group of Americans who left by train for a two- or three-day trip to Belgium, and Hoover appeared to have been a principal leader of the group with the President (McCormick Diary, pp. 104–9). Either Hoover had forgotten this event by 1951 or the meeting mentioned in *Memoirs* took place after June 20. Actually Hoover saw Wilson also on June 23 with McCormick, who gave no indication that Hoover again exposed weaknesses in the treaty although he records that the three spoke of Russia and the recent sinking of German ships (McCormick Diary, p. 111). Possibly McCormick left before Hoover did and it was then that the heated exchange with Wilson over the terms of the treaty took place. However, neither the McCormick Diary nor *Ordeal* nor *Memoirs* suggests any such confrontation so near June 28—the day Germany signed the peace treaty. On June 22 the Germans made one final plea that the Allies agree to at least a consideration of revision within the next two years. The sharp refusal of the Big Four was actually written by Wilson himself on the evening of June 23. The late enemy yielded completely—just in time to stave off the movement of Foch's armies against them (*World Settlement*, vol. 2, pp. 518–19).

Paris, 4 June 1919

My dear Mr. President:

In this most critical moment, I know you will not take it amiss if I express my views somewhat more fully than is possible at such a conference as that of Tuesday morning. I, of course, have had no part in the Treaty making and, for this reason and the independent sources of information which I have enjoyed, I have had perhaps a useful opportunity in objective observation. I do wish you to feel that whatever the course you may choose I am, for what I am worth, prepared to stand by.

I am convinced the Germans will not sign the Treaty without considerable modification. I do not feel that strict justice is now in question, for no adequate punishment of German crimes is possible or is even dealt out in the present draft treaty, nor that some points even relate to this issue. From an American point of view, we have been fighting autocracy and militarism and I feel that the paramount issues now are to secure stability of government in Europe, to secure the establishment of democracy in Germany and of a League of Nations, which may be able to further correct the international wrongs which have accumulated over centuries and deter them in the future, and give security to the many nations that have been re-created.

I feel that even if Germany signed the present terms, we would not secure stability and that if she refuses we will have extinguished the possibility of democracy in favor of either Communism or reaction, and that we will have wrecked the very foundation of the League of Nations.

To secure the signature of the Treaty by blockade or the bombing of German towns would itself guarantee a later revision of the Treaty by the moral shock to the world. Military occupation, I am convinced, will be welcomed by the Germans as an alternative to the Treaty in its present form, for occupation would be a guaranty of the survival of the German people at the expense of the Allies.

I feel that many issues in the Treaty which prevent its acceptance have been pressed into the draft in forms against what you and your American colleagues have consistently contended was far-sighted statesmanship. There has been a tendency to yield on these points because of the belief that the very survival of 200 million people revolved around early conclusion of these negotiations and the return of these populations to production, and that time and economic forces would remedy the worst phases. I see in the present British change of heart a tendency to recognition of the wisdom of your original positions and this fact offers an opportunity not only to remind them of these original positions, as you have done, but to state to them that we are glad that they have come to a realization and are ready to support important modifications which affect themselves as well as others. If such modifications do not secure signature, it will have at least demonstrated our faithfulness to your high objectives.

Faithfully yours,
Herbert Hoover

Memorandum on the Peace Treaty

[Paris] 5 June 1919

In any discussion of the draft treaty, I think it must be accepted as a promise [*sic*] that real justice can never be meted out, for no adequate punishment of German crimes is conceivable or even compossed in the present draft treaty. Therefore, if we strip the subject of questions of punishment and also of all humanitarian views toward the Germans (which to me are at least illogical in discussion of the other factors involved) the impression I get from a study of the situation is as follows:

A

The objectives desired appear to me to be:

I. To take all the economic surplus of Germany for a generation. This premise necessarily assumes that it is not desired to claim more than the surplus for in such a case the population will either (*a*) die, (*b*) migrate, or (*c*) plunge into economic chaos that will engulf Europe, and in either case yield no surplus.

II. To effect such regime and control as will strip Germany of the power of political and military offensive. This premise assumes that it is desired to establish stable democracy in Germany, for otherwise she will turn either to Communism or to Reaction, and will thereby become either militarily or politically on the offensive.

III. To secure signature to and acquiescence in the treaty by the German people. This premise necessitates that the signature should be obtained without either (*a*) blockade, (*b*) bombing of towns, or (*c*) military occupation. I assume that a treaty signed under either blockade or bombing would be revised within twelve months under the recoil of the moral shock to the world, and I also assume that military occupation means not only further enormous sacrifices to the Allies but also developing political entanglements amongst themselves. Furthermore, it is not at all certain that it would be unwelcomed by a very large part of Germany as a guaranty of food, industrial recuperation and protection of private property, for under any occupation the population must be fed and put to production, and this will be at least at the initial expense of the Allies.

B

As I weigh the draft treaty on these premises, and alternatives, I am convinced that: (*a*) the demands made are greater than the economic surplus; (*b*) that the regime and controls are such as endanger stable democracy in Germany; and (*c*) that the Germans will never sign the treaty in its present form. The present Government in Germany is the only alternative to either Reactionary or Communistic Government and if it fails we have political debacle in any event. As they do not intend to sign the treaty in its present form, we are faced with either modification or the alternatives above.

C

I am not unaware that criticism is easy, nor am I unaware that the problem involved is the most difficult that statesmen have been confronted with, because it resolves itself into the degree with which all the objectives above can be imposed and still not create the adverse currents to which I have referred. Nor am I unaware of the fact that every statesman will have a different view as to the degree with which these demands can be imposed with success.

The point I would like to make is, however, that many of the demands in the draft treaty which I believe are impossible either of acceptance or, if accepted, will not obtain the results expected, have been included against the protests of the President and his colleagues, but yielded by them because of their belief that the very survival of 200 million people revolved around the immediate conclusion of these negotiations and the return of these populations to production, and with the anticipation that time and economic forces would remedy the worst phases.

D

I see in the present British change of heart a tendency to the recognition of the President's original propositions and it appears to me that it offers an opportunity for the President now to definitely insist from an American point of view that these modifications should be carried out.

E

I am not sure how far we ought to sacrifice the United States to the objectives of the European Allies. To me, from an American point of view, we have been fighting autocracy and militarism and it has been destroyed. I feel that the paramount issues are now to secure stability of government in Europe, to secure the establishment of democracy in Germany, to secure a League of Nations that may be able to further correct the international wrongs which have been accumulated over centuries and deter the repetition of such wrongs in the future, to give security to the many nations that have been re-created, to secure to the Allies any practicable reparation.

If tested by this touchstone alone, even great modifications in the proposed treaty will not involve or jeopardize these points, whereas the failure to make immediate stable peace does jeopardize them. These are the high objectives which the President has held constantly before him as in the interest of the world as a whole, and I feel that the opportunity is arriving for the President to absolutely insist on his original contentions, even at the risk of disruption of the Conference. I believe this disruption is the least of evils; I do not believe it will happen. We will be used as a foil for every European politician any way. Therefore, there will be very little good will toward us no matter what conclusions are come to.

Herbert Hoover

Feeding Undernourished Children

Paris, 6 June 1919.

Dear Mr. President:

As you are aware, under your approval I set up very early in this general relief work in Europe a plan and organization for special feeding of children sub-normal because of under-nourishment. In this matter, we defined sub-normal children as those already showing the disease effects of under-nourishment and therefore in a much worse state than what is usually considered in the United States as under-nourishment. It appeared at the time, and has since been demonstrated, that the furnishing of rough staples to large massed populations under the difficulties of distribution in weak governments was more or less a hit or miss as to whether the children, especially of the poor, would receive sufficiency of such staples. Furthermore, in order to bring them back to normal they required special types of food which no available finance could provide for the population as a whole.

This situation arose primarily from the failure of milk supplies, which in turn is due in a few localities to the loss of dairy herd, but mainly through the war, blockade and loss of shipping, there is an acute famine in feeding stuffs for all European cattle. This, it is expected, will correct itself with the summer feed and imports of feed after peace.

The plan of organization was in each of some twelve countries to set up a structure of national committees of women and physicians, with local sub-committees. These committees have established canteens, either independently or at the school houses, and dispensed one meal a day of specially prepared foodstuffs from special imports for such children as have passed doctor's inspection as coming within our category. We placed enough American[s] who had previous skill in handling this problem in Belgium and Northern France, in each of these countries, together with assistants, to erect the organization and see that the administration was carried out on sound lines, the objective in organization being to stimulate self-help and continued action among these communities. We now have literally thousands of committees and upwards of three million such children under food treatment. We are importing the special food required for their supply; they themselves pay the cost of local organization and, in some countries, even subscribe to our funds.

I have undertaken to give this service of imported food as a matter of charity from the American people and have not demanded governmental obligations of repayment. Some of the money has been found by public charity in the United States and locally; we have found some from the residue of the Five Million Dollar fund which you have placed at my disposal, and I have found some from the Hundred Million dollar appropriation of Congress. We also have a contingent fund in the Grain Corporation which I will describe later, on which I am expecting to draw for some of this cost.

As you are aware, the Hundred Million Dollar appropriation ceases to be effective and will, in fact, be exhausted on the 30th of June and there seems little hope of getting this great mass of child life back to anything like normal for some months yet. We are fundamentally fighting a milk famine by the import of American condensed milk and other equivalent foods in the hope of redeeming child life, and I feel that it must go on for some four or five months at least after the broad relief measures of Europe have been relaxed owing to the arrival of the harvest. I am, therefore, greatly concerned over the question of finance, as it represents an expenditure of Two to Three Millions of Dollars a month.

In the course of our operations in Europe, we have been constantly faced with the possibilities of large losses if there should be a break-down in the political situation on the enormous stocks of food afloat and in warehouse. We have, therefore, in the sale of these foodstuffs, provided a small margin for insurance to cover such an eventuality, thus having gradually built up the contingent fund before referred to. We are approaching the end of our large shipping campaign, and I now have hopes that we will get through without such a loss. I take it that the books of the Grain Corporation or the Relief Administration must not show a profit made out of this winter's necessities of Europe, and the object of this communication to you is to ask your approval for my developing some plan by which any such surplus can be diverted into that part of our organization conducted under the fund which you furnished to us and used in continued Child Relief, for such a time as it may afford resource or by such supplement of public charity as we may be able to secure.

The reaction which I receive from all over Europe indicates that we have touched the heart of the populations at large as much by this baby feeding department as in any form of American intervention in Europe, and its continuation for some months will, to my mind, contribute to smooth out those ruffled feelings which are bound to arise from the political settlements. It is obvious that no single country in Europe is going to obtain what its politicians want, and that there will be, until they awaken to more rational sense than most of them display at the moment, a tendency for them to blame the United States for failure to secure each and every one his objectives against the other.

Beyond all this, of course, is the infinitely more important, intrinsic question of the saving of child life by such widely organized and wholesale methods as will meet the necessities of Europe at the present time.

Faithfully yours,
Herbert Hoover

Approval of Plan for Children

[Note handwritten by Wilson]

[ca. June 6, 1919]

My dear Hoover,
    I entirely approve the proposal you here make.

                                                    Woodrow Wilson

French Military Force against Budapest

Béla Kun was proving to be a much more durable force than Hoover
and the Allies had anticipated. The telegram from Alonzo Taylor
underscored the strength of the Hungarian leader's military might
backed by Lenin's Communist government. Another Hoover adviser
in Vienna, T. C. Gregory, urged stronger measures, even the use of
military force, to dethrone the Bolshevik leader. For months Hoover
had stood firmly against such action to put down the many turbulent
forces that arose throughout Europe upon the cessation of hostilities
in November 1918. Seven months later, however, he felt reluctantly
compelled to agree that the French forces in Yugoslavia should be
allowed to advance on Budapest. He continued to favor this policy
for several weeks, but by June 26 he considered it more desirable to
encourage the forces inside Hungary to take action to replace Béla
Kun with a more representative and responsible government. He
conveyed to the Hungarians that food supplies could hardly be supplied while the Communist leader was in power. By August 1, Kun
had fled by plane and eventually reached Russia; soon Hoover began
to send large supplies of food into Hungary. Kun continued his revolutionary activities until 1939 when he became a victim of Stalin's
purge (*F.R., P.C.*, vol. 6, 20–26, and vol. 10, 259–60, pp. 348–49;
Memoirs, vol. 1, pp. 397–400).

                                                    June 9th, 1919.

Dear Mr. President:

    With regard to the condition of Central Europe I wish to call
your attention to the attached telegram that I have just received
from Dr. Alonzo Taylor, in which he again emphasizes this most
critical situation. Neither Dr. Taylor nor Mr. Gregory, whose letter I
sent you yesterday, are given to exaggeration, and I must agree with
them that unless something can be done to the Hungarian situation
and at once, the adjacent orderly Governments will fall into chaos.

As much as I dislike to suggest it, I can see but one solution and that is for the French troops which are now in Jugo-Slavia to advance on Budapest without delay. Otherwise, it appears to us, that both the Czecho-Slovakian and German-Austrian Governments will surely fall.

Faithfully yours,
[signed, Hoover's secretary]

Appropriation for Food Administration

Paris 9 June 1919.

My dear Mr. President:

It appears that the Food Administration appropriation will exspire [sic] by law the 30th of June. As you are aware, the Administration has been demobilized down to a very small staff who are necessary to continue the prosecution of some profiteering cases and to collect the data incident to preparing the final report and to take care of the still undetermined destination of buildings and files in Washington. It will probably cost us $50,000 to $100,000 to completely wind this matter up, and I would like to have your permission to use this sum from the appropriation of the Presidential Fund which you gave to me for general administration expenses and emergency measures, as I think I can squeeze enough out of the residue to take care of this matter also.

Faithfully yours,
[signed, Hoover's secretary]

Approval of Plan for Food Funds

Paris, 10 June, 1919.

My dear Hoover:

In your letter of June ninth you ask if you have my permission to use from fifty to one hundred thousand dollars of the sum from the "President's Fund" assigned to you for general administrative expenses and emergency matters. You certainly have, if you can squeeze it out. I am glad you think you can.

Cordially and sincerely yours,
Woodrow Wilson

Wilson Concern over Central Europe

Paris, 10 June, 1919.

My dear Hoover:

Dr. Taylor's letter, added to Mr. Gregory's, makes a deep impression on me. We are studying that Czecho-Slovak-Hungarian situation now and are deeply perplexed what to do, because we feel it might be very important to send the forces of the neighboring countries into Hungary. You may be sure that we realize how very critical the whole matter is.

Cordially and faithfully yours,
Woodrow Wilson

New Blockade of Germany

The action against Budapest discussed in Hoover's letter of June 9 appeared to some Allied leaders as a suitable means to force the Germans to sign the treaty. But Hoover objected and on June 17 Wilson accepted Hoover's suggestion that such action cease. Wilson brought the matter before the Big Four at 4:00 P.M. He stated that he had told Hoover to protest the detention of American ships since he did not wish to deprive the people of Czechoslovakia and Poland of needed supplies. Clemenceau seemed unconcerned but Lloyd George telephoned London immediately after the meeting and had the American ships released (*F.R., P.C.*, vol. 4, pp. 532–33). Hoover spoke personally with Wilson at about the same time—whether it was before or after this meeting cannot be ascertained. On June 17 at 10:30 P.M. he boarded the train with Wilson for a two- or three-day trip to Belgium. Thus we may presume that Hoover had the gratifying news of Lloyd George's action directly from the President.

Paris, 16 June 1919.

My dear Mr. President:

I quote below a message which I understand has been delivered to all vessels in the port of Hamburg (and probably also at Bremen and other German ports) by a British cruiser:

Vessels which have discharged cargoes are to leave German ports before Monday 16th June p.m. Those include merchant vessels chartered by Allied and Associated Governments or merchant vessels. Other ships of similar denomination partly discharged or fully loaded are to get steam at short notice and be ready to leave German waters.

The cruiser has been told to tell the American Food Relief at Hamburg to try and get them to participate in message to Emden [?], Staten, Dantzig [*sic*], Bremen and Bremerhaven. These steps are taken as a precaution and every endeavor is being made to prevent Germans detaining any tonnage. No other food ships are being sent to German ports from the U.K. and those arriving from over-seas will be detained when they reach British ports.

I am greatly alarmed at this, as it appears to me an absolute and positive blockade of Germany, and so far as I am aware, this has been done without any authority from the council of four.

I should be very glad, if it is in accord with your views, that this order be rescinded.

> Faithfully yours,
> [signed, Hoover's secretary]

Rice Millers and Controls

> Paris, June 17, 1919

My dear Mr. President:

I beg to submit herewith a Proclamation releasing from license the rice millers of the United States. This is in accordance with the policy of releasing license regulations as quickly as conditions allow. With the signing of this Proclamation the only food control remaining in the United States relates to cereals, cereal products and sugar.

If you return the original of this Proclamation to me I will have it forwarded to Washington and presented to the State Department for sealing and filing.

> Faithfully yours,
> [signed, Hoover's secretary]

Czechs, Coal, and Munitions

Austria was almost entirely dependent on its neighbors for coal and many other commodities needed to stave off famine, let alone to reestablish its economy. When actual hostilities ceased, these neighbors kept the natural flow of such essential products cut off as a punitive action against Germany's recent ally. Within a week after Hoover arrived in Europe in November 1918, he prevailed on a reluctant President Masaryk of Czechoslovakia to lift his blockade on coal for Austria (*Memoirs*, vol. 1, pp. 392–93). But this brought only a temporary show of cooperation. On July 20, 1919, Colonel William G. Atwood, an army railway expert borrowed by Hoover for relief work, received a plaintive message from Lieutenant Colonel W. B. Causey, another ARA man in Vienna. Causey underscored the lack of cooperation between Austria and Czechoslovakia regarding coal. In desperation he wrote, "I have about come to the conclusion that the only way to handle the whole situation in central Europe is to use military dictatorship" (*Organization*, p. 644). This message was written a month after Causey and Gregory telegraphed Hoover on the same matter, and Hoover sent the telegram to Wilson on June 17 (see the following note). There is no evidence that Wilson gave Hoover a written response. However, the two had a private interview on June 17 and then left Paris together for a two- or three-day tour of Belgium; Hoover also consulted with the President on June 23. Thus the subject could have been discussed on several occasions.

Paris 17 June 1919.

My dear Mr. President:—

The matter mentioned in the telegram which I quote below seems to me of such urgent importance that I raise it to your attention.

The Czechs are insisting upon agreement that German Austria turn over to them at once munitions in exchange for coal. Czechs will not agree to supply coal unless a certain amount of munitions are delivered. Political situation in Vienna is so delicate that it is impossible for Government to turn over munitions. The Czechs have the idea that if the Entente will order the German Austrians to deliver munitions in exchange for coal, that the Austrian Government will then be relieved of responsibility and can then ship the munition to the Czechs without fear of political difficulties in Vienna. Can you handle this question in Paris as indicated? German Austria, Czechs and Poles are in conference. Colonel Goodyear at Ostrau today. CAUSEY, GREGORY

Faithfully yours,
[signed, Hoover's secretary]

Final Closing of Food Administration

Paris, June 17, 1919.

My dear Mr. President:

Referring to my letter of June 9th with regard to the final closing up of the United States Food Administration.

I am now informed by the Washington office of the Food Administration that about $40,000. still remains from the Appropriation made by you from your National Security and Defense Fund of 1919 for the contingent expenses of the Food Administration. This sum can only be made available to pay our small expenses after June 30th if you will authorize me to draw out the balance of this Appropriation before June 30th to my personal credit for the purpose of closing up the Food Administration. I understand that substantially the same course has been taken with regard to the Fuel Administration. Expenses of the Food Administration will amount to approximately $5,000. per month.

If you approve of this, I should be glad to have you indicate your approval at the foot of this letter.

Faithfully yours,
Herbert Hoover

Approved. *and authorized*
Woodrow Wilson

Proclamations on Wheat Matters

Paris, June 20, 1919

My dear Mr. President:

In behalf of Mr. Julius H. Barnes, United States Wheat Director, I submit herewith for your approval two proclamations and one executive order with regard to the Administration of the Wheat Guaranty [*sic*] Act of March 4, 1919. These documents were prepared in the United States under Mr. Barnes' direction and were cabled to me. I have dated these documents of different dates in order that there may be no confusion in referring to them.

The first proclamation requires a license to be taken out by all persons engaged in the storage and distribution of wheat and the manufacture, storage, distribution of wheat flour and [*sic*] by manufacturers of bakery products. In this respect it continues the license control with regard to these commodities which was in effect under the Food Administration, and which is essential to an adequate control of the wheat flour markets.

The second proclamation prohibits the import and export of wheat and wheat flour, except under license from the Wheat Director. This will continue the present export and import control exercised by the War Trade Board whose power will soon come to an end under their own act.

The executive order raises by two cents the price of wheat at Gulf points without changing the wheat level in other parts of the United States. This is an adjustment which in Mr. Barnes' opinion promises an equable flow for export purposes, without the burden on transportation and other market facilities which occurred last year.

If you approve these orders and return the original to me signed, I will see that they are forwarded to the State Department for filing.

Faithfully yours,

[signed, Hoover's secretary]

Situation in Armenia

The historical boundaries of the region and ancient kingdom of the Armenians have varied considerably over the centuries. Today these people live in the northeastern part of Turkey and in the Armenian Soviet Socialist Republic, one of the fifteen Russian republics. The Russian Armenians also border on Georgia, another Russian republic. The Armenians took advantage of the exhaustion of Turkey and the revolution in Russia to establish an independent nation. It was recognized on August 10, 1920, and President Wilson was to establish its definitive boundaries. But within months Russia and Turkey obliterated the young country and absorbed the people within their territories. In 1951 Hoover penned a pitiable picture of the Armenians as he recalled 1919 and his relief work in Europe (*Memoirs*, vol. 1, pp. 385–89). As for his request in the following letter, the British troops were allowed to remain in Armenia a few weeks longer. In the meantime he wrote Wilson another letter that resulted in establishing better conditions for relief in Armenia (see letter of June 27).

Paris 20 June 1919

Dear Mr. President:

The situation in Armenia is today and has been for the last four months infinitely the most distressing famine in Europe. In addition to the indigenous population there are about 700,000 Armenian refugees in Russian Armenia and our sole route of access to them is the railway from Batoum to Riflis, which traverses the territory of the New Georgian Republic. These areas have been up to the present time, in occupation of the British Army, under whose directions [*sic*] the railways have been operated. Owing to the shortage in railway rolling stock we have only been able to transport some 1200 tons of foodstuffs a week from Batoum into Armenia, and on this ration the refugee population is dying at the rate of thousands daily. The British authorities have made Herculean efforts to improve the situation and it is, in fact, now showing considerable improvement, and we had lately hoped that we could cope with it.

The recent decision, however, that the Italian authorities will occupy this territory in replacement of the British authorities, has already had one result and will have another of most appalling character. The immediate situation is that the Georgian Government is demanding of us a large supply of foodstuffs in consideration of allowing us to traverse the railways, as they seem to anticipate less vigorous military control. There is no starvation in Georgia and they have sufficient foodstuffs to get through with and every pound that they exact from us means that many dead Armenians.

The other, and more discouraging factor is that if one Army is to evacuate and another take its place, the railways will be solely employed on military work and we shall have a period of a month or two months when there will be practically no food transported into this section. Our people estimate that there are already 200,000 deaths from starvation and that unless we can have a rigid control of this railway under the British authorities and unless we can stop the piracy of the Georgian Government, and unless we can have no interruption by military change, we shall certainly lose another 200,000 lives.

I do not wish to burden you with the heart-breaking details of the whole Armenian situation. The daily reports that we have not only through all our own agencies at work here but as well as through the British agencies are of the most appalling that have yet developed out of the war. I need only mention that the eating of the dead is now general. We have large stocks of foodstuffs lying in Batoum and I am confident that everything has been done both on our part and on the part of the British authorities that could have been done so far, but these impending interruptions can mean nothing but total break-down.

With the arrival of harvest about the end of August, the situation will be much ameliorated.

If it were possible for you to discuss this matter with your colleagues it might be that some arrangement could be made that the change in armies could be delayed and that the British authorities could take a more emphatic and rigid control of the railways than they now hold, and that emphatic notice be given the Georgian Government. A change in occupation after the end of August could probably be made without such a disaster as will certainly overtake us at any time prior to that date. The matter is of the most urgent order.

Faithfully yours,
Herbert Hoover

Funds for Food Administration

Paris, 21 June, 1919

My dear Mr. Hoover:

The President asks me to return to you herewith your letter of June 17th, on which the President has indicated his approval and authorization of the allotment of the balance of about $40,000, still remaining from the appropriation made by the President from the

National Security and Defense fund for 1919 for the contingent expenses of the Food Administration.

Sincerely yours,
Gilbert F. Close
Confidential Secretary to the President

Withdrawal of Germans from Baltics

> The problem presented in this letter was taken up by the Big Four on June 23 when Wilson presented the points made by Hoover in his communique. The President pressed Hoover's arguments. Finally the question was turned over to the commission on Baltic affairs which filed a report incorporating the substance of the last paragraph of Hoover's letter to Wilson (*F.R.*, *P.C.*, vol. 6, pp. 621–22, 672–73, 680–81).

21 June 1919.

Dear Mr. President:

The recent direction given by the Heads of State to Marshal Foch that he should demand the withdrawal of the Germans from certain portions of the Baltic States will require some extension or preparatory arrangement or it will result in the starvation of the population. The Germans are withdrawing the whole of the railway rolling stock from that area. They claim this rolling stock is their own. This apparently is literally, although not morally right. The Germans changed the gauge of the railways from the broad Russian gauge to the German standard gauge at the time of the German invasion of Russia, and equipped the railways with German rolling stock as part of their military operations.

The matter is one of a great deal of urgency and possibly could only be settled in event of the Allies agreeing to return the equivalent amount of the rolling stock acquired or to be acquired under the Armistice as against material to be left in the Baltic States by the Germans.

Faithfully yours,
Herbert Hoover

Proclamation on Rice Millers

Paris, 21 June, 1919.

My dear Mr. Hoover:

The President asks me to return herewith the original of the proclamation releasing from license the rice millers of the United States, in accordance with your letter of June 17th.

Sincerely yours,
Gilbert F. Close
Confidential Secretary to the President

Hoover View of Russian Situation

> Immediately after the signing of the treaty, President Wilson was due to leave Paris for the United States. Therefore, there is a sense of urgency in the following letter from Hoover in which he asks the President to establish an economic commission for Russia to reorganize its currency, production, transportation, and distribution. But Wilson was not disposed to accept the proposal. In the afternoon of June 23 Hoover came to see the President just as McCormick was leaving. Hoover asked him to stay and the three Americans discussed the Russian situation. Wilson expressed fears that it would be impossible for an inter-Allied body to give economic aid without getting involved in Russian politics. He added that the Russian people must solve their own problems, observing that it had been a mistake for European powers to have interfered in the French Revolution; however hard this would be for the present generation, it would mean less distress for Russia. McCormick agreed with Wilson (McCormick Diary, p. 111).

Paris, 21 June 1919.

Dear Mr. President:

Before the present Joint Councils of the Heads of States dissolve by your departure, I wish to lay before you earnestly what appears to me (after Peace) the greatest outstanding situation in the world insistent for solution, and that is Russia. Nor do I wish to approach it from any point of view other than purely its economic phases.

Sooner or later the Bolshevik Government will fall of its own weight or it will have swung sufficiently right to be absorbed in a properly representative government. Already about one-half of the area of the old Russian Empire is under non-Bolshevik influences. No government of any character can stand in this country without an economic reorganisation [sic]. Such reorganization primarily revolves on two positive factors, first, currency, and second, transportation. Even the governments of Holtchak [sic] and Denikin are both likely to fail at any moment, due to the practical break-down in the distribution of commodities. There is in both of these areas not only ample foodstuffs for their populations but an actual surplus and yet there is here actual starvation.

I attach one single telegram out of a host as indicating the character of the situation, and in this special case of the Donetz Basin there is ample wheat not 500 miles distant if there were some form of currency in which the population could have confidence, and transportation with which to expect exchange of coal for wheat. This is only typical of many other instances.

By and large, there can be no hope of stable government unless these two primary things can be solved. It is already the defeat of Bolshevism and will be the defeat of any government that takes its place. The re-establishment of currency, transportation, the stimulation of production, and the normal flow of distribution, is sheerly a matter of some sort of economic dictatorship, backed by sufficiently large financial and moral support of the Allied Governments. These appropriations would need to be expended fundamentally in commodities and railway rolling stock for import into Russia and for the establishment of a currency, I do not believe that the sum involved is extraordinarily large if such an economic dictatorship could have command of the resources already in Russia.

Furthermore, it appears to me that some such an economic commission, if placed upon an economic and not a political basis, could if conducted with wisdom, keep itself free from conflicting political currents and allow a rational development of self-government in Russia. I have no idea that such self-government can develop over night in a nation totally inexperienced and without tradition, but there can be no foundation on which such government can emerge so long as populations are mad from starvation and unemployment and the lack of the very necessities of life.

This matter becomes of immediate importance if America is to have any hand in the matter, as the resources and organization at our disposal come to an end either upon the signing of Peace with Germany, or, alternatively, on the first of July with the expiration of the Acts with which you are familiar.

I wish to add one suggestion to you in organization of such a commission. It is utterly impossible that it would be organized on the basis of any Inter-Allied Commission with all the conflicting financial and trade interest that lies therein. It is necessary to set up one government as the economic mandatory, with the support of the other governments, and to set up some one man as the head of such a commission, who should choose his own staff for the great administration that will be involved. Such a staff could with judgement be composed of representatives of each nationality, but they must be definitely responsible to the head of such a commission and not independently responsible to different governments.

Faithfully yours,
[signed, Hoover's secretary]

Funds for Continued Relief Work

Paris, June 22, 1919

My dear Mr. President:

In accordance with your request to the Treasury of December 16th, five million dollars from your National Security and Defense Fund was paid on that date to the Food Administration Grain Corporation for the purpose of paying the expenses of the Food Administration's relief activities in Europe, partly for administration, and partly for the furnishing of supplies.

On February 13th you approved my proposal that this fund be turned over for administration to the new American Relief Administration. This fund has been practically indispensable in meeting emergency situations in Europe, and in permitting us to act promptly in many cases without waiting for the completion of the formalities incident upon other available funds.

It is impossible at present to determine what amount of this fund may be reimbursed, but to avoid any misunderstanding, I now propose that such balance of the fund as there may be, should be disposed of in the following manner:

First, that you authorize the transfer to my personal credit, or that of the Food Administration Grain Corporation, at my option, of one million dollars, to cover the expenses of administering such relief work in Europe as may be necessary after June 30, 1919, relating principally to liquidation and the Armenian and Baltic areas.

Second, that the balance be used in the immediate purchase of food, including particularly children's relief food to create a small reserve which we may have available after June 30th to meet special situations.

My final report will of course include the details of these expenditures, as of those previously made.

I should be indeed pleased if you could indicate your approval of this expenditure.

Faithfully yours,
Herbert Hoover

Approved and authorized:
Woodrow Wilson

Proclamation for Wheat Guarantee Act

Paris, 23 June 1919

My dear Mr. Hoover:

The President has signed the two proclamations and the executive order with regard to the administration of the Wheat Guarantee Act of March 4th, 1919, enclosed with your letter of June 20th. I am returning the originals to you herewith.

Sincerely yours,
Gilbert F. Close
Confidential Secretary to the President

Ending Food Administration

This letter on Hoover's retirement refers to a June 23 conversation in which he told Wilson of his desire to resign as head of the Food

Administration on July 1. Other letters on his retirement were written on January 23, March 25, and August 2, 1919.

June 24th, 1919.

Dear Mr. President:

Since speaking to you yesterday, I have reconsidered the matter as to closing my career as Food Administrator.

The Food Administration is in fact ended, except in the sense that the Relief of Europe represents its final phase. In this sense I think if you approve, I will remain in office until I get home with this last phase completed.

Faithfully yours,
Herbert Hoover

Approved
Woodrow Wilson

Economic Plan for Southeast Europe

Paris, 24 June 1919.

Dear Mr. President:

Before you leave I would like to know if I could have your informal approval to the following:

In addition to food activities, I am, under a "mandatory" given to me by the Supreme War Council, a sort of a Receiver for the whole of the railways in the Austrian Empire, and I likewise enjoy the same "high" office in respect to the coal mines of the Austrian Empire and Poland. These very great matters have been carried with indeed great ability by the corps of American officers whom I have had in charge in these countries. As the result of their success in maintaining economic life in this area of political dissension | all | [we][1] enjoy a great deal of prestige with all the six or eight different governments that nest around Southeastern Europe. At some moment after the signing of peace it will be necessary for us to withdraw all of these services. What these countries will want above all things will be some kind of economic inter-arrangement among themselves as to railway management, coal distribution, customs conventions, the common working of their telegraph and telephone systems, etc. I therefore have the notion that the opportunity may arise when I can go into this area and call a convention of economic delegates representing these different governments at some central point under my chairmanship, and on the ground that we were about to withdraw we should set up the preliminaries of their necessary co-operation. On this basis I have the feeling that I might produce substantial results in the solution of these vital problems.

I do not want to undertake these things without at least your approval. On the basis of simply arranging for withdrawal of our organization we will avoid jealousies of the other great governments and will, I am convinced, be able to perform a service that cannot otherwise be accomplished.

Faithfully yours,
Herbert Hoover

---

1 | all | changed by hand to [we].

Approval of Hoover Plan

Paris, 25 June, 1919.

My dear Hoover:

What you propose in the enclosed letter, which I take the liberty of returning with this answer, meets with my entire approval, and I am glad that you thought of so interesting and serviceable a scheme.

Cordially and sincerely yours,
Woodrow Wilson

International Economic Conference

This letter with the enclosed memorandum was sent to Wilson the day before the treaty was signed. It appears that the conference here proposed was also the subject of Hoover's cables to Wilson of July 12 and August 2.

Paris, 27 June 1919

My dear Mr. President:

You will please find enclosed herewith a memorandum which I propose to introduce to the Supreme Economic Council in reply to the memorandum of the various other Governments demanding the erection of some continuing economic body. I trust this is in accord with the understanding which we reached a few days ago.

I am deeply impressed with the necessity for coordinated action within the United States in connection with the granting of private and public credits and in the supplying of raw material and food to various countries in Europe. That is, it would seem to me to be a disaster if we allowed our merchants and bankers to expend either American private or public credits to Governments in Europe who did not maintain stability, who did not cease hostilities and who do not busy themselves with sound economic reconstruction and return to production. I would like to lay before you for consideration whether it would not be desirable to set up some sort of an economic committee in the United States representing the different departments of the Government and such other persons as you might select, and who would in a general way pass upon the policies to be pursued by the American Government and people in these matters. Such a council could quite well have relations with similar Councils set up in other countries and could no doubt affect [*sic*] a great deal of constructive order towards rehabilitation in Europe without submerging American policies in these matters in those of foreign Governments. I have discussed this matter with Mr. Davis who will no doubt take it up with you on the steamer enroute home.

Faithfully yours,
Herbert Hoover

Memorandum

Paris, 27 June 1919

The American Delegates on the Supreme Economic Council, being as they are, officials for the period of war only, have felt that the establishment of some form of international conference on economic matters must rest for decision, so far as the United States is concerned, with the permanent departments of the Government. In conference with the President on this matter, he has taken the same view and feels that on his own authority alone he could not establish such an American representation in a body of this character as would make it an effective organ from the American point of view.

The matter therefore requires to be laid before the leading officials in the Government at Washington and their views obtained. It is my understanding that this will be undertaken. I also understand that the present Council in any event continues until the end of July pending the signature of peace with the Governments with whom the Entente have been at war. It seems to the American Delegates undesirable that the present Council should continue after such a date lest it should give the impression to the world of an economic block of the Governments who have been aligned in war.

Plan for Armenia

At 11:00 A.M. on June 28, just hours before the signing of the treaty, the Big Four met at Wilson's Paris house in the Place des Etats-Unis. Several matters were discussed, including the following letter presented by Wilson. His proposal was accepted and General James G. Harbord was made chairman of an investigation team. During the meeting Hoover was introduced but appears not to have spoken (*F.R., P.C.*, vol. 6, pp. 741, 743–44). In August Hoover recommended that Colonel William N. Haskell be appointed as high commissioner for Armenia. For the next year he carried on Hoover's relief work there (*Memoirs*, vol. 1, p. 388; *Ordeal*, p. 229).

When the question of mandates was considered previously, the Allies proposed to Wilson that the United States accept Armenia as a mandatory. The President was not opposed to the idea. Hoover, however, confided to Colonel House in mid-May that Armenia as it then stood was not a viable country, and he felt Armenia would need a strong American garrison for protection against its fierce enemies. Nonetheless, Wilson—without proper consultation—later proposed to the Senate that the United States accept Armenia as a mandate. The upper chamber rejected his recommendation on June 1, 1920 (*Ordeal*, pp. 225–29, n. 12).

Paris 27 June 1919

Dear Mr. President:

In accordance with your discussion with Mr. Morgenthau and the several discussions with myself in connection with Armenia, we make the following joint recommendations to be brought to the attention of the Chiefs of State before your departure.

1) We suggest that a single temporary resident Commissioner

should be appointed to Armenia, who will have the full authority of the United States, Great Britain, France and Italy in all their relations to the de facto Armenian Government, as the joint representative of these Governments in Armenia. His duties shall be so far as he may consider necessary to supervise and advise upon various governmental matters in the whole of Russian and Turkish Armenia, and to control relief and repatriation questions pending the determination of the political destiny of this area.

2) In case the various Governments should agree to this plan, immediate notification should be made to the de facto Governments of Turkey and of Armenia of his appointment and authority. Furthermore, he will be appointed to represent the American Relief Administration and the American Committee for Relief in the Near East, and take entire charge of all their activities in Russian and Turkish Armenia.

The ideal man for this position would be General Harboard [*sic*], as I assume under all the circumstances it would probably be desirable to appoint an American. Should General Harbord be unable to undertake the matter, I am wondering whether you would leave it to us to select the man in conjunction with General Pershing.

I assume that the personnel of this Mission would be necessarily comprised of army and navy officers who would retain their rank and emoluments and I understand from the Commission for the Near East that they would be prepared to supply such funds as were required for incidental expenses until such other arrangements could be made.

Faithfully yours,
[signed, Hoover's secretary]

Haskell as Commissioner for Armenia

> As indicated in the introduction to the preceding letter, Hoover was successful in providing relief for Armenia through the means proposed in the following cablegram. The blank spaces in the text of the letter may represent words or phrases that the decoder in Washington could not interpret. This typed copy is found in the Wilson collection at the Library of Congress; presumably the message reached the President in this form.

Paris

The President.

July 5; 10 p.m. After receiving General Harbord's views and discussion with the peace mission, we have concluded that there are temporary measures necessary to strengthen relief and _____ in Armenia would be separated from the problems involved in repatriation and expulsion of present trespassers, _____ permanent pacification of the territory. We therefore recommended the appointment of Colonel William N. Haskell, at present in charge of relief measures in Roumania to be a temporary commissioner as proposed by us to you and accepted in principle by the heads of state, and we trust he will not be recalled by the War Department. The broader question of repatriation requires an examination as to the measures and force necessary successfully to cope with the _____ and will require Congressional action to provide sufficient funds and forces. We therefore recommend that the mission should immediately be sent to Armenia headed by General Harbord, who should choose his own assistants to investigate this question, together with the general political and economic problems involved in setting up the new state of Armenia. Such investigation as a basis of determination of policy is, in our opinion, necessary before even the repatriation of refugees can be _____. We believe General Harbord could be persuaded to undertake such a mission. Hoover, Morgenthau.

We endorse the statements made in the above telegram.

Economic Situation of Europe

On June 20 Hoover was in Paris again after a brief stay in Belgium with the President's entourage. On June 23 he spoke personally with Wilson as President for the last time. The following day Hoover left for London and on June 25 was awarded an honorary degree by Oxford. In the afternoon of June 28 the Treaty of Versailles was signed in the Hall of Mirrors and Hoover was present for the historic occasion. Later that day he bade farewell to Wilson at the railroad station. On June 29, the President boarded the *George Washington* at Brest for America, reaching Hoboken, New Jersey, on July 8. On July 10 President Wilson addressed the Senate on the treaty and presented that document and the Covenant of the League of Nations.

In the meantime, Hoover returned to Paris and relief work for a prostrate Europe. The following lengthy report was sent off on July 5 to Wilson, who was aboard the *George Washington* in the mid-Atlantic. Hoover cabled Wilson another long report on August 2 requesting in conclusion that his oral resignation of June 23 be accepted as effective on the previous July 1. Wilson apparently did not respond so it may be presumed that the President simply let Hoover's June 24 letter determine his status with the Food Administration. The August 2 cable was in general a message of gloom and Wilson probably considered this newest resignation to be merely a by-product of Hoover's discouragement.

Paris, July 5th, 1919.

Dear Mr. President:

In a liesure [*sic*] moment you may find the opportunity to read the enclosed memorandum in which I have tried to sum up my views on the economic situation on this side.

Faithfully yours,
Herbert Hoover

Enclosure

3 July 1919.

MEMORANDUM ON THE ECONOMIC SITUATION OF EUROPE.

The economic difficulties of Europe as a whole at the signature of peace may be almost summarized in the phrase "demoralized productivity." The production of necessaries for this 450 million population (including Russia) has never been at so low an ebb as at this day.

A summary of the unemployment bureaus in Europe will show that 15 million families are receiving unemployment allowances in one form or another and are in the main being paid by constant inflation of currency. A rough estimate would indicate that the population of Europe is at least 100 million greater than can be supported without imports and must live by the production and distribution of exports, and their situation is aggravated not only by lack of raw materials imports but by low production of European raw materials. Due to the same low production, Europe is today importing vast quantities of certain commodities which she formerly produced for herself and can again produce. Generally, not only is production far below even the level of the time of the signing of the armistice, but far below the maintenance of life and health without unparalleled rate of import.

Even prior to the war these populations managed to produce from year to year but a trifling margin of commodities over necessary consumption or to exchange for deficient commodities from abroad. It is true that in prewar times Europe managed to maintain armies and navies, together with a comparatively small class of non-producers, and to gain slowly in physical improvements and investment abroad, but these luxuries and accumulations were only at the cost of a dangerously low standard of living to a very large number. The productivity of Europe in pre-war times had behind it the intensive stimulus of individualism and of a high state of economic discipline, and the density of population at all times responded closely to the resulting volume of production. During the war the intensive organization of economy in consumption, the patriotic stimulus to exertion and the addition of women to productive labor largely balanced the diversion of man power to war and munitions. These impulses have been lost.

II.

It is not necessary to review at length the causes of this decrease of productivity. They comprise in the main as follows:

The industrial and commercial demoralization arising originally out of the war but continued out of the struggle for political rearrangements during the armistice, the creation of new governments, the inexperience and friction between these governments in the readjustment of economic relations.

The proper and insistent demand of labor for higher standards of living and a voice in administration of their effort has unfortunately become impregnated with the theory that the limitation of effort below physical necessity will increase the total employment or improve their condition.

There is a great relaxation of effort as the reflex of physical exhaustion of large sections of the population from privation, mental and physical strain of the war.

To a minor degree considering the whole volume, there has been a destruction of equipment and tools and loss of organization and skill due to war diversions with a loss of man power. This latter is not at present pertinent in the face of present unemployment.

(The demoralization in production of coal in Europe today is an example in point of all these three forces mentioned above and promises a coal famine and with industrial disaster unless remedied. It is due to a small percentage from the destruction of man power or the physical limitation of coal mines or their equipment. It is due in the largest degree to the human factor of the limitation of effort.)

The continuation of the Blockade after the armistice has undoubtedly destroyed enterprise even in open countries, and of course prevented any recovery in enemy countries. The shortage in overseas transportation and the result of uncertainties of the armistice upon inter-national credits have checked the flow of raw materials and prevented recovery in the production of commodities especially needed for exchange for imports from overseas. The result of this delay has been unemployment, stagnation, absorption of capital in consumable commodities to some extent all over Europe.

From all these causes, accumulated to different intensity in different localities, there is the essential fact that unless productivity can be rapidly increased, there can be nothing but political, moral and economic chaos finally interpreting itself in loss of life on a scale hitherto undreamed of.

III.

Coincident with this demoralization in production, other disastrous economic phenomena have developed themselves, the principle [*sic*] one of which is that the very large wage paid special workers and the large sums accumulated by speculation and manufacture during the war have raised the standard of living in many individuals from the level of mere necessities to a high level of luxuries. Beyond this class there is a reflex in many other classes from the strenuous economies against waste and the consumption of non-essentials in all countries, and as a result there is today an outbreak of extravagance to a disheartening degree.

Another economic change of favorable nature from a human point of view, but intensifying the problems of the moment, has been the rise in the standard of living in large sections of the working classes through the larger and better wage distribution, separation allowances, etc., during the war. Parallel with these classes are those of fixed income, the unorganized workers, the unemployed to whom the rising cost of living is inflicting the greatest hardship.

IV.

During some short period, it may be possible for the Western Hemisphere, which has retained and even increased its productivity, to supply the deficiencies of Europe. Such deficiencies would have to be supplied in large degree upon credits; but aside from this the entire surplus productivity of the Western Hemisphere is totally incapable of meeting the present deficiency in European production if it is long continued. Nor, as a practical fact, could credits be mobilized for this purpose for more than a short period, because all credits must necessarily be simply an advance against the return of commodities in exchange, and credits will break down the instant that the return of commodities becomes improbable. Further, if such credits be obtained in [sic] more than temporary purposes, it would result in economic slavery of Europe to the Western Hemisphere and the ultimate end would be war again.

The solution, therefore, of the problem, except in purely temporary aspects, does not lie in a stream of commodities on credit from the Western Hemisphere, but lies in a vigorous realization of the actual situation in each country of Europe and a resolute statesmanship based on such a realization. The populations of Europe must be brought to a realization that productivity must be instantly increased.

V.

The outcome of social ferment and class consciousness is the most difficult of problems to solve. Growing out of the yearning for relief from the misery imposed by the war, and out of the sharp contrasts in degree of class suffering, especially in defeated countries, the demand for economic change in the status of labor has received a great stimulus leading to violence and revolution in large areas and a great impulse to radicalism in all others. In the main these movements have not infected the agricultural classes but are essentially a town phenomena.

In this ferment Socialism and Communism has embraced to itself the claim to speak for all the downtrodden, to alone bespeak human sympathy and to alone present remedies, to be the lone voice of liberalism. Every economic patent medicine has flocked under this banner. Europe is full of noisy denunciation of private property rights necessarily being exploitation. Considerable reliance upon some degree of Communism has been embraced by industrial labor even in non-revolutionary countries. Its extremists are loud in assertion that production can be maintained by the impulse of altruism alone, instead of self-interest. Too often they are embracing criminal support and criminal methods to enforce their ideals of human betterment. Every country is engaged in political experimentation with varying degrees of these hypothesis [*sic*] and so far every trial has reduced production. The Western Hemisphere with its more equitable division of property, its wider equality of opportunity still believes that productivity rests on the stimulus from all the immutable human qualities of selfishness, self-interest, altruism, intelligence and education. It still believes that the remedy of economic wrong lies not in tampering with the delicate and highly developed organization of production and distribution, but in a better division of the profits arising from them. It still believes in the constitutional solution of these problems by the will of the majority while Europe is drifting toward the domination of extremist minorities. The Western Hemisphere's productivity is being maintained at a surplus over its own needs.

The first and cardinal effort of European statesmanship must be to secure the materials and tools to labor, and to secure its return to work. They must also secure a recognition of the fact that whatever the economic theory or political cry it must embrace the maximum individual effort for there is no margin of surplus productivity in Europe to risk revolutionary experimentation. *No economic policy will bring food to those stomachs or fuel to those hearths that does not secure the maximum production. There is no use of tears over rising prices; they are, to a great degree, a visualization of insufficient production.*

VI.

During the period of reconstruction, and recovery from reduced productivity, the conservation in the consumption of nonessential commodities is more critical than any time during the war. The relaxation of restriction on imports and on consumption of articles of this character since the armistice is disheartening in outlook. It finds its indication in the increased consumption of beverages and articles de luxe in many countries, even above a prewar normal. Never has there been such a necessity for the curtailment of luxury as exists today.

VII.

The universal practice in all the countries at war of raising funds by inflation of currency is now bringing home its burden of trouble and in extreme cases the most resolute action must be taken, and at once. In other countries of even the lesser degree of inflation, such currency must be reduced and included in the funded debt or alternately the price of wages, living and international exchange must be expected to adjust itself to this depression. The outcry against the high cost of living, the constant increase of wages and the fall in exchange that is going on, is in a considerable degree due to this inevitable readjustment.

VIII.

The stimulation of production lies in the path of avoidance of all limitations of the reward to the actual producer. In other words, attempts to control prices (otherwise than in the sense of control of vicious speculation) is [sic] the negation of stimulation to production, and can only result in further curtailment of the total of commodities available for the total number of human beings to be fed, clothed and housed. There still exist in Europe great bureaucracies created from the necessity of control of price and distribution by the conditions of the war who are loath to recognize that with world markets open no such acute situation exists and that their continued existence is not essential except in the control of speculation. The argument so much advanced that world shortage may develop and justifies continued control of distribution and price is based upon the fallacious assumption that even if the world markets are freed of restraint that there is a shortage today in any commodity so profound as to endanger health and life. From any present evidence, thanks to the high production outside Europe, no shortage exists that will not find its quick remedy in diminished consumption or substitution of other commodities, through minor alteration and price. All attempts at international control of price, with view to benefitting the population in Europe at the cost of the producer elsewhere, will inevitably produce retrogression in production abroad, the impact of which will be felt in Europe more than elsewhere. A decrease of 20 percent of Western Hemisphere wheat would not starve the West, it would starve Europe. It must never be overlooked that control of price and distribution cannot stop with a few prime commodities, but once started its reprocussions [*sic*] drive into a succeeding chain of commodities and that on the downward road of price control, there can be no stoppage unless all commodities have been placed under restriction, with inevitable stifling of the total production. It is also often overlooked by the advocates of price control that whereas the high level of production was maintained during the war even under a restraint of price, this high production was obtained by the most vivid appeal to patriotic impulse on both sides of the front. This stimulus to production and distribution no longer maintains and the world must go back to the prime impulse, and that is the reward to the individual producer and distributor.

That body of advocates who have deduced from war phenomena that production and distribution can be increased and maintained by appealing to altruism as the equivalent of patriotism or self-interest should observe the phenomena of Russia where the greatest food exporting country is today starving.

IX.

It must be evident that the production cannot increase if political incompetence continues in blockade, embargoes, censorship, mobilization, large armies, navies and war.

X.

There are certain foundations of industry in Europe that no matter what the national or personal ownership or control may be they yet partake of the nature of the public utilities in which other nations have a moral right. For instance, the discrimnatory [*sic*] control of ships, railways, waterways, coal and iron in such a manner as to prevent the resumption of production by other states will inevitably debar economic recuperation and lead to local spats of economic chaos with its ultimate infection abroad, to say nothing of the decrease in productivity. These mis-uses are already too evident.

XI.

The question of assistance from the Western Hemisphere during a certain temporary period, and the devotion of its limited surplus productivity to Europe, is a matter of importance and one that requires statesmanlike handling and vision. It is but a minor question compared to those stated above and it is in a great degree dependent upon the proper solution of the factors already touched upon. It is a service that the Western Hemisphere must approach in a high sense of human duty and sympathy. This sense will, however, be best performed by the insistence that their aid would not be forthcoming to any country that did not resolutely set in order its internal financial and political situations, that did not devote itself to the increase of productivity, that did not curtail consumption of luxuries and the expenditure upon armament and did not cease hostilities and did not treat their neighbors fairly. If these conditions were complied with, it is the duty of the west to put forth every possible effort to tide Europe over this period of temporary economic difficulties. Without the fulfillment of these conditions, the effort is hopeless. With Europe turned toward peace with her skill and labor aligned [sic] to overcome the terrible accumulation of difficulty, the economic burden upon the West should not last over a year and can be carried and will be repaid. To effect these results the resources of the Western Hemisphere and here must be mobilized.

HERBERT HOOVER

International Economic Organization

On July 12 Hoover and John Foster Dulles, counsel to the American delegation to the Peace Conference, sent the following cable from Paris to the State Department. In it they set forth the resolutions adopted on July 10 by the Supreme Economic Council relative to the establishment of an international organization for continued consultation on economic matters. Hoover and Dulles recommended that the United States agree to participate and suggested the reply Wilson might make if he approved of the plan. The cablegram was received at the State Department on July 13 and sent to Wilson. The President's power to appoint an American representative to such an international body was questioned. A typewritten copy of the cable carries this scribbled note: "Is there any reason why Pres. should not appoint a rep—?" The initials are illegible. In any event, Undersecretary of State Frank L. Polk presented the question to L. H. Woolsey, solicitor for the State Department.

Woolsey answered Polk on July 17, noting that during his career in the department the question of the President's power to appoint "such Commissioners" without congressional authority had arisen several times, and "it has been decided that the President has authority to make these appointments except that only Congress could provide the salary." The solicitor added that there was available money for this purpose in either the President's fund or in his emergency fund.

Woolsey noted that a congressional act of March 4, 1913, had indeed forbidden the President "to participate in any international conference, congress, or like event, without first having specific authority of law to do so." But he concluded that in his opinion "the enactment of this law is quite outside the powers of Congress and that they cannot control the power of the President to conduct international relations, by limiting his power of appointment for the purpose of conducting those relations." On July 18 Polk sent Woolsey's letter to Wilson, adding his assurance that the President was free to implement the recommendation of Hoover and Dulles. The final chapter in this episode is contained in the message Hoover sent Wilson on August 2. (For copies of the Polk and the Woolsey letters, see Pre-Commerce Papers.)

Paris, July 12, 1919.

For the President. Supreme Economic Council July 10th passed the following resolutions [and] proposed organization for carrying into effect international consultation in economic matters pending the formation of the League of Nations. The Council of the principal Allied and Associated Powers at their meeting on the 28th June decided as follows: "That in some form international consultation in economic matters should be continued until the council of the League of Nations has had an opportunity of considering the present acute position of the economic situation and that the Supreme Economic Council should be requested to suggest for the consideration of the several Governments the methods of consultation which would be most serviceable for this purpose. [*Continues*] the subcommittee of the Supreme Economic Council appointed to report upon the means of carrying into effect the above decision makes the following recommendations. One. An International Economic Council shall be formed to consult together on economic matters and to advise the various Governments concerned pending the organization of the League of Nations. On the termination of the Supreme Economic Council, the Interallied organizations then existing which have been previously responsible to the Supreme Economic Council shall report to the International Economic Council.

Two. The membership of the International Economic Council

shall comprise two delegates of ministerial or High Commissioners rank from each of the nations represented on the Supreme Economic Council, viz. United States, British Empire, France, Italy, Belgium with the addition after the first session [of] one delegate each of the same rank from four other Governments to be invited by the International Economic Council.

Three. The Council may in its discretion, invite a representative of any other country to sit as a member at any meeting of the Council during the consideration of matters specially affecting the interests of that country.

Four. The Council shall normally meet once a month in London, Paris, Washington, Brussels or Rome according as the Council may decide.

Five. The Council shall have full authority to create the necessary organization and machinery to carry on its work.

Six: The first session of the Council shall be held at Washington not later than the 15th of September. In respect to the above, we would like to lay before you our views:—

First. That it is desirable that the American Government should show no disinclination to join in any real world necessity of an economic character.

Second. In order that coordinate, efficient and disinterested action can be taken by the United States, it is desirable that some kind of Committee be created within the United States comprised of the head of the Departments bearing on creditors and foreign relations, such a committee to determine the broad policies to be pursued in economic assistance to Europe.

Third. We have the feeling that if these matters are left solely to an organization of bankers, it will create distrust both at home and in Europe and may be charged with Economic exploitation no matter how wise its intentions.

Fourth. Such a Governmental committee could coordinate our economic support so as to maintain political stability in Europe without stifling individual initiative.

Fifth. If this plan were adopted such a committee could extend an invitation to similar departmental heads in Europe to a conference such as outlined in the above resolutions of Supreme Economic Council. If this suggestion should meet with your views it would seem desirable to reply somewhat as follows to each of the representatives of the above Governments at Washington.

"With respect to the recommendations of the Supreme Economic Council the American Government is giving consideration to the creation of a committee comprising the necessary Cabinet Ministers and other officials who will direct the American Policy in economic relationship to Europe so far as this may prove necessary or possible and this committee will extend an invitation to the Governments mentioned by the Supreme Economic Council and such other countries as may be determined by these governments to a general conference on world economic matters and it would seem to the American Government that questions of permanent organization should be left to determination by this conference." Hoover, Dulles.

AMERICAN MISSION [Hoover and Dulles]

Sugar Control in United States

> The Sugar Equalization Board, an agency of the Food Administration, controlled sugar and had contracts with Cuban and American producers that could not be liquidated according to existing law before the end of the sugar crop year. Hoover believed that trade should be returned to normal as soon as possible, but he realized that continued restrictions on sugar might be necessary. In the following cablegram (sent through Barnes to the President) Hoover wrote that if the board reached this conclusion Wilson would need to appoint a new chairman to shepherd the needed legislation through Congress, since he himself would be detained in Europe for some time.

Paris, 23 July 1919

FOR BARNES July 23. Please transmit the following to the President as a cable from me:

"It is necessary to take important decisions as to the sugar control in the United States in order to anticipate the marketing of the new beet harvest and to settle policy with Cuba for the next year. You will recollect that last July I presented to you the view that either in event of continued war and the consequent shipping isolation of the East Indies sugar, or in the event of peace and the opening of new demands, there would be a world sugar shortage in the year Nineteen [1919]. I recommend that we form the Sugar Equalization Board to purchase the Cuban sugar crop jointly with the Allies and to arrange for equalization in marketing with the domestic sugar in order to assure American supplies at reasonable prices and to eliminate speculation and profiteering, and that the Board should secure a small margin in handling Cuban sugar to cover losses in the event of reverse on Atlantic shipping and to equalize freight and distribution costs. These things were done and today the United States is the only large nation possessing liberal supplies for the entire year and at a saving of four cents per pound under the world price, or equal to about twenty-five million dollars per month saving to the consumer. These courses of action grew out of war disruption of supply and distribution. Decision must now be made as to whether Congress should be recommended to legislate authority for the continuation of these measures over the year Nineteen Twenty providing again for the purchase of the Cuban crop and the control of domestic production, Stabilization of price and distribution. The intrimele [sic] situation is by no means clear as to the prospect of supplies, and it is argued by many that there will be a continued shortage over the year Nineteen Twenty with attendant speculation and profiteering unless action is taken.

"The matters to be considered are (a) the crop prospects of the world in which there is undoubtedly an increase over pre-war in the Western Hemisphere and East Indies, but the European beet production (outside Russia) will be apparently twenty-five percent short of pre-war average, and although the Russian situation is unknown there are no exports likely; (b) the probable consumption of the world as to which there is an undoubted increase outside of Europe, especially in the United States, but with regard to Europe the limited buying power during the next year (unless there is very rapid economic recovery) will tend to restrain the non-essential use of sugar.

"The problem is also effected [sic] by (a) whether European governments will continue their national buying and with national finance be in position to contract for national supplies for long periods in advance to the prejudice of a free market and the ability of normal commerce to purchase on the same terms. This will probably depend upon whether the United States will allow credits to foreign countries to be used for such form of purchase; (*b*) whether in the long view the adjustment of production to world necessity will not be more rapid [with] free operation of supply and demand although there may be great fluctuations in the process of readjustment; (*c*) whether, from a social point of view, it is desirable to perpetuate a great governmental control in commerce now that the war interference of supply through short shipping, the necessity of control of cargoes, etc., has largely disappeared even though speculation and profiteering may result. Any continuation of control will require action by Congress and it must embrace appropriations, the continuation of power and embargo, control of speculation, profiteering and distribution. The alternative course to any action of the above character is for the Sugar Equalization Board to announce its cessation of control at an early date prior to the marketing season of domestic beet and cane sugars and to dispose of the remaining stocks from the old crop purchased by them at the market prices from day to day until they are exhausted. Owing to the delays in the Austrian Treaty it seems impossible for me to withdraw American control of railways, coal mines and transport of food in Central Europe before the middle of September without producing absolute chaos in that area, and therefore I will not be able to arrive home before that date. The determination of the sugar policies requires immediate consideration, and my lack of intimate knowledge of American situation after eight months' absence and my inability to leave here renders it impossible for me to be of useful service in the matter. I therefore suggest you request Professor Taussig, Mr. Zabriskie and the other members of the Sugar Equalization Board to present you their recommendations in the matter independent of myself. If, as a result of your councils, you should decide to propose to Congress that the control be continued, it is imperative that a new Chairman should be chosen in my place at once in order that he may be of assistance to Congress in legislation, and that he should be in charge from the beginning as I must, in any event, retire this autumn. If it be decided that there should be no extension of control I would be glad to be relieved anyway as I wish a rest, but if this should be inconvenient to you I would of course continue until the Board is wound up this fall."

1919, August / 209

Resignation as Food Administrator

Hoover had informed Wilson (see letter of June 24) that he intended to resign as Food Administrator on July 1. In the following cable, sent through Barnes, he reminds the President of his resignation. He advises Wilson that problems remain in the area of food production that may require new legislation by Congress to legalize action in solving these problems. (See letters of March 25 and January 23). This cable was probably sent by Hoover from Paris through a representative of the U.S. government in London. At least two other cablegrams for August 2 and 3 were also sent from London by Hoover.

As suggested in the introduction to Hoover's letter of July 5, Wilson probably did not accept Hoover's new resignation and allowed his term to run until his return to the States in mid-September.

London [?], 2 August 1919

FOR BARNES, RICKARD, Aug. 2. Please forward the following to the President as a cable from me:

"The degeneration of the world food supply situation during the last month, the outbreak of speculation and profiteering all over the world, due partially to this but principally to a moral slackening in all avenues of life, and the action as shown in my cable today of the Allies, through which they propose in effect to restore collective buying which should reduce speculation, but unless controlled on our side may work great hardship on the American farmer, seem to me to necessitate at least the laying of the position before Congress for it to decide whether protection is needed both for consumer and producer.

"There has been a steady degeneration of the cereal crops during the last thirty to sixty days, and the promise of marginal supplies, the weight of which would control speculation, has greatly diminished, and while there is sufficient balance to meet the world's needs during the next year if properly distributed, but margins are sufficiently narrow to create great danger of speculation and profiteering. In respect to wheat, the indications now are that while the price might remain near the guarantee during the heavy marketing period, under free world prices it would probably rise very materially before the next harvest. In the matter of pork products and fats generally, the margins over the world's needs are very narrow, but as the surplus production of the United States comes with a rush during a short period, combinations of European buying, unless they are controlled, may result in depreciation of price below cost of production, and unless some control is exerted either through provision by Congress for accumulation of surplus for subsequent distribution or through the control of European credits by which righteous prices may be insisted upon as a condition of such credits, there is great danger, first to the producer in [if] the heavy marketing ceases, and second to the consumer through subsequent rises in price under uncontrolled speculation.

"In order to clear the decks, it seems to me desirable to brush away the remains of the old Food Administration. In my view, if it were decided to take interest in the matter, nothing could be done without new legislation because, although the present Food Act is technically in force, it will expire at any moment with the ratification of peace: it is based on war powers, and even if extended, its legal foundations could be attacked in peace. It should be noted also that the Act taken alone would have been entirely ineffective against profiteering, for the success of the previous administration was based not on the Act, but on voluntary co-operation of the trades, the form of which would be illegal in peace without specific legislation. In any event, acting under your original instructions, we demobilized the food administration as rapidly as possible after the Armistice. By the end of March the largest part of its activities were brought, in my view prematurely to an end under pressure of the Cabinet, and all those functions still outstanding have been finally completed within the last thirty days by the setting up [of] the Wheat Directorate, the only outstanding matter being the liquidation of the sugar continuation of Food Administration must finally indicate the desire for its suppression. With regard to the sugar contracts, I have telegraphed you separately, but, in any event, and if temporary use of the Food Act is necessary for this purpose it can be delegated to the President of the Board by Executive Order. In order that the last vestige of the old administration may be eliminated, I would be glad if you would consider that my oral resignation as Food Administrator, given to you before leaving Paris, should be considered as effective as from that date, i.e., July 1st. I will, of course, if you desire, continue as Director General of Relief, until completion of its accounting.

"In conclusion, it seems to me that Congress should give careful consideration as to whether legislation is needed and the erection of such new administration as may be necessary. I do not feel that, after eight months' absence, I am sufficiently in touch with the American conditions and sentiment to advise as to methods to be pursued, but I feel it my duty to point out the conditions which are likely to obtain during the next twelve months."

HOOVER

Dropping International Council

> This cablegram should be read along with the Hoover-Dulles message to Wilson of July 12 and the Davis-Hoover cablegram sent from London on August 3. The latter cablegram seems to contain a matter discussed by the Allies on the same day that they considered a joint plan for the purchase of food, a plan Hoover immediately rejected (see his August 3 message to Wilson). The Hoover-Dulles proposal of July 12 for an international economic council was substantially altered by the Allies on August 2, whereupon Hoover apparently recommended that the idea be dropped. Wilson concurred (*Epic*, vol. 2, p. 226).

London, 2 August 1919

Secretary of State, Washington
For President

Mr. Dulles and myself recently sent you a joint recommendation that an invitation should be extended to the Finance and Commerce Ministers of the various Allied countries to come themselves to Washington to conduct the first meeting of the International Economic Council sometime in September. It developed at a meeting of the Supreme Economic Council today that the various Cabinet Ministers have decided that they could not themselves come in person, but could only send Delegates. Inasmuch as this suggestion was made purely for the purpose of visualizing the world's necessities and being able to exchange views first-hand between the principal Cabinet Ministers of the world on the situation, it does not appear to me that anything would be gained by having such a conference without the presence of these men, and therefore as the original suggestion was based on Cabinet Ministerial representation which was at that time considered possible by all of the Governments, I would like to recommend to you that the matter be dropped and that in any event until peace has been ratified by the Senate it would not be apropos to call any meeting in Washington.

Hoover

Proposed Joint Food Purchase

> Hoover sent this cable to Barnes and Rickard in New York with instructions that it be dispatched to Wilson. One draft of the cable was marked "most secret," although this copy carries the word "secret." In his *Epic* (vol. 2, p. 225) Hoover printed the relevant part of this cable with an August 2 date. This suggests that it was dispatched from Paris on August 2 to a representative in London who on August 3 transmitted it to the State Department, and from there it went on to the President. The copy printed below was sent from Paris by Norman Davis of the Treasury Department. After June 28 he and Hoover were the only two Americans who continued to attend the meeting of the Supreme Economic Council. The views of Davis and Hoover on the matter were identical, but in his *Epic* (vol. 2, pp. 225, 226) Hoover states that he sent the cable. He adds that he was unaware of any reply from Wilson on the proposal of the Allies.

August 3rd London 4.25 pm

Secretary of State, Washington   Important
Secret

Please present following to the President from me.

At Supreme Economic Council today France, England, Italy, produced and adopted in principle a plan providing for restriction of cooperation in purchase of foodstuffs. We took the attitude that we have no authority to even discuss the matter, but advised them that it was not to the world's interest to use such powers to the detriment of the farmers of the world or they would decrease the world's production and starve themselves, but that they should seek to place it on a basis of cooperation with the United States or otherwise, they would create in the mind of the American producer the impression of such combinations against him. Further, that if the impression of such combinations was to gain currency it would destroy the hope of Allied credits in the United States. We stated that the American people would sympathize with any plan for dealing with speculation and profiteering.

It was finally decided by[1] the other Governments [to][2] propose to you for acceptance a plan to be further amplified by a Committee on which we decided we would not be represented.

Davis

---

[1] | by | changed to typewritten | that |, restored by hand to "by."
[2] Handwritten insertion.

Haskell and U.S. Army in Armenia

In his letter to Wilson of June 27 (the day before the treaty was signed and before the President left for the States) Hoover made a proposal for handling the situation in Armenia. It was accepted. Then on or about August 12, he dispatched the following recommendation to Wilson through Edgard Rickard, who sent it to the President through Tumulty. Colonel William Haskell, recommended by Hoover to head the Armenian mission, was accepted by the Council of Five and took charge in mid-August. His work was successful amid much tribulation, as Hoover's letter of November 11 indicates. Soon after the Americans withdrew, Armenia was taken over by the Communists and ultimately became a republic of Russia.

Since Hoover was on a tour of central Europe from August 7 to August 21, it is not known where he actually composed this letter. It is conjectured that he telegraphed it to his central office in Paris where it was coded and then dispatched to Washington through Rickard.

Paris, August 12, 1919.

Joseph Tumulty, White House, Washington

Hoover asks that following cable be transmitted to President soon as possible and trust early action can be taken. "In order to maintain the relief in Armenia after the withdrawal of Food Administration measures it was agreed by Council of five that Colonel Haskell, US Army, should be appointed High Commissioner in Russian Armenia, representing all the allies jointly, and this has been done and Colonel Haskell is on the ground now. He is being supported by stocks of food which I have provided and by funds from the Near East Relief Committee. Owing to the demobilization of the reserve army he will in a few days be without staff and the entire Administration will break down. The only solution is to allow us to secure volunteers from the regular army and navy officers here and have Pershing and Knapp authorized to transfer them to Haskell in name of war and navy departments. The continuance of this service is absolutely necessary and entirely outside General Harbords [*sic*] commission of examination as he only expects to remain a month in the country. The question has also arisen of providing the new government in Eastern Europe with technical advisors on transportation and other questions and who will be paid by these governments. Many of these positions can be best filled with officers from the regular army who have already been conducting these services under my administration. It appears to me no better experience or service could be gained or no more constructive work done by the American army and navy than to fill these positions. In order to cover both issues your approval to war and navy departments is necessary. I trust you can see your way to recommend these matters to them for prompt action. Signed Hoover."

Edgar Rickard

Relief for Armenia and Poland

On August 7, 1919, Hoover began a two-week tour through central Europe. He returned to Paris on August 21 and found hundreds of letters from friends in the United States urging him to consent to be the Republican candidate for the Presidency in 1920. After spending a few days closing the Paris office of the American Relief Administration, he made a trip to Belgium on August 26. Clemenceau bade him farewell on September 5 and thanked him for his many services during the Peace Conference. In London, Lloyd George expressed his appreciation on September 6. That day Hoover sailed on the *Aquitania* for New York City and arrived there September 14. Wilson was in the midst of a country-wide tour appealing directly to the people over the heads of the Senate for acceptance of the treaty. On September 25 he collapsed after a speech at Pueblo, Colorado, and was immediately taken back to Washington. In the White House on October 2 he suffered a stroke that paralyzed his left side. For several weeks the medical bulletins were bland and seemed calculated to keep an anxious and alarmed world unaware of the true state of the President's health. Thereafter much of the executive business appears to have been conducted by a triumvirate consisting of Mrs. Wilson, Joseph Tumulty, and Dr. Cary Grayson, Wilson's personal physician. It is significant that Hoover's letter of November 11 was addressed to Tumulty and that he asked if Wilson's secretary could "transgress on the President's condition for a moment to get him to sign a simple direction" in order to get badly needed flour to Armenia and Poland. Tumulty may have complied but there appears to be no subsequent letter from him or from Wilson on this matter.

This letter of November 11 seems to be Hoover's first message to Wilson since August 12. This gap is partly explained by Hoover's tour of Europe and by the heavy tasks incident to the closing of his Paris office. Events after September 6 made communications virtually impossible, for Hoover was on the high seas and Wilson was traveling across the nation in his crusade for the League of Nations.

The cable he enclosed was from Colonel James A. Logan, chief of the Paris ARA staff; it was a message from Paderewski handed to Hugh Gibson, American minister to Poland. The Haskell telegram that Hoover mentioned is not now among the Hoover or the Wilson papers.

New York City, November 11, 1919.

My dear Tumulty:

I enclose you herewith copy of telegram from Colonel Haskell, who has charge of the relief work generally in Armenia on joint behalf of my own organization and that of the Near East Committee. I also send you herewith a copy of a telegram from Paderewski.

The delay in getting settlement of peace and [for] Armenia is making this position absolutely desperate. I have raised some $750,-000 charitable money for food, other than flour, for Armenia and I think I can secure from private sources the money with which to pay the freight on 35,000 tons of flour. I cannot, however, finance the flour, and Mr. Barnes agrees with me as to the urgent necessity of the Grain Corporation selling this flour on credit to the Armenian Government. It requires, however, a direction from the President to Mr. Barnes.

There is also waiting at the White House a direction from the President to Mr. Barnes to sell flour to the Polish Government on credit from the Grain Corporation. This is an equally desperate situation.

These situations are so very urgent that I am wondering if you could transgress on the President's condition for a moment to get him to sign a simple direction to Mr. Barnes to sell say 35,000 tons of flour to the Armenian Government and say up to 500,000 tons to the Polish Government, on credit.

I am going to Buffalo tonight to see if I can secure from a convention of Poles that I have called there the resources with which to pay freight on the flour to Poland, as there is no provision in the Grain Act that will allow the Grain Corporation to pay overseas transportation, even if the President decides that he can give the direction as above. I do not know of anything that impresses me more in its urgency than the above, both from a humane and a political point of view, and I am appealing for your assistance to get it before the President at an early moment.

Faithfully yours,
[signed, Hoover's secretary]

Enclosure

Paris, November 8, 1919, 4:24 p.m.

Food 61 for Hoover from Gibson Warsaw from Paderewski
Present truly crucial situation and excessive suffering. Urban people compel me address myself once more for help to you our true friend who [sic] humanity never found wanting. Poland needs 300,000 tons wheat and rye half of which amount in shape flour also 3,000 tons pure lard. In view of critical most dangerous conditions 1,000 tons of lard are required immediately. Long term credit covering cost supplies freight marine insurance indispensable on account war forced upon Poland on Eastern fronts and resulting obligations. Short term notes could not be met and our only hope lies in you who gave us already so many proofs your magnanimity and your generous country with heartfelt gratitude.

LOGAN

Food for Austria and Hungary

On the first page of this letter are the words, "Ackd. Dec 27 1919." As far as can be ascertained, no such acknowledgment was sent to Hoover by the White House then or at any other time. Therefore, it is fair to conclude that this notation refers to a letter sent to Hoover by the Hungarian food minister; Hoover enclosed this letter in his own, asking the President "to write an acknowledgement" of it.

New York City, November seventeenth, Nineteen hundred nineteen. Dear Mr. President;

In carrying out, in the newly-created countries, the child-feeding operations which were initiated with your approval in the early part of the year, we have experienced some difficulty in securing the necessary finance for meeting the appalling conditions in Austria and Hungary, for which our government funds were not available. My associates in America have succeeded in stimulating the feeling of responsibility in the foreign-born populations in America to support the children's feeding in the country of their affiliation.

In the case of Hungary, for which we had no funds whatever available, we have succeeded in securing from a Hungarian committee in New York a guarantee that they will assume the entire responsibility of the child-feeding program in Hungary during the coming winter, at an expense considerably over half a million dollars. They have already come forward with cash donations of over a hundred thousand dollars, and we are very anxious to give them all of the ammunition possible for approaching their own people. We have just received a letter for transmission to you from the Hungarian Food Minister, which is particularly heart-rending, and I am wondering whether we could not trespass upon your time to write an acknowledgment of this letter in order that we might use the incoming and outgoing letters for publicity purposes.

Faithfully yours,
Herbert Hoover

Industrial Conference

The industrial conference mentioned in this letter received a brief treatment by Hoover in 1952 in his *Memoirs* (vol. 2, pp. 30–32,

102). He recollects that in October 1919 Wilson called such a conference representing labor, management, and the general public to search for remedies for the growing industrial conflict. Hoover observes that the conference "broke up in a general row and got nowhere" (ibid., p. 30). Shortly thereafter many public groups and the cabinet recommended that Wilson call another meeting. The President responded with his letter of November 19 announcing, without consulting any of his appointees in advance, that the second conference would convene in Washington on December 1.

Some fifteen members were included in the conference. Although the Secretary of Labor was elected chairman, he was unable to devote sufficient time to meetings and thus Hoover as vice-chairman usually presided. For the next four months work of the conference went on continuously. In its report, the conference recommended collective bargaining, the growth of unions, the right to strike, decreased hours of work, better housing, restrictions on child labor, and old-age insurance. Both the extreme right and the extreme left received such recommendations coldly. On March 24, 1920, Hoover explained them to the Boston Chamber of Commerce. He recalls that "the applause would not have waked a nervous baby" (ibid., p. 31). Later, as Secretary of Commerce, Hoover worked hard to achieve the goals of the conference (ibid., pp. 102–8).

As for the President's letter, it is significant that the Wilson signature is definitely slanted upward to the right suggesting that Mrs. Wilson or an aide guided his hand as he formed the characters in his name.

Washington, 19 November, 1919.

My dear Mr. Hoover:

In accordance with the suggestion given me by the Public Group of the recent industrial conference, I am calling a new body together to carry on this vitally important work, and I trust you will give me the pleasure of naming you as one of its members.

Guided by the experience of the last conference I have thought it advisable that in this new body there should be no recognition of distinctive groups, but that all of the new representatives should have concern that our industries may be conducted with such regard for justice and fair dealing that the workman will feel himself induced to put forth his best effort, that the employer will have an encouraging profit, and that the public will not suffer at the hands of either class. It is my hope that this conference may lay the foundation for the development of standards and machinery within our industries by which these results may be attained.

It is not expected that you will deal directly with any condition which exists today, but that you may be fortunate enough to find such ways as will avoid the repetition of these deplorable conditions.

The conference will meet at a place to be hereafter designated in this city on the 1st of December next.

Cordially and sincerely yours,

Woodrow Wilson

Acceptance of League Reservations

The covenant of the League of Nations was drawn up in Paris in early 1919 under the personal direction of President Wilson, and on his insistence it was incorporated into the Treaty of Versailles. It was a short concise document of 26 articles with Articles 10–17 containing the League's basic idea, collective security with certain procedures for peaceful settlement of disputes. Since the covenant had been embodied in the treaty, membership of the United States in the League depended on Wilson's success in winning the affirmation of two-thirds of the Senate.

At the time of Wilson's return from Paris on July 8, 1919, a fairly distinct alignment already existed in the upper chamber. A small minority of fifteen resolute isolationists, mainly Republicans, adamantly opposed the treaty in any form as long as it contained the covenant. Since they dominated the Foreign Relations Committee, they were able to put heavy pressure on Henry Cabot Lodge, chairman of this committee. These 15 "irreconcilables" were outnumbered by some 34 Republican senators who favored ratification of the treaty provided certain changes were made in the covenant to safeguard American interests. Most of these Republicans were called "strong reservationists," the others "mild reservationists." Among the Democrats at least 43 of the 47 in the Senate were willing to follow Wilson's demand that the treaty and the covenant be accepted without adding any amendments or reservations.

All the reservationists had misgivings about the covenant's provisions for involving the United States in international disputes without the prior consent of Congress. Article 10 in particular invited their criticism; it called on all League members to guarantee the integrity and political independence of each member state against aggression. The reservationists amended it to require that American implementation of Article 10 could be affected only by a joint resolution of Congress. Thirteen other amendments affecting the covenant and/or the treaty were proposed by Lodge on November 6. It soon became evident that ratification of the treaty and the covenant were doomed unless Wilson would accept at least some of the proposed reservations. Such prominent figures as Bernard N. Baruch and David Hunter Miller, the person who helped draft the covenant, had already urged Wilson to compromise on the matter. On November 17, Gilbert M. Hitchcock of Nebraska, Democratic leader in the Senate, visited the ailing President in his bedroom and found that he was resolutely opposed to the Lodge modification of Article 10, since in his mind it constituted a virtual nullification of the treaty.

In the meantime, Hoover had in several public addresses urged acceptance of the treaty along with agreement to United States membership in the League, but he realized that senatorial approval was impossible unless Wilson permitted his loyal followers in the Senate to vote in favor of at least some of the Lodge reservations. It appears that shortly before November 19, Hoover tried in vain to carry his plea personally to the bedside of the President (*Ordeal*, p. 282). On the morning of November 19 he wired Wilson in the hope that he might convince his stricken chief to give Democratic solons an approving nod in the few hours remaining before the crucial Senate vote. The message in this wired communique was also put into a letter and sent off the same day.

Evidence from material in the archives of the Hoover Presidential Library shows that on November 19 Hoover sent the identical message to Democratic leaders in the Senate (HH Public Statements, Oct. 1919–Jan. 7, 1920, box 6). It would appear to be rather bold action to go over the head of the President in this manner, but he may have done just that; the letter below could have been written for a group of persons as well as for one man. Moreover, the same source contains an identical message dated November 12, which was presumably sent by wire from New York City on that day. (Actually Hoover was in Buffalo for an address on November 12, arriving there at 9:55 A.M. Even if it were impossible to reach New York City that night, Hoover might have had the telegram sent over his name from his Manhattan office.) Then Hoover, receiving no answer from the White House and having been denied a personal interview with the President, may have on the morning of November 19 sent the wired message again to Wilson and at the same time wired an identical message to the Democrats in the Senate. There is one final possibility: Hoover could have composed the telegram on November 12 and kept it from release for a week. Years later, in reviewing the episode, Hoover mentions only his letter of November 19, observing that he received no response and that Wilson was perhaps too ill even to read it.

New York City, November 19, 1919.

My dear Mr. President:
  Confirming my wire today:
  "I take the liberty of urging upon you the desirability of accepting the reservations now passed, except for the removal of objectionable provisions in the preamble and in addition with such other changes in their text as can be obtained by compromise without running the great dangers of voting the treaty out.
  "Some of the reservations are constructive particularly in rendering it clear that the war power must be invoked by Congress. Others are interpretive in line with the original intent of the Covenant. One arouses the amour propre of a great many American people, the raising of which should not have been inflicted on us by the British Government. The others of the voted reservations are in part form undesirable but taken as a whole they do not seem to me to imperil the great principle of the League of Nations to prevent war.
  "I have the belief that with the League once in motion it can within itself and from experience and public education develop such measures as will make it effective. I am impressed with the desperate necessity of early ratification.
  "The delays have already seriously imperiled the economic recuperation of Europe. In this we are vitally interested from every point of view. I believe that the Covenant will steadily lose ground in popular support if it is not put into constructive operation at once because the American public will not appreciate the saving values of the Covenant as distinguished from the wrongs imposed in the Treaty. These wrongs will day by day become more evident to the entire world and will be confused with the Covenant itself. For instance, it can only be days until actual starvation begins in Vienna for which the insistence by England, France and Italy upon the political isolation of Austria from Germany must bear the fundamental responsibility.
  "We must recognize that if Europe is to survive it must import an enormous quantity of supplies from the United States, that these supplies can only be found on credit, that already the existing supplies show exhaustion in many parts of Europe, that no credit facili-

ties or commercial machinery for meeting this situation can be erected until ratification is over.

"On the other hand we have large surpluses of commodities in the United States, the damming back of which within our shores will sooner or later inflict great hardships on our own people particularly our farmers and endanger our production.

"If we have the great misfortune of the Treaty becoming a political issue in Presidential election it will become confused with our own domestic issues, our own racial prejudices, the constant blame of every difficulty in Europe upon the Treaty. It will be impossible to secure the clear voice of the American people on the Covenant itself. Moreover the shades of difference between Democratic and Republican reservations are too fine for alignment of public opinion.

"My own feeling is therefore that this great constructive effort is mainly accomplished as it stands and its operation can repair mistakes in its building and that the world issues are so great as not to warrant the risks involved in delay of getting it into service in the hope of securing a few percent more ideal structure."

Faithfully yours,
Herbert Hoover

Conference Appointment Accepted

20 November, 1919

My Dear Mr. President:

I beg to acknowledge your note of the 19th of November in respect to the new industrial Conference. I am always glad to be of any service to yourself or the community and will join the conference.

Faithfully yours,
[signed, Hoover's secretary]

1920

Rebuke for Hoover Interview

Although on November 19, 1919, the Senate had apparently given an irrevocable "nay" to the treaty and America's membership in the League, public sentiment throughout the country was generally strong for ratification. Thus the Senate felt compelled to agree to a reconsideration of their action of the previous fall; the critical vote came on March 19. Two days earlier the press inexplicably released to the public a letter that Hoover had written to Wilson on April 11, 1919, when both were heavily engaged in matters affecting the treaty and the reconstruction of Europe (*Post*, Mar. 18, 1920, p. 1; *Times*, Mar. 17, 1920, p. 1). In this letter Hoover recommended that after the Peace Conference the United States should discontinue its membership on the various commissions that had been established during the Conference; Hoover explained that by cutting itself free from these commissions, the United States would be free to participate more effectively in the League of Nations. Other portions of the letter taken out of context could be read as a treatise on the dangers of international alliances and thus appeared to constitute arguments against participation in the League. Naturally the "irreconcilables" seized on Hoover's words and used them as grist for their propaganda mill. For the Wilson forces this press release burst like a time bomb just as the Senate prepared for the vote on March 19. Senator William Borah read it into the Congressional Record, adding his own gloss that the letter constituted an opinion of a highly placed official recommending America's withdrawal from Europe, "lock, stock and barrel." (See Hoover's letter of April 11, 1919.)

The *Times* (Mar. 17, 1920, p. 1) observed that the letter had "created the greatest interest" since it was rumored that Hoover was "Wilson's candidate" for the Democratic nomination for the Presidency; now the letter would dispose of that idea. But the *Ledger* (Mar. 17, 1920, p. 1), which had first published the letter, observed that many other Democrats were delighted that Hoover had provided "rallying ground" for overcoming the stubborn position of

Wilson which would lead them, so they feared, to abysmal defeat. On the other hand, many Republicans commented that the letter "regularized" Hoover as a genuine Republican. Indeed, Hoover's party affiliation had never been strong, but by supporting Wilson's plea for a Democratic Congress in 1918, he had quite disaffected most stalwart Republicans.

It should be noted that the letter of rebuke came from Tumulty and does not carry Wilson's signature. It is possible that the President was unaware of the incident. Or he may have been well enough to read the newspaper accounts which orchestrated the affair. If so, it is possible that he either dictated the letter or informed Tumulty of his sentiments, which his secretary then put in letter form. In any event, the pique of the White House ostensibly came only from Hoover's interview which followed the publication of the letter. Tumulty makes no mention of the untimely release to the press or of the contents of Hoover's communique of April 11, 1919. It should be recalled that on April 15, 1919, Wilson responded and told Hoover of his approval of the recommendations with one exception; he felt that the United States would be virtually forced to keep a representative on the reparations commission to act as a kind of arbiter. In an interview of March 18, Hoover explained that he himself had changed his views and endorsed such representation as a definite necessity.

It is well to note that in his New York interview, Hoover protested that the letter of April 11, 1919, was a private one and should not have been released without the permission of both himself and the President. He denied that he had released it and said he was sure the White House had not done so (*Post*, Mar. 18, 1920, p. 1). This latter statement apparently piqued Tumulty and provoked his ill-humored letter—strange as such reaction might seem. Possibly the White House suspected that Hoover, in spite of his disavowal, had been privy to the letter's publication or had even released it himself for some personal political gain. But lacking proof of such action by a man of high honor and integrity, Tumulty could only grasp at straws in venting his irritation at Hoover.

Washington, 17 March 1920

My dear Mr. Hoover:

I would not be frank with you if I did not tell you that in your statement your secretary has been good enough to send me, with reference to the Public Ledger interview article, it really was unnecessary to say that the White House had not issued the statement. Of course, the White House, even if it knew of this statement, would not have given it publicity because of its disastrous effect upon the

Treaty situation at this time. We had a similar experience some weeks ago with reference to another alleged interview, where it was made to appear that you differed with the President on the question of reservations. At that time your secretary telephoned the White House to find out if we had given this statement out.

An intimation that the White House had given out either of these statements is tantamount to a charge of treachery on our part which I know you did not intend.

Sincerely yours,
Joseph Tumulty
Secretary to the President

Hoover Regrets Misinterpretation

New York City, March 19, 1920.

My dear Tumulty:

I am sorry that you should have taken amiss the inquiry that was made from you with regard to the publication of correspondence with the President. I was, perhaps, over-anxious in the matter of unauthorized publication of documents that would be distorted by its enemies into opposition to the League, the establishment of which I am as anxious to see as anyone, although I may differ as to the merits or demerits of the reservations proposed by the mild reservationists.

Yours faithfully,
Herbert Hoover

Note on Shipment Address for Wool

This brief note to Hoover carries no signature or other identification of the sender. Since it was written on White House stationery, one might conclude that it came from Tumulty, Mrs. Wilson, or some lesser figure in the executive mansion. The mention of "wool" invites further conjecture: it might have been intended for use in the United States or for shipment overseas for distribution as a gift from the Salvation Army. If the latter conjecture is true, one might further surmise that the Salvation Army's director of publicity was anxious to see that his organization received proper credit for the charitable deed. When the letter reached Hoover, someone, apparently a secretary, jotted across the top these words: "wrote Leffingwell, 6/8/20," probably indicating that Leffingwell had been informed that the wool had been or was to be sent as the White House directed.

Washington, May 29, 1920.

Mr. Hoover:

When the wool is shipped, please see that it is marked as follows:

> Elmore Leffingwell,
> Director of Publicity,
> Salvation Army Headquarters,
> 120 West 14th Street,
> New York City.

Unspent Food Administration Budget

New York City, June 21, 1920.

Dear Mr. President:

I enclose herewith Grain Corporation check for $1,660,573.74, being the unexpended balance of the $5,000,000 which you on December 16, 1918, authorized the Secretary of the Treasury to pay to the Food Administration Grain Corporation, from your fund for National Security and Defense, for relief in Europe. I also enclose auditor's statement.

Final accounting has not hitherto been possible, owing to prolonged delays in settling accounts as between the Grain Corporation, the Shipping Board, and the War Department.

> Yours faithfully,
> [signed, Hoover's secretary]

Statement on Children's Fund

Neither the Wilson nor the Hoover papers reveal any communication containing the President's approval of the plan mentioned in the following letter. Perhaps it has been lost or possibly Tumulty used the telephone to send Wilson's approval—if so, it would be a rare departure from ordinary practice.

June 26, 1920

Dear Mr. President:

You will recollect that on June 6, 1920, you approved the plan whereby the "contingent margin" reserved for losses and administrative charges in fixing the prices for the supply of foodstuffs to various countries through the different organizations subsidiary to the Supreme Economic Council should, in final liquidation of their accounts, and in order that no profits be taken from relief, be appropriated to continue the support of the organizations engaged in feeding undernourished children in Europe after the exhaustion of the $100,000,000 appropriation by Congress of February 25th, 1919. This plan was ratified by agreements with the Governments of Germany, Austria, Poland, Czecho-Slovakia, Roumania, Lithuania, Esthonia, Latvia, Serbia, and Finland, who were the purchasers of supplies under the relief operations above mentioned.

The enclosed statement exhibits the operations of the European Children's Fund since August 1, 1919. As soon as possible after August 1st next we shall issue an audited statement of accounts. During the year, the Fund has organized the support of the following numbers of children:

COUNTRY	CHILDREN FED
FINLAND	90,000
ESTHONIA	84,000
LATVIA	80,000
LITHUANIA	40,000
POLAND	1,400,000
AUSTRIA	350,000
SERBIA (Jugo Slavia)	150,000
HUNGARY	125,000
CZECHO-SLOVAKIA	600,000
GERMANY	500,000
GRAND TOTAL	3,419,000

You will observe from the statement that in addition to the "marginal reserve fund" for relief purposes we have raised $10,-000,000 by charity and other resources. In addition to these funds again the local European governments and local European charities have contributed about equal amounts. There is still some cash in hand and there are current stocks of food in warehouses in Europe, which will enable the work to be continued for a few months longer. We are extending the organization if [sic] view of further mobilizing public charity in an endeavor to maintain the service over next winter. The extensive personnel of the Fund is shown in the enclosed statement.

Assuming the Treasury will in due time pay certain vouchers against the $100,000,000 appropriation, the question now arises of final accounting between the European Children's Fund and the Grain Corporation (who have handled the accounts on behalf of the various parties concerned). There now remains in the hands of the Corporation in addition to payments to date of $22,553,205.99, a further $2,554,106.15 in cash after meeting all damages, out of pocket expenses, etc., and the question outstanding is that of the proper charge by the Grain Corporation to cover a right proportion of the overhead administrative expenses of the Corporation for commercial conduct of these operations. The total operations for which the Corporation did the commercial handling amounted to $371,139,603.61, the largest portion of which were [sic] for cash from various European governments through the arrangements made under the Supreme Economic Council.

It was your direction that no profits should be earned by our government organizations in lending their machinery to this work. Naturally my desire is, in American interest, that we should continue to show a sympathetic interest in European poverty over the next winter, and the lower the Grain Corporation charge is placed the larger the resources of the organization will be for this battle with misery during the next twelve months. On the other hand, we must necessarily desire to treat government agencies with entire equity. Mr. Barnes, representing the Grain Corporation, considers that if the Corporation received one-fourth of one per cent on the entire operation and undertook out of this to settle a few contingent liabilities, it would be an equitable covering of Grain Corporation services. This would allow the further payment to the European Children's Fund of approximately $1,600,000. My own view is that this would be a fair settlement and it is my purpose, on behalf of the Fund, to agree [to] this sum with Mr. Barnes. I trust that this basis of settlement has your entire approval.

Yours faithfully,
[signed, Hoover's secretary]

Acknowledgment of a June Letter

Tumulty speaks of a Hoover letter, with an enclosure, of June 28. Actually no letter to Wilson for that date seems to have been written. There is, however, a June 26 letter and it is possible that the overworked Tumulty made a mistake. His remark that Hoover's letter had been called to the President's attention is somewhat difficult to interpret because of the uncertain condition of Wilson's health at the time.

Washington, July 10, 1920.

My dear Mr. Hoover;

I beg to acknowledge the receipt of your letter of June 28th, with enclosure, and to say that it has been brought to the attention of the President.

Sincerely yours,
J. P. Tumulty
Secretary to the President

Epilogue

As far as can be ascertained, the letters of June and July 1920 are the final pieces of correspondence between the President and Hoover, who worked so diligently to help solve the complex problems during and after World War I. Much has been written about Wilson's break with such notable intimates as Colonel House, Robert Lansing, and Joseph Tumulty. There is no account of any such dramatic break with Hoover. A few incidents produced a certain coolness between the Director of American Relief and the President. At Paris in early June 1919, Hoover protested against the terms of the peace treaty. In a private interview with Wilson, Hoover spoke vigorously and the President interrupted with sharp rejoinders. Hoover implies that after this unpleasant encounter Wilson's intimacy visibly declined. Yet for the next several months an exchange of a few letters bore every mark of cordiality and mutual respect.

When Hoover returned to America in September 1919, Wilson was engaged in a bitter fight over the treaty and membership of the United States in the League. Hoover became a fellow combatant and spoke on several occasions in favor of the new world organization. But he was realistic and soon understood that the Senate would reject American participation unless the President would compromise somewhat (see introduction to Hoover's letter of June 19, 1919). The message of the June 19 letter was scarcely calculated to warm the heart of the stubborn President.

The following March 17, 1920, there was an unfortunate publication of a letter that Hoover had written to Wilson on April 11 the previous year. Although the President had replied on April 15, 1919, that excepting one point he entirely agreed, the letter was made to appear by certain propagandists as containing anti-League sentiments long harbored by one of Wilson's most trusty lieutenants (see

Rebuke for Hoover Interview). Tumulty's testy letter of reprimand may have reflected the official attitude toward Hoover that prevailed within the small coterie at the White House.

Moreover, a strong current of support for Hoover as a presidential candidate in November on either the Democratic or Republican ticket had now developed. In spite of his weakened physical condition and even while the base of his support was crumbling away, Wilson seems to have entertained some hopes of running for a third term. Thus the growing prospects of Hoover would have been watched with a jealous and suspicious eye. When, on July 6, 1920, James M. Cox, Governor of Ohio, was chosen to be the standard-bearer of the Democratic party, Wilson insisted that the campaign be a "great and solemn referendum on the League." It became in many minds just that plus a referendum on Wilsonianism itself.

The Republicans had on June 12 picked Senator Warren Harding as their candidate. He was pressed hard on all sides—by the irreconcilables, the strict reservationists, and the mild reservationists —to take a firm stand on the League, and his ambivalent statements kept the nation guessing as to his own true convictions. Hoover was soon won over and supported Harding's candidacy, but he and others (including Charles Evans Hughes, Elihu Root, and William Howard Taft) kept the vacillating candidate from abandoning the world organization altogether. Thus the election was not really a great referendum on the League. In a private letter of September 29, 1920, Hoover seems to have stated the real situation quite precisely: "Since the Armistice, the present administration has been a failure by all the tests that we can apply. It has obstinately held up the peace of the world for eighteen months, with a fearful cost to ourselves and to the world. It has woefully neglected and failed upon great reconstruction and administrative measures that are critically necessary as the aftermath of the war. . . . The responsibilities of government should now, therefore, be transferred" (*Harding*, pp. 68–69).

The sentiments expressed in this letter indicate a break in relations between Hoover and Wilson at least several weeks prior to the elections of November 1920. On December 9, 1920, nearly five weeks after the election, Wilson wrote to a high government official that Hoover "is no friend of mind [*sic*] and I do not care to do anything to assist him in any way in any undertaking whatever" (*Aftermath,* p. 22, n. 56). It is not known if Hoover ever heard of this remark.

On February 23, 1921, Hoover accepted Harding's offer of a cabinet post as Secretary of Commerce and the severance became complete.[1]

Four months after Wilson's death, Hoover dismissed all incidents involving the President's strained relations with former intimates as aberrations flowing from the stroke he had suffered. Hoover preferred to blot them out of his mind and to cherish the memory of the real Wilson, the prophet and spiritual leader of the world (Hoover to H. A. White, June 13, 1934, HPL).

On March 4, 1921, Woodrow Wilson left the White House never to enter it again. When Harding was sworn in at noon as President, Wilson became a private citizen, and, as such, took up residency in Washington at 2340 S Street. About the same time the Hoovers moved into a home in the same block at 2300 S Street. It would be comforting to end this book by recording that a number of pleasant chats took place in the next three years between these two neighbors, who as great heroic figures had once worked so closely together to make the world a better and a safer place for people to live in. But there are no such chats or visits to record.

On Friday, February 1, 1924, it was publicly announced that Wilson's life was near an end. The following morning, Hoover, like many other notables, dropped by at 2340 S Street and left his card. On the following day the former President died and was laid to rest in a side chapel of Washington National Cathedral. The ordeal of Woodrow Wilson had come to an end. His great dream was shattered. Harding soon publicly stated in unequivocal language that there was no sentiment in America for the League of Nations; then the country's lawmakers, having rejected the peace treaty, officially ended hostilities with Germany by a joint act of Congress.

But some vindication would eventually come for the work of the two great internationalists. A short distance from their homes on S Street is Dumbarton Oaks, the estate where, four decades after Wil-

---

[1] Hoover implies that he did speak with Wilson at some length a few months after Wilson left the White House (*Ordeal,* p. 265), but there is no record of such.

son's death, the great global powers sent representatives to draw up proposals leading to the establishment of the United Nations.

Hoover lived for another forty years, experiencing his own share of the agony and the ecstasy of public life. He died in 1964 and was buried on the grounds of the Hoover Presidential Library at West Branch, Iowa.

Glossary

Alexander I, 1888–1934. Son of Peter I of Serbia. King, 1921–1934, of the new state which was created in December 1918 as the "Kingdom of the Serbs, Croats, and Slovenes," named Yugoslavia in 1929. Alexander was assassinated in 1934.

Andrews, E. C. An American connected with the merchants in St. Louis. Mentioned in a Hoover-Wilson communication of March 26, 1919, as the sender of a telegram to Hoover. Not otherwise identified.

Atwood, William G., 1872–1948. Army colonel borrowed from the army by Hoover in 1919 for his relief work in central Europe.

Auchincloss, Gordon, 1886–1943. Lawyer, Democrat, and son-in-law of Colonel Edward M. House. Secretary to House at Paris, 1918–1919.

Baker, Newton Diehl, 1871–1937. Secretary of War, 1916–1921. Fought for the League of Nations and against American isolationism.

Baker, Ray Stannard, 1870–1946. Author and journalist. Supply commander for the Department of State in France, Great Britain, and Italy in 1918. Director of the Press Bureau of American Commonwealth to Negotiate Peace, at Paris 1919 to 1926. Author of many books, including authoritative works on Wilson during the war and at the Peace Conference.

Bakhmetev, Boris, 1880–1951. Russian university professor. A leader of the Menshevik faction—as opposed to the Bolsheviks—in Russia's Social Democratic Labor Party, founded 1898. In July 1919 he was named an envoy to the United States by the Kolchak government.

Balfour, Arthur James, 1848–1930. British statesman. Born in Scotland. Became leader of Conservative Party and Prime Minister in 1902. Opposed Irish home rule, 1910–1911. Resigned as Conservative leader in 1911. Foreign Secretary in Coalition government, 1916–1919. Chief British representative to the League of Nations Assembly in 1920.

Barnes, Julius H., 1873–1953. Member of the Cereal Division of the U.S. Food Administration. Traveled to Paris with Hoover in November 1918. Named U.S. wheat director in 1919.

Baruch, Bernard M., 1870–1965. A U.S. representative on the Reparations Commission of the Paris Peace Conference. Close Wilson adviser, member of President's Committee of Economic Advisers and of Supreme Economic Council. During the war he was director of the War Industry Board.

Benson, William Shepherd, 1855–1932. Admiral in U.S. Navy. Appointed Chief of Naval Operations, May 11, 1915. Naval representative in drawing up naval terms of armistice. Adviser to American Commission to Peace Conference. Provided valuable assistance to Hoover in recruiting navy men for his European relief work. Stood firmly with Hoover against continued food embargo on Germany by Allies.

Bliss, Tasker Howard, 1853–1930. U.S. Army general. One of the five plenipotentiaries on the American delegation at the Paris Peace Conference.

Borah, William Edgar, 1865–1940. U.S. Republican senator from Idaho, 1907 to 1940. A frequent critic of Hoover from 1917 to 1920 and an opponent of the Versailles Treaty and the League of Nations. His leadership was an important element in the Senate's rejection of both.

Boysen, Fran D. L. Mentioned in a letter to Hoover by Wilson's confidential secretary, March 17, 1919.

Brown, Philip Marshall, 1875–1952. Teacher of international law at Harvard and Princeton. Prior to World War I he served in several different diplomatic posts. In 1919 he was on the food mission to Vienna gathering information for Hoover's relief program.

Bullitt, William C., 1891–1962. Attaché to the American Commission at the Paris Peace Conference, 1919. Chief of the Division of Current Intelligence Summaries of the U.S. State Department. Member of a special mission to Russia, 1919. U.S. Ambassador to Russia, 1933–1936.

Causey, William B., 1865–1936. U.S. Army lt. colonel. A prewar railway man who assisted Hoover with railroad matters in 1919 during reconstruction of Europe, especially in Austria. He remained in Austria for five years after the war and helped greatly in building up that country's economy.

Cecil, Lord Robert, 1864–1958. British statesman. Assistant Secretary of State for Foreign Affairs in 1918. Minister of Blockade, 1916–1918. At the Peace Conference he was one of the chief architects of the Covenant of the League of Nations. Awarded the Nobel Peace Prize in 1937.

Clemenceau, Georges, 1841–1929. French Premier and Chairman of the Paris Peace Conference. He had visited the United States shortly after the Civil War. He first served in the French National Assembly in 1871 and kept eternally alive the bitter memory of the humiliation suffered in that year at the hands of Bismark. This accounts for much of the vindictiveness he displayed in 1919 toward Germany.

Clémentel, Étienne, 1862–1936. French Minister of National Economy from 1916 to 1920.

Close, Gilbert F., 1881–1952. Born in Pennsylvania. Confidential secretary to President Wilson at the Paris Peace Conference. Previously he had been confidential secretary to Josephus Daniels, then Secretary of the Navy.

Coolidge, Archibald C., 1866–1928. American university professor. Served at several different diplomatic posts prior to World War I. At the Paris Peace Conference he was a special assistant to the State Department. In 1919 he was a member of the Vienna food mission. In 1921 he joined the American Relief Administration in its work to provide food for Russia.

Cotton, Joseph P., 1875–1931. Lawyer and diplomat. U.S. representative in London to the Inter-Allied Council on War Purchases and Finance. Representative of the American Food Administration in London, 1918. Under-Secretary of State in the Hoover administration.

Cox, James Middleton, 1870–1957. U.S. Democratic congressman, 1909–1912. Governor of Ohio, 1913–1915. Unsuccessful Democratic candidate for President in 1920.

Cravath, Paul D., 1861–1940. Lawyer. In December 1917 he represented the U.S. Treasury on the "House Mission" to the Inter-Allied War Conference at Paris. He was advisory counsel of the American mission to the Inter-Allied Conference on War Purchases and Finance held in London and Paris in 1918.

Crespi, Francisco. During World War I, Italian food controller and one of the Italian members on the Reparations Commission at the Peace Conference.

Davis, Norman H., 1878–1944. Representative of the Treasury Department at Paris; member of the President's Committee of Economic Advisers at the Peace Conference.

Denikin, Anton Ivanovich, 1872–1947. Military commander in the Russian army. Leader of the White Army in the Civil War of 1918–1920. Upon defeat he left Russia; he died in the United States.

Dulles, John Foster, 1888–1959. Captain and major in U.S. Army Intelligence Service, 1918–1920. Counsel to the American Commission at the Peace Conference. Member of Reparations Commission and Supreme Economic Council. Republican U.S. senator from New York, 1947–1949. Secretary of State, 1953–1959.

Ebert, Friedrich, 1871–1925. German. Chairman of Social Democratic Party. Elected President of the Weimar Provisional Government in February 1919, a position he held until 1925.

Elmore, A. A. President of the Joint Organization of the Farmers Union and State Grange of the States of Washington, Oregon, and Idaho.

Elmore, A. Robert. Born in London, England. Served as a lieutenant in the U.S. Navy in World War I. Was a recruiting officer for the U.S. Navy and also served in its purchasing department. He died in 1937.

Foch, Ferdinand, 1851–1929. Grandson of an officer of Napoleon I and a close friend of Clemenceau. A resourceful French marshal throughout the war, he was named Supreme Commander of the Allied forces in April 1918.

Fotieva, Lydia. As secretary of the Council of Peoples Commissars in 1923, she was one of three Soviet officials who signed a scroll of thanks for the food Hoover sent the starving Russians through the American Relief Administration.

Francis Ferdinand, 1863–1914. Austrian Archduke and heir presumptive to the crowns of Austria and Hungary. His assassination on June 28, 1914, at Sarajevo, Bosnia, precipitated World War I.

Gibson, Hugh, 1883–1954. For many years a member of the U.S. diplomatic service. Served under Hoover in Europe with the American Relief Administration from November 1918 to April 1919. Prior to that he was First Secretary to the American Legation in Belgium where he became well known to Hoover. Wilson did not appoint Gibson as Minister to Czechoslovakia, as Hoover requested, but three weeks later on April 16, 1919, he became Envoy Extraordinary and Minister Plenipotentiary to Poland. On March 18, 1924, he was named to the same post in Switzerland. During World War II he collaborated with Hoover on books dealing with means to preserve peace between nations.

Glasgow, William. Chief counsel of the U.S. Food Administration. Chosen by Hoover to be his substitute on Wilson's War Council—"War Cabinet" —when Hoover was in Europe in July 1918.

Glass, Carter, 1858–1946. Democratic member of U.S. Congress, 1902–1918. Secretary of the Treasury 1918 to February 2, 1920. U.S. senator, 1920–1936, 1942–1946. Declined an appointment by President Franklin D. Roosevelt to serve as Secretary of the Treasurer.

Goodyear, Anson C., 1878–1964. Member of Hoover's relief and reconstruction organization as chief of the coal mission to eastern Europe.

Gorbunov, Nikolay Petrovich, 1892–1944. Lenin's personal secretary. One of the three Russian officials who in 1923 signed the long scroll of thanks sent to Hoover for bringing relief to the Russian people. Died in prison in 1944.

Gore, Thomas Pryor, 1870–1949. U.S. Democratic senator from Oklahoma, 1907–1921, 1931–1937. A frequent critic of Hoover during the war and the Peace Conference.

Gray, Prentiss N. A representative of the Shipping Board on the committee which assisted the Food Administration during Hoover's absence in Paris.

Grayson, Gary T., 1878–1938. In 1916 named medical director of the navy with rank of rear admiral. Personal physician of President Wilson.

Gregory, T. T. C. Lawyer and captain in the U.S. Army. Closely associated with Hoover's relief work in Europe in 1918 to 1919, especially in Austria and Hungary.

Harbord, James G., 1866–1947. U.S. Army lt. general. Appointed on May 14, 1917, to Chief of Staff of American Expeditionary Force in France. In June 1919 he was named chairman of a team to investigate the unsettled conditions in Armenia prior to the extension of Hoover's relief to that country.

Harding, Warren G., 1865–1923. U.S. Republican senator from Ohio, 1915 to 1921. President of United States, 1921–1923. He appointed Hoover to Secretary of Commerce in 1921.

Harries, George Herbert, 1860–1934. U.S. brigadier general, N.A.

Harstone, P. Englishman. Writer of a letter to Hoover, March 19, 1919. Otherwise not referred to again or further identified.

Haskell, William N., 1878–1952. U.S. Army colonel recommended by Hoover as higher commissioner for Armenia where he carried on American relief for approximately one year from August of 1919.

Heath, Mrs. Julian. An American who in 1918–1919 was leader in the National Housewives League in New York City.

Hitchcock, Gilbert M., 1859–1934. U. S. Democratic congressman from Nebraska, 1903–1905, 1907–1911. U.S. Senator, 1911–1923. In 1919 and 1920, as minority Senate leader, he was compelled to lead the Wilsonian senators down to defeat on ratification of the Treaty and the League after he failed to convince Wilson to accept some of the more modest reservations.

Holtchak. A name used once in a letter by Hoover who probably meant "Kolchak," a Russian general in the White Army. (q.v.).

Hoover, Herbert C., 1874–1964. Mining engineer. Organized and headed the Commission for the Relief in Belgium, 1914–1917. U.S. Food Administrator, 1917–1919. General director of the Relief and Reconstruction Commission established in Paris in 1919. Organized and directed the American Relief Administration for aid principally to Austria, Hungary, Armenia, and Russia, 1919–1923. Secretary of Commerce, 1921–1929. Thirty-first President of the United States, 1929–1933. Author of many books, mainly on his relief work and his political career.

House, Colonel (honorary) Edward Mandell, 1858–1938. Born in Texas, he was an intimate confidant of President Wilson from 1912 to the end of the Peace Conference when this "strangest friendship in the world" palpably cooled. At the Conference, House was one of the five plenipotentiaries on the U.S. delegation and acted as Wilson's personal deputy whenever the President was ill or absent.

Houston, David F., 1866–1940. Secretary of Agriculture, 1913–1920, and of Treasury, 1920–1921.

Hughes, Charles Evans, 1862–1948. American jurist and statesman. Governor of New York. U.S. Supreme Court justice, 1911–1916. Unsuccessful Republican candidate for the presidency, 1916. Secretary of State, 1921–1925. Appointed Chief Justice of Supreme Court by Hoover, 1930–1941.

Hurley, Edward Nash, 1864–1933. Chairman of U.S. Shipping Board and president of Emergency Fleet Corporation, July 24, 1917–July 31, 1919.

James, Arthur Curtis, 1867–1941. American merchant and capitalist.

Kamenev, Lev Borisovich, 1883–1936. Russian political leader and Communist Party official. In 1923, as the president of the Council of People's Commissars, he signed an elaborate scroll which expressed to Hoover the gratitude of the Soviet government for the food he had provided for the famished Russians. He was executed in 1936.

Károlyi, Count Mihály, 1875–1955. Hungarian political leader who as a liberal aristocrat took over as president of the short-lived democratic republic after the abdication of the Hapsburg Emperor Charles. Ruled from January to March 1919. He escaped abroad in July 1919 and thereafter spent many years in exile. He returned to Hungary in 1946 and served as Hungarian Ambassador to France from 1946 to 1949.

Kellogg, Frank B., 1856–1937. Secretary of State, 1925–1929. U.S. senator from Minnesota, 1917–1923. Ambassador to Great Britain, 1924–1925. A member of the Senate Foreign Relations Committee and voted against the Versailles Treaty in 1919. Special assistant to the U.S. Attorney General under President Theodore Roosevelt and became one of the most noted "trust busters." Awarded Nobel Peace Prize, 1929.

Kellogg, Vernon L., 1867–1937. Zoologist. An official in 1915–1916 in Hoover's organization for feeding Belgium and Northern France. Also served in the American Relief Administration in Europe in 1919.

Kerensky, Aleksandr Feodorovich, 1881–1970. Russian political leader. Head of the provisional government in the revolutionary period from July to November 1917. Upon the Bolshevik uprising, he fled to London, France, and, finally, New York.

Keynes, John Maynard, 1883–1946. English economist. Adviser to the Treasury of the British government at the Peace Conference. Also a member of the Reparations Commission. Protested vigorously against the harsh terms of the Versailles Treaty.

Knapp, Harry Shepherd, 1856–1923. Rear admiral in U.S. Navy. An adviser at the Peace Conference, 1919. Placed in command of the U.S. Navy in European waters, 1919.

Kolchak, Aleksandr V., 1875–1920. Admiral in Russian navy. On November 18, 1918, he led a rebellion against the Bolshevik government and proclaimed himself supreme ruler of Russia. His cause collapsed and he was executed by a Bolshevik firing squad on February 7, 1920.

Kun, Béla, 1886–1939. Hungarian who joined the Communists while a prisoner of war in Russia. Sent by the Soviets to Budapest, he seized control of the Hungarian government in March, 1919. Overthrown August 1, he fled to Russia. Killed in the 1939 purge of Stalin.

Lansing, Robert, 1864–1928. American lawyer and diplomat. Secretary of State, 1915–1920. Member of American peace delegation at Paris Peace Conference. Opposed League of Nations. Because of this and other differences with Wilson, he was forced to resign from the cabinet on February 12, 1920.

Leffingwell, Elmore C., 1880–1942. Publicist and newspaper man.

Lenin, Nikolai, 1870–1924. Russian Bolshevik who seized power in 1917 and held it till 1924.

Link, Arthur S., 1920–. Professor of history and author, Princeton. Foremost scholar and writer on the life of Woodrow Wilson.

Lloyd George, David, 1863–1945. Prime Minister of Britain's Coalition government, 1916–1922. Leader of British delegation at the Peace Conference.

Lodge, Henry Cabot, 1850–1924. U.S. Republican congressman, 1886–1893; U.S. senator, 1893–1924. A persistent critic of Wilson. Led opposition to the League of Nations till its rejection by Senate in March 1920. A critic of Hoover since 1914, when he charged that the chairman of the Commission for Relief in Belgium was violating the Logan Act, which prohibited private citizens from attempting to influence U.S. foreign policy by dealings with a foreign country.

Logan, James A., Jr., 1879–1930. Lawyer, diplomat, and soldier. Colonel in the army. After the Armistice, he became chief of the Paris staff of the American Relief Administration and Hoover's principal assistant in the work of feeding Europe. During the war he was an assistant Chief of Staff to General Pershing. For several years after the war he was an unofficial U.S. observer at nearly every international conference.

McAdoo, William Gibbs, 1863–1941. American statesman from Georgia. Supported Wilson for the presidency in 1912 and was named Secretary of the Treasury in 1913. During the war he became director general of the government-operated railroads. His second wife was Wilson's daughter, Eleanor. A prominent candidate for the presidency in 1920 and 1924. U.S. senator from California, 1933–1939.

McAlpin, Charles W. For many years secretary of Princeton University and close friend of President Wilson. Mentioned by Wilson's confidential secretary in his letter to Hoover, March 15, 1919.

McCormick, Vance C., 1872–1946. Newspaper publisher and Democratic political leader on the national and state (Pennsylvania) level. Adviser to President Wilson at the Peace Conference. A U.S. representative on the Reparations Commission at the Conference. Member of President's Committee of Economic Advisers and of Supreme Economic Council.

Mannerheim, Baron Carl G., 1867–1951. Finnish marshal and statesman. Served in Russian army during World War I. Returned to Finland in 1917 upon outbreak of Russian Revolution and organized the White Guards, who fought in Finnish Civil War of 1918. As an anti-Communist he built the defenses in Karelia between the Soviet Union and Finland in 1933. President of the Finnish government for a short time, 1940–1941 and 1944–1946.

Martin, Thomas S., 1847–1919. Served as a cadet in Confederate Army. U.S. Democratic senator from Virginia, 1895 to 1919.

Masaryk, Thomas Garrigue, 1850–1937. A philosopher, Czechoslovak patriot, and first President of Czechoslovakia. Mainly through his efforts the allied government in June, 1918, recognized the cause of Czechoslovak independence. He served as president of the new republic for several years after November 14, 1918. He resigned in December 1935.

Mayer, Arno J., 1926–. Professor at Princeton. Author of books, principally on World War I and the peace-making efforts which followed.

Maximilian, Prince of Baden, 1867–1929. Appointed October 3, 1918, by the Kaiser, William II, to be Chancellor at the head of the ministry, responsible to the Reichstag.

Miller, David Hunter, 1875–1933. New York lawyer and diplomat. Member of the "Inquiry" under Colonel House which in 1917–1918 prepared data for the Peace Conference. Special assistant to the State Department. Helped in writing the final draft of the covenant of the League of Nations, along with Sir Cecil Hurst of the British Foreign Office.

Morgenthau, Henry, Jr., 1891–1967. Born in New York. During World War I he was sent to France as an agricultural expert. Also served in U.S. Naval Reserve. From 1933 to 1945 he was Secretary of the Treasury under President Franklin D. Roosevelt. After World War II he proposed a plan to divide Germany into a few deindustrialized, agrarian states.

Morris, Ira Nelson, 1875–1942. Diplomatist, author. American Minister to Stockholm, 1914–1922.

Nansen, Fridtjof, 1861–1930. Norwegian polar explorer and humanitarian. Championed independence of Norway from Sweden in 1905. Held several diplomatic posts. Won Nobel Prize for Peace in 1922 for repatriation of nearly half a million war prisoners in Russia and for other humanitarian work in that country. From the first he represented Norway at the League of Nations.

Nitti, Saverio, 1868–1953. Minister of the Italian Treasury, 1917–1919. Became Prime Minister in June 1919.

Orlando, Vittorio Emanuele, 1860–1952. Italian and fourth member of the Big Four at the conference. He and the Italian delegation were interested almost exclusively in acquiring the territories promised them by the 1915 secret pact of London. The Italian delegation withdrew from the conference on April 25, 1919, after Wilson publicly denounced their demands. But, according to Hoover, Orlando did not criticize the President. President Wilson was bitter that the French and British failed to give him their public support on the Italian question as promised. Orlando returned to Paris to sign the treaty, including the League covenant, on June 28, 1919.

Paderewski, Ignace, 1860–1941. Polish pianist, composer, and statesman. Highly instrumental in having Poland restored as an independent country. On January 17, 1919, he formed its first new government with himself as Prime Minister. He resigned from that position on November 27, 1919.

Parker, Edwin B., 1868–1929. A Texas judge. During World War I he helped organize the War Industries Board. In 1918–1919 he was chairman of the U.S. Liquidation Commission which settled the claims of the Allies against the United States for war matériel.

Penrose, Boise, 1860–1921. Pennsylvania lawyer and U.S. Republican senator, 1897–1921. A highly controversial political figure in Philadelphia politics.

Pershing, John Joseph, 1860–1948. U.S. Army general and commander of American Expeditionary Force in France in World War I.

Pichon, Stéphen, 1857–1933. French diplomat, physician, journalist. Minister of Foreign Affairs in Clemenceau's cabinet at the time of the Peace Conference. At the conference, he contended vigorously for France's security. Defended the Allied invasion of Russia in 1919 and constantly opposed all plans to treat with the Bolsheviks.

Pittman, Key, 1872–1940. U.S. Democratic senator from Nevada, 1913–1940.

Polk, Frank L., 1871–1943. Acting Secretary of State, December 4, 1918–July 18, 1919, during the absence from Washington of Secretary of State Robert Lansing.

---

244 / Glossary

Redfield, William C., 1858–1932. Democratic congressman from New York, 1911–1913. Secretary of Commerce, 1913 to November 1, 1919.

Reed, James A., 1861–1944. U.S. Democratic senator from Missouri, 1911 to 1929. A persistent Hoover critic during the war and the Peace Conference.

Rickard, Edgar, 1874–1951. Internationally known mining engineer. Born in France in 1874. Educated in America. Associated with Hoover in the work of the Commission for the Relief in Belgium, 1914–1917. During the war he was a member of the U.S. Food Administration. Thereafter, he was closely associated with a number of Hoover's activities.

Robinson, Henry M., 1870–1937. Banker, economist, and confidant of Presidents Wilson, Coolidge, and Hoover. Member of President Wilson's Committee of Economic Advisers and of the Supreme Economic Council at the Peace Conference. During World War I he was on Wilson's Council of National Defense. He declined offers of cabinet posts made by three different presidents but served them in many other capacities.

Root, Elihu, 1845–1937. Secretary of War, 1899–1904. Secretary of State, 1905–1909. Republican U.S. senator from New York, 1909–1915. Awarded the Nobel Peace Prize in 1912. Appointed by Wilson in 1917 to head a special U.S. mission to Russia.

Ryan, T. R. U.S. Army colonel. Associated with Hoover in the work of the American Relief Administration in Europe, 1919.

Sazonov, Sergei D., 1861–1927. Russian diplomat and statesman. Played a direct and major role in leading Russia into World War I. Appointed Russian Ambassador to London in March 1917 and dismissed in May 1917. He thereupon moved to Paris where he acted as foreign minister for the short-lived Kolchak counterrevolutionary government.

Scheidemann, Philip, 1865–1939. German Social Democrat. With Friedrich Ebert he set up a German democratic republic on November 9, 1918. First provisional chancellor of the Weimar government of February 1919. Resigned rather than sign the Versailles Treaty on June 28, 1919.

Sharp, William Graves, 1859–1922. Member of Congress for 14th Ohio District, 1909–1915. Ambassador Extraordinary and Plenipotentiary to France, 1914 to 1919.

Sherley, Joseph Swagar, 1871–1941. Kentucky congressman, 1903–1919.

Snyder, F. S. Member of the Meat Division of the U.S. Food Administration.

Stimson, Henry L., 1867–1950. American statesman. He was made Secretary of War in 1911 by President William Taft. He was not in government service under Wilson but was Secretary of State under President Hoover from 1929 to 1933. Secretary of War, 1940–1945.

Straus, Oscar S., 1850–1926. Diplomatist and author. Secretary of Department of Commerce and Labor, 1906–1909. Member of The New York Commission for Relief in Belgium, 1915–1918. A representative in Paris of the private organization, the League to Enforce Peace, 1919.

Strauss, Lewis L., 1896–1975. Personal secretary to Herbert Hoover at Paris Peace Conference and previously in Washington, 1917–1919.

Taft, Robert A., 1889–1953. Son of President William Howard Taft. Member of the legal staff of the Food Administration, 1917–1918. Hoover's legal adviser at Peace Conference. U.S. Republican senator from Ohio, 1939–1953. Unsuccessful in 1952 for the Republican nomination for the presidency. An isolationist after 1945, opposing U.S. participation in NATO and similar organizations.

Taft, William Howard, 1857–1930. Twenty-seventh President of the United States, 1909–1913. He held a large number of other highly important public positions. He was Secretary of War under President Theodore Roosevelt and Chief Justice of the Supreme Court from 1921 to 1930.

Talbot, J. S. Unidentified writer of a letter mentioned by Wilson's secretary in his letter to Hoover, May 28, 1919.

Tallents, Sir Steven, 1885–1958. British publicist. Fought with Irish Guards in 1914–1915 during World War I. In 1919 he was chief British delegate for the relief and supply of Poland and from 1919 to 1920 British Commissioner for the Baltic Provinces. From 1922 to 1926 he served as Imperial Secretary of Northern Ireland.

Taussig, Frank W., 1859–1940. Harvard professor of political economy. In 1920 he supported Hoover as a highly desirable nominee for the presidency.

Taylor, Alonzo E., 1893–1949. Professor at Stanford University. Member of the American War Trade Board, 1917–1919.

Troubridge, Sir Ernest C. T. Admiral in the British navy and chairman of the Inter-Allied Danube River Commission.

Tschakste, Jan, 1859–1927. President of the Council of State of Latvia and president of the Lettish Delegation at the Paris Peace Conference, 1919. Elected as first President of the Republic of Latvia in 1922 and served until his death in 1927.

Tumulty, Joseph Patrick, 1879–1954. Personal secretary of President Wilson from 1910 to 1921. Remained in Washington during the Peace Conference.

Ulmanis, Karlis, 1877–?. Latvian political leader. In November 1918 he was made head of the Latvian provisional government by Latvian patriots who at the same time proclaimed the independence of Latvia. He subsequently became Prime Minister, a post he held for a number of terms. Because of pressure from overwhelming Soviet military forces, he was compelled to resign the presidency in June, 1940. Shortly thereafter he was arrested and deported to Russia.

Vix,————. Lieutenant colonel in the French army. In 1919 head of the Allied military mission in Budapest.

Walscheid, Otto W. Identified only as the writer of a January 1919 letter to Wilson.

Watson, Grant. Representative of the British government at Libau, Latvia.

White, Henry, 1850–1927. Diplomat. One of the five plenipotentiaries on the American Commission at the Paris Peace Conference.

White, John Beaver. Representative of the War Trade Board on the committee which assisted the Food Administration during Hoover's absence in Paris.

Whitlock, Brand, 1869–1934. Author, diplomat. U.S. Minister to Belgium, 1913–1919, and Ambassador, 1919–1922.

Whitmarsh, Theodore F., 1870–1936. Merchant. Member of the U.S. Food Administration and acting chairman during Hoover's absence in Paris. As joint director of the American Relief Administration, he helped supervise a $100,000,000 appropriation of Congress for European relief after World War I.

Wilson, Woodrow, 1856–1924. Twenty-eighth President of the United States, 1913–1921. Democratic Governor of New Jersey, 1910–1912. President of Princeton University, 1902–1910. Prior to that, professor of history and political economy at Bryn Mawr, Wesleyan, and Princeton, 1885–1902. Author of many books on American history and political science. Head of the U.S. delegation to the Peace Conference, 1919. Awarded Nobel Peace Prize, 1919.

Wood, Robert E., 1879–1952. U.S. colonel and brigadier general, N.A., in World War I. Acting Quartermaster General of U.S. Army, 1918–1919. Assisted the U.S. Food Administration as representative of the War Department.

Woolsey, Lester H., 1877–1937. International lawyer and former partner of Robert Lansing, Wilson's Secretary of State. Tactical delegate to the Paris Peace Conference. Lawyer in the State Department, 1909–1920.

Zabriskie, George A. Member of Hoover's American Relief Administration connected with the New York office.

Index